Full of Character

of related interest

Character Toolkit for Teachers
100+ Classroom and Whole School Character
Education Activities for 5- to 11-Year-Olds
Frederika Roberts and Elizabeth Wright
Foreword by Kristján Kristjánsson
ISBN 978 1 78592 490 3
eISBN 978 1 78450 879 1

The Moral Heart of Public Service
Edited by Claire Foster-Gilbert
Foreword by the Dean of Westminster
Afterword by Stephen Lamport
ISBN 978 1 78592 255 8
eISBN 978 1 78450 540 0

The Forgiveness Project
Stories for a Vengeful Age
Marina Cantacuzino
Forewords by Archbishop Emeritus Desmond
Tutu and Alexander McCall Smith
ISBN 978 1 78592 000 4
eISBN 978 1 78450 006 1

The Spirit of the Child, Revised Edition
David Hay
ISBN 978 1 84310 371 4
eISBN 978 1 84642 473 1

Full of Character

A Christian Approach to Education for the Digital Age

Frances Ward

Jessica Kingsley *Publishers*
London and Philadelphia

First published in 2019
by Jessica Kingsley Publishers
73 Collier Street
London N1 9BE, UK
and
400 Market Street, Suite 400
Philadelphia, PA 19106, USA

www.jkp.com

Library of Congress Cataloging in Publication Data
A CIP catalog record for this book is available from the Library of Congress

British Library Cataloguing in Publication Data
A CIP catalogue record for this book is available from the British Library

ISBN 978 1 78592 339 5
eISBN 978 1 78450 660 5

Printed and bound in Great Britain

For Tilda, Jonty,
Theo and Hsuan, Hugh and Sam

Contents

Acknowledgements

This book was written during six months spent with the College and Community of the Resurrection at Mirfield in West Yorkshire, UK. It was conceived before that, though, while I was Dean of St Edmundsbury in the Diocese of St Edmundsbury and Ipswich in the county of Suffolk. I am grateful to everyone I lived, prayed and worked with there over the last seven years, in that beautiful cathedral.

Mirfield offered so much: a deep river of prayer and discipline in which I have been immersed, finding expansive space to think, read and write. I've been alongside my husband Peter as he trained for priesthood and put up with the light going on too early in the morning, as I've turned those liminal anxieties into something tangible, in the hour or two before Mattins.

I wouldn't have thought it possible to have been welcomed so warmly by the College Principal, Fr Peter Allan, the staff and other ordinands, who are a great group of people and will make even greater priests.

I'm grateful to Natalie Watson, who has been an inspiring and patient editor, and after she left JKP, the other staff there, Alex Holmes, Hannah Snetsinger and Simeon Hance.

Without the following, with whom I have discussed the ideas over recent years, or who have read and commented on drafts, this book would have been greatly impoverished: Geoff Barton, Matt Bullimore, Carla Carlisle, Mark Cazalet, Sarah Coakley, Elizabeth Cook, Trevor Cooling, Jennifer Cooper, Andrew Davison, Vivienne Faull, David Ford, Nigel Genders, Penny Graysmith, Malcolm Guite, George Guiver CR, John Hall, David Ison, Judith Maltby, Jessica Martin, Edmund Newey, Richard Peers, Martin Seeley, Jane Sinclair, Tim Stevens, Francis Spufford, Richard Sudworth, Vanessa Ward, Flora Winfield.

My thanks, particularly, to Lillias August RI, for the image used for the cover. Thanks, also, to Francis Spufford, and Faber and Faber, for permission to use the passage from his *Unapologetic* on pages 76–7, and to Malcolm Guite and Canterbury Press, for permission to use the sonnet, *Good Measure*, on page 203.

New Year's Eve, 2018 – Setting the Scene

Between Christmas and New Year, Maddy and Craig binge-watched back episodes of *Black Mirror*, reminding themselves of previous series, in preparation for Series 5. As soon as Emily had had her bedtime story and was asleep, they turned on Netflix and watched until they could watch no more.

Craig enjoyed the tension, the drama. Deeply satisfying stuff. Maddy was left alarmed, anxious in a way she hadn't really felt for ages. Craig told her not to worry. It was only TV. But it touched a raw nerve in her. Most of the episodes did. Whether it was *Be Right Back*, with that android up in the attic, waiting to respond to Martha's grief, or the awfulness of *15 Million Credits*, the reduction of life to day after day on the bike producing energy, only to watch crap entertainment, the image of Abi, trapped into porn. Or *White Christmas*, part two particularly, with its portrayal of consciousness copied and tortured into submission as a slave. Maddy was disturbed. She was impressed too. Charlie Brooker – a prophet for today. *The Waldo Moment*, so clever on the rise of populism. Brooker had even predicted Trump.[1]

Maddy was left with big questions. What happens when we're able to build cyborgs, and you really can't tell the difference? What about the future of work, if robots take all

---

1   www.telegraph.co.uk/on-demand/0/black-mirrors-charlie-brooker-predicting-donald-trump-love-story

our jobs? She could hardly bear to watch *Arkangel*. Its theme of parental anxiety was just too close to the bone, when she thought about Emily and the dangers she could face as she grew up. Charlie Brooker was brilliant. He'd captured the zeitgeist, tapping into the fears she felt but couldn't articulate.

New Year's Eve, and Craig and Maddy had some friends around. Just close friends – Sam and Natalie, Benji and Dan, Caz and Jonty. At theirs, so they could settle Emily and enjoy the evening. None of the others had kids yet, though Benji and Dan were considering surrogacy. They'd know each other a while – Craig had trained as a horticulturalist with Sam. Natalie and Caz were at uni together. Jonty and Benji taught in the same school. They often met, with friendship built up over the years. Knew, pretty much, what each would say and where the fault lines were.

As 2018 became 2019, the conversation inevitably turned to their hopes and fears.

Hopes and fears

Let me summarise the way the conversation went, as they ate sweet potato and bean chilli and sticky toffee pears. Maddy, as ever, got things going. She shared her excitement that this year Emily would start school. That felt massive. But it just seemed that the education system that would hold Emily for the next 12 years or so was fraught with politics and different ideologies. Would it prepare her for the future world?

She went through the questions on her mind, in no particular order. There was work and how automation would impact it. Then, would Emily know the difference between truth and post-truth? Would school give her emotional and moral knowledge, rather than just knowing how to get information from the internet? Help her to be thoughtful, kind and wanting to contribute to making a better world? Maddy hoped for something deeper and more community-minded than seemed to be on offer. It all seemed so individualistic and knowledge-light.

Benji mentioned a blog he followed that he thought Maddy might enjoy, called 'The Traditional Teacher'.[2] And then the conversation moved on to how things felt more generally – fragile, with a lot of anxiety around. It was hard to feel hopeful. The dominant stories through the media left a bleak sense of being out of control. They talked about 'post-truth'. Jonty Googled it. It was the *Oxford English Dictionary* word for 2016.[3]

Sam had heard of a study that proved false retweets travelled faster and farther than true ones, which take six times longer to reach 1,500 people.[4] Benji said how difficult it was at school for students to tell the difference. Everything was based on what was attractive, what felt good. It was hard to get the children to see when they were being manipulated. Dan had been reading about how Cambridge Analytica used data from Facebook, extensive and lengthy hacking of emails and misinformation to impact the election in the USA in 2016 (and who knows where else), the Brexit referendum too – making it all the more difficult to know what to trust.

But 'post-truth' was just one aspect of a changing world. Maddy, who read a lot of reviews, remarked on the enormous number of books that were published over the previous couple of years, most expressing anxiety at the state of things, nationally and internationally.

In the middle of the night

Natalie talked about what kept her awake in the middle of the night. She worked in journalism. She described the political and social divisions of many Western nations, with the rise of populism against established systems that seemed out of touch. How the financial crash of 2008 was an ongoing problem, with

---

2   http://thetraditionalteacher.wordpress.com
3   'Relating to or denoting circumstances in which objective facts are less influential in shaping public opinion than appeals to emotion and personal belief.' https://en.oxforddictionaries.com/definition/post-truth
4   *The Economist*, 10 March 2018, p.80.

grievances and inequality still growing. She thought the world was suffering alarming levels of unpredictability and threat, of power re-alignments, violence and war, with both China and Russia effectively dictatorships, and Western liberalism in retreat (Luce 2017).

For Craig it was the environment. Climate change now a reality affecting everyone, and especially the poorest communities of the world.[5]

Climate change

Craig outlined his deep anxiety. How the environment faced the accelerating impact of climate change. The Paris COP21 Agreement of 2015 saw 195 countries adopt the first-ever universal, legally binding global climate deal. The agreement set out a global action plan to put the world on track to avoid dangerous climate change by limiting global warming to well below 2°C. It all seemed so hopeful at the time. Then in June 2017 Trump withdrew the US from the Paris agreement; convinced, with a wide section of his fellow Republicans, that climate change wasn't happening. The Paris Agreements had taken back seat within a Europe and the UK overwhelmed by preoccupation with Brexit, so it all seemed stalled.

They'd heard it before from Craig, but his passion carried him on – describing how global warming was melting the ice caps – and not just polar ice, but also vast regions of tundra. How the sea was becoming more acidic, and polluted – with plastics. Craig didn't need to remind them of David Attenborough's albatross and her hungry young chick.[6]

He said the challenges were in at least four major areas, as he saw it, including the radical changes in climatic patterns. He was worried about the major extinction of species, caused

---

5   See the reports of the UN Intergovernmental Panel on Climate Change report at http://ipcc.ch

6   www.radiotimes.com/news/tv/2018-03-08/blue-planet-2-plastic-waste-final-episode

by deforestation as the land was converted to agricultural monocrops, as the oceans were subjected to industrialised deep-sea fishing, and by the increased use of pesticides and herbicides in modern agricultural systems. Then pollution was a real problem in the oceans, rivers, air and land, caused by industrial and chemical wastes and residues. Fourth, soil erosion and desertification were causing increasing shortages of drinkable water and other natural resources and 'commons'.

Craig was almost in tears as he described how the environment was under threat as never before. Instead of moving towards greater global co-operation on issues that require global solutions – on the environment, on security, on poverty – he saw everything becoming more tribal, with nationalism and regionalism on the increase.

He said the best global leadership in recent years had been offered by the Pope in his encyclical *Laudato Si* of May 2015. It was excellent on the threat of climate change, showing the global reach of the Catholic Church.[7] But otherwise the nations of the world were retreating from international co-operation into silo mentalities, and undermining international collaboration. Maddy said that they both wanted Emily not to grow up completely over-anxious and scared about the future of the planet. That she wanted school to help her to know and love the natural world, deeply and intimately, cherishing the environment around her. George Monbiot was brilliant – the way he talked about rewilding the child.[8]

The Trump phenomenon

Then, of course, they got onto Trump. Natalie described the discontent that turned voters out in 2016, both for Trump, and to vote in the European Union (EU) referendum in the UK, to demand something different, someone different, and how social

---

7   http://w2.vatican.va/content/francesco/en/encyclicals/documents/papa-francesco_20150524_enciclica-laudato-si.html

8   www.monbiot.com/2013/10/07/rewild-the-child

media shortcut more traditional, constitutional decision-making processes and voting patterns. She saw a swing away from representative democracy to referendum democracy with its populist appeal, helped in both campaigns by clever digital means to target voters.[9] How Trump appealed to the people with a series of promises, half-truths and prejudices in a way dictators have done since time began, and how, since he'd been in the White House, he'd undermined the usual constitutional checks and balances of Western liberalism that curtail arbitrary power: the rule of law, the elected houses, the judgement of trained advisors and counsellors, the civil service.

Sam disagreed. He thought Trump brought a fresh exciting energy to a tired old establishment that needed a good shake up. Natalie came back at him – a moment of real tension. She argued forcefully that Trump impacted the global world by intensifying the threat of world power re-alignment, and pouring fuel on existing hotspots, particularly in the Middle East and Syria, making them more dangerous than ever. She'd recently read *The Economist*'s articles on 'The Future of War' that outlined the increasing threats of Russia and America modernising their nuclear forces at huge expense and China enlarging its nuclear arsenal.[10] Existing nuclear-arms-control agreements were fraying; the protocols and understandings that helped avoid Armageddon during the Cold War had not been renewed. It wasn't just nuclear arms that were the problem, though. The use of chemical weapons was on the increase, too. Trump's promise to introduce trade tariffs on steel and aluminium would disrupt the rules and regulations that keep the global economy going.

They agreed that Trump's popular appeal was definitely a sign of how insecure many people were. Since the recession of 2008 there were fewer prospects of well-paid jobs. Society was polarising, with the wealthiest becoming ever richer, and the poorer struggling more, and a clear hollowing out of the middle

9   www.nytimes.com/2018/03/19/technology/facebook-cambridge-analytica-explained.html
10   *The Economist*, 27 January 2018.

classes who were the backbone of a cohesive society.[11] Natalie talked of an uber-rich class now, able to fund and influence politics in ways unaccountable through traditional political means. How bad it was when constitutional democracy lost its basis in rational debate and decision-making, and lobbying becomes entrenched, and tribal.

Little, brittle Britain

They stayed clear of Brexit, treading carefully; aware that one or two had voted Leave. They all recognised, though, that it had left UK society divided and bitter. The UK government was preoccupied with leaving the EU, distracted from other, crucial issues, including proper attention to universal credit, to the National Health Service and its future.

Benji talked of the mindfulness courses his school ran to help with anxiety. Craig brought it back to Emily and how he was worried she faced a future of real anxiety and social divisions which were going to deepen further. Mindfulness was all very well, but things hadn't really recovered since the 2008 crash. Growth and productivity wasn't back to where they were before, and the outlook was grim. Austerity, in the UK, was biting deep. The number of rough sleepers in England had risen;[12] the GIG economy didn't help as people with irregular incomes and zero-hours contracts found it difficult to budget properly to pay rent and save.

All of them had seen the realities of poverty. They lived outside Manchester and knew the North-South divide was real

---

11   For more, Robert Peston (2017) and Martin Ford (2016) are the place to start. Edward Luce (2017) is good too.

12   Official figures, based on a single-night snapshot estimated by local authorities each November puts them rising from 1,768 in 2010 to 4,751 in 2017. Researchers at Heriot Watt University put the total figure in Britain at about 9,000 and expect the number to rise by 75 per cent over the next decade unless action is taken. *The Economist*, 10 March 2018, p.30.

in the UK.[13] Maddy wanted Emily to learn at school not that she was 'a unique child' (and Maddy dug out a recent leaflet from the school that put 'the unique child' at the centre of everything – 'How self-centred is that?' she said) but that she belonged to the whole of humanity.

Natalie – ever provocative – came back to Brexit, with its nostalgic dream of stand-alone Great Britain. How it ignored the realities of current global threats, cyber-attack and energy black-out. She said she was worried about security and how much better it was to stay within the European Union than outside and alone. They remembered the Manchester Arena attack of May 2017.

It was Russia that concerned Natalie, though. Already there had been a number of assassinations of British citizens on UK soil, using deadly nerve agents. She thought that Russia had been handled really badly by Europe since Glasnost and that she wouldn't be surprised if, once Brexit happened, Russia moved to colonise Britain. The others pooh-poohed it, but she went on about how much of London's wealth and property was owned by Russian oligarchs and how little transparency there was. How transatlantic communication lines were vulnerable to sabotage.[14] The UK military had been underfunded for decades, reducing capacity. Cyber-war was a growing reality, with Russia targeting UK systems. Imagine, she said, if Russia decided to colonise the UK, once we had left the EU. Imagine the Special Relationship with the USA, as unreliable as in Churchill's Darkest Hour. She argued that the British Government, post-Brexit, was doing its very best to make the UK as weak and vulnerable as possible, based on a fantasy of the former glory of the British Empire. Little, brittle Britain – no longer one nation, no longer a world power, with its one great strength – finance – a chimera when examined too closely.[15]

---

13   www.childrenscommissioner.gov.uk/publication/growing-up-north-time-to-leave-the-north-south-divide-behind

14   www.wired.com/2015/10/undersea-cable-maps

15   As Robert Peston points out in *WTF* (2017), particularly chapters 6, 7 and 8.

When it comes down to it, said Maddy, I want Emily to be someone who sees life as a gift. Honest and open. Resourceful, with a good sense of humour, despite our grim fears. At home in a diverse world where character counts more than identity – so it doesn't matter that she and I are black, or what gender you are, but it does matter what sort of person you are. Where confidence comes from a rich hinterland of cultural literacy, so she knows traditions of music, poetry and literature and can grow in emotional and moral wisdom. Already she was enjoying a wide range of books and poetry, really loving learning things off by heart. More than anything, said Maddy, that she knows how to tell the difference between what's true and what's not. When she mentioned this, Benji mentioned a school he'd heard of in London where all the children learned three poems off by heart each year in secondary school, and discipline was really strict. He said he was intrigued and wanted to visit.[16]

The latest revolution

The meal extended into the early hours. As time went on, they each became aware of this as one of those special events that they would all remember. It felt really significant, as they covered an enormous amount of ground, trying to anticipate the New Year with a gathered sense of what their generation faced in the future.

Sparked by watching Brooker's *Be Right Back*, and *The Entire History of You*, Maddy wanted to know what everyone thought about the relationship between human and robot. Dan and Jonty had read a lot on the latest artificial intelligence (AI) revolution. They knew the questions: will AI overtake human intelligence, as some are predicting, into a great Singularity (Kurzweil 2014, 2016)? Are we entering Life 3.0 (Tegmark 2017)? The age of the *Homo Deus* (Harari 2015)? What if you

---

16   He's talking about Michaela Community School (http://mcsbrent.co.uk). See also Birbalsingh 2016.

can't tell the difference between a robot and a human? Or the two become hybridised, as a cyborg? Or the human person is simulated to such an extent that the distinction no longer is meaningful?

This latest revolution. Humanity had seen revolutions before – the industrial, the technological – and Caz argued that this is simply the next, bringing hoped-for advances and unpredicted costs in its wake. Jonty agreed that all revolutions stir anxiety, but this one had some disturbing aspects. It meant facing deep questions about what it means to be human. 'That is, if humanity, and indeed planet earth, survives,' said Craig.

The digital age is upon us

Dan pointed out just how much wealth was created by the revolution in communication and digital technology. Google, Amazon, Facebook, PayPal – all produced capital beyond the wildest of dreams, largely because labour costs were minimal, or non-existent. This was wealth unregulated and untaxed by national governments which couldn't get a grip on multi-national figures and companies that were always a step ahead, attracting the best brains.

Dan said he thought this was going to impact on economic systems in ways no one was really thinking through properly. Well, some were. Michael Sandel for one.[17] Neo-liberalism: The market society was struggling with productivity, with the failure to create enough jobs for everyone, with a lack of sustainable growth.[18]

And that's before the big hard hitter of automation kicks in. Dan talked about the McKinsey Global Institute, which had recently produced a report called 'Jobs lost, jobs gained: Workforce transitions in a time of automation'. A staggering 75 million, perhaps even as many as 375 million people around

17   www.bbc.co.uk/programmes/b01nmlh2/episodes/downloads
18   http://bigthink.com/in-their-own-words/the-vital-difference-between-a-market-economy-and-a-market-society

the world may need to change occupational categories and acquire new skills by the year 2030, their jobs automated away. That's 14 per cent of the global workforce.[19] The first to go will be predictable, routine jobs, but it won't stop there.

Dan said, 'Think of a skills pyramid rather than a skills ladder. The tide of automation is rising; the pyramid is not floating. In the world to come, you're safer if you're a hairdresser, a teacher or a carer. Better to work with people than in accountancy, or as a legal researcher, or a programmer.' He told Jonty and Benji, '"Work with people, rather than in front of a screen" is the advice to give your kids at school.'

He explained how computers are cleverer and faster and now deep learn, turning their AI inwards. Many now programme themselves. 'Algorithm' is a word to know.[20] They are becoming increasingly clever and self-learning.

Automation bites in a divided world

So on top of the lack of any real rise in wages since the turn of the century, work is disappearing, and that's only going to get worse as automation bites more deeply.

Dan didn't talk about the other ways in which AI will change the workforce. How in 2018 Amazon was granted a pair of patents for wristbands that monitor warehouse workers' exact location and track their hand movements in real time, providing information that will allow the company to gauge their employees' productivity and accuracy – just one example of how invasive workplace surveillance is and will increasingly become. Most employment contracts in America give employers blanket rights to monitor employees and collect data about them, although few workers are aware of it. Europe has stronger privacy laws, but privacy concerns and

---

19   www.mckinsey.com/global-themes/future-of-organizations-and-work/how-will-automation-affect-jobs-skills-and-wages

20   It's a process or set of rules to be followed in calculations or other problem-solving operations.

surveillance can only leave employees increasingly vulnerable and potentially violated.[21]

Income from work? Or Universal Basic Income?

Dan had read Noah Yuval Harari's book *Homo Deus*, how Homo sapiens would be surpassed by highly intelligent algorithms, dividing humankind into 'a superhuman caste that will treat normal human beings no better than nineteenth-century Europeans treated Africans' (Harari 2015, p.350). Martin Ford too, who also described a massive job polarisation, where the rich who control the benefits of a digital age are ever richer, and those who have routine, predictable jobs risk losing their employment to automation. The middle classes will not be safe, either, as more non-routine, non-predictable work is taken over by machines that learn with increasingly speed and adaptability (Ford 2015).

Many other contemporary writers – like Max Tegmark, Robert Peston, George Monbiot – all worry about how people can survive a jobless future (Monbiot 2017; Peston 2017; Tegmark 2017). Digital automatisation threatens the world of work in ways that will devastate, dividing further the rich from the poor.

Dan was with those who, in anticipation of this world, wanted to see the introduction of Universal Basic Income (UBI). He explained how UBI is being considered seriously in many countries around the world and piloted in Ontario, Canada; Finland; Utrecht in the Netherlands; Nairobi; Sao Paulo in Brazil.

In the UK, the Royal Society for the Arts (RSA) produced a paper in December 2015 advocating UBI, and also commending an interim Universal Basic Opportunity Fund.[22] The RSA argue that UBI would enable people to be creative citizens, freed from

---

21   *The Economist*, 31 March 2018, 'Special Report GrAIt Expectations: AI in Business', pp.10–11.

22   www.thersa.org/discover/publications-and-articles/rsa-blogs/2017/10/universal -basic-services-or-universal-basic-income

the necessity of earning an income. Relieved of the worry of how to support themselves, everyone would be able to look for work, or retrain, or do voluntary work for the common good, or take risks as entrepreneurs. He said that it was worth reading the RSA paper entitled *Creative Citizen, Creative State*.[23] UBI would alleviate homelessness and poverty overnight. It would also give people the resources to develop fruitful occupation.

Maddy thought of Emily facing all this. Automation was already changing work enormously. How could her education help her grow up resourceful, with a love of learning that continued through her life?

Dan said that it seemed to him the main question was how the best of humanity is carried through the latest revolution. One of the best aspects of being human is our care and compassion for others and our ability to forget self as we imagine what others around us feel, and need, so they too can lead fruitful and fulfilled lives. What might it mean for robots to learn from humanity about what it is to be humane, he wondered? So that the digital future doesn't just value super *intelligence*, but super *wisdom* too?

Automated weapons systems

Digital advances run through life today. Maddy, Craig and the others remembered how drones replaced fireworks at the Winter Olympics in South Korea – a beautiful, clever display.

Having watched the *Black Mirror* episode *Hated in the Nation*, Maddy said how much drones scared her. They scare experts too, especially those who see the threat of automated weapons systems (AWS). These are weapons that can be remotely controlled, with the potential to kill humans, independent of a human programmer or control. This is of such concern to over 1,000 digital scientists and researchers, including the late

---

23   https://medium.com/pathways-to-universal-basic-income/creative-citizen-creative-state-a3cef3f25775

Stephen Hawking, that in 2015 they launched an international campaign 'Stop Killer Robots'. Digital scientists are usually future-optimists. If they are worried, AWS are a serious threat. Charlie Brooker had again hit the spot. Maddy said this was the stuff of nightmares, automated drones that use face recognition to destroy individuals or whole groups, to then self-destruct, leaving no trace. Imagine wiping out all black children, or a particular ethnic group, like the Kurds: genocide with very little cost or control (Tegmark 2017). Cyber warfare was a risk, too.

Brain change

Jonty talked about the amount of time everyone spent in front of screens. How we live in an age of distraction, seduced by the virtual realities and instant gratification. As a teacher, he saw it all the time and worried that too much screen time was changing our brains, our ability to think and concentrate.

They talked of someone they all knew, how Mike was addicted to online gambling. Games, pornography – on the increase. Caz remarked: 'When it comes to the web, we think we're spiders, when really we're flies.'[24] They had all seen Brooker's *Playtest*.

The friends hadn't read Will Storr (2017) or Jean Twenge (2014, 2017), who describe the self-obsessed culture of 'selfie' hyper-individualism, and the iGeneration. Nor do they know of Matthew Crawford (2015) and Nicholas Carr's (2015)

---

24   There's a blog by Ben Myers (www.faith-theology.com), who is a theologian based in Brisbane, Australia, that's known by avid followers for its aphoristic wit and wisdom. He posted this in November 2016:
  • When it comes to the web, we like to think we are spiders when in fact we are flies.
  • What's the difference between a care home for people with dementia and a Starbucks full of people with iPhones and laptops? You'll find more interpersonal skills among folk in the former.
  • Street-wear tee shirts for the dwindling number of those whose iPhones aren't prosthetic: the inscription reads 'Watch where I'm going, apphole!'
  • How would I describe the social imaginary of people addicted to social media? As an anti-social imaginary, or an imaginary imaginary.

work on how, if we become too reliant upon digitalisation and automation, we lose skills. Crawford and Carr argue that humanity needs to continue to engage with and attend to the real world, out there, that offers friction to make us adapt and grow, and that children need an education that teaches skills that use their bodies as well as their minds, learning and interacting in reality as well as in virtuality.

Hope is not easy optimism

It was nearly 4 am. Maddy said Emily would soon be waking up. They needed some sleep to be on the ball for a good New Year's Day walk – maybe even up to Top Withens – and a pub lunch. She said how good the conversation had been. The best she could remember. Craig thanked them: their friendship sustained hope in the face of the fears and challenges they all felt.

Maddy proposed that they met more often like this as a New Year's resolution. Formed themselves into a reading group where they took something engaging each time and read it together. She had heard of a book called *The Master and his Emissary* (McGilchrist 2010), and that it was worth reading. The others agreed it was a good plan, though wanted some time to think about it, to check out the book. Maddy said it just helped, meeting and talking like this. Helped keep her hope alive.

It seemed the right time to head off into 2019.

At the Heart of This Book – Human Flourishing

Experienced fullness, joy and fulfilment

Steven Pinker, in *Enlightenment Now* (2018), puts human flourishing at the top of the list of reasons to live. Evidence to corroborate what the philosopher Charles Taylor (2007) claims, that regardless of religious faith or non-faith, all of us have a sense of something more, something that inspires us out of ourselves, that leads us to yearn for fulfilment.

What is it to flourish?

It might look something like this: We want to have a good, happy and secure family life, with a continuing network of friends. We want fulfilling work that feels worthwhile. We want to make a difference to human welfare, to the common good. And often people will also say they want a life that enables loss and darkness to be held, so that we are not overwhelmed with a sense of chaos, or collapse. To flourish is to be able to acknowledge the depths of the human condition, its bleak places and sad times, within a greater sense of fullness.

This book

This book is written to provoke a deeper thoughtfulness about education and how it can be enriched today. How can parents and educators do more to help young people flourish as well-rounded and imaginative human beings who are full of character, and who care for others and the environment? It is written with the digital generation in mind – children and young people who are comfortable interacting with AI.

This book is not a how-to manual for teachers. It doesn't offer strategies to enhance leadership, or performance, or provide the know-how to run a Multi-Academy Trust (MAT). It doesn't explain what mentoring is or commend consultancy to over-stretched head teachers. Nor does it have a linear argument, presented in an accessible style with text boxes, different examples and anecdotes.

What it does do is wonder aloud about what education is for in today's highly complex and rather scary world. The temptation, when things are complex and scary, is to keep on keeping on, addressing the next thing that needs sorting, fire-fighting the crisis that's looming. There's no time, or opportunity, when you're faced with the pressures of too much work, to think, or reflect, or wonder. To read books and engage with big questions. How-to manuals are reassuring. They offer the solutions that are required here and now, with strategies and tactics to cope with this problem that's just presented itself, ways to drill down into the finances and access sources of funding, how to manage under-performance of that particularly difficult member of staff.

I'm offering something different.

The book argues that the progressive educational theories of the last half-century haven't focused enough on the importance of acquiring a rich hinterland of cultural knowledge. Nor have they enabled children to practise and learn habits of the heart that hard-wire us to be thoughtful, kind, truthful, generous and engaged socially with other people.

Here, the main educational emphasis is on deep learning that comes through deliberate practice – learning stuff off by heart. The sort of deep learning which, strangely enough, is causing the latest revolution in AI.

Humane?

'Humane' usually means being kind to animals. I'm extending the word so the kindness is not only for animals, but also for other human beings and the natural environment. It has another meaning, too. 'Humane' can mean civilising and civilised, so you can talk of a humane education, or as I do here, a humane future. I think being civilised is a good thing: that we are more human the more humane, kind and civilised we are. In a world of digital generations, humanity needs to be compassionate, tender and true to each other and in the world. It needs to be humane and civilised.

Cultural literacy

Humane compassion for others can only grow on the basis of a good understanding of other cultures and languages. Cultural literacy means a good knowledge of our own culture and the cultures around us, so we understand and can translate from culture to culture. It's crucial to a humane future.

E.D. Hirsch (1988, 2006) has argued powerfully and carefully through his long career for cultural literacy as the bedrock of a good education. He commends reading from an early age, to build a rich, cumulative hinterland of cultural knowledge that helps children make sense and meaning of all the school subjects, and their life experience, and live humanely with others.

As Maddy and Craig want the best for Emily in the years ahead, they will look to her teachers to enable her to grow on the foundation they have established. Already Emily enjoys reading and learning about a rich cultural heritage that embraces her black heritage (her grandmother came over from Barbados as part of the Windrush generation in the 1950s) and Craig's Scottish ancestry, but also that of her friends from the diverse Asian heritage cultures that live all around her in the Northern town on the outskirts of Manchester. Emily and her friends at school will need a diverse but common cultural heritage, bringing them together as they grow in moral and emotional knowledge, consolidating their knowledge of that heritage and its riches over the years in a systematic and coherent way.

The fear that Maddy has is that, instead of a knowledge-rich education, Emily will be taught transferable skills and strategies, in an over-instrumental education system. That's why Maddy wants to read Iain McGilchrist's book *The Master and His Emissary* with her friends.

The Master and His Emissary

Iain McGilchrist's seminal 2010 work reflects his experience as a consultant psychiatrist at the leading UK Bethlem Royal and Maudsley Hospital and his research in neuroimaging at Johns Hopkins University Hospital in Baltimore, USA, and also his teaching English at Oxford as a fellow of All Souls. He comes with credibility across a number of academic fields. The title of his book comes from a legend, told by Nietzsche, about a ruler whose emissary becomes contemptuous, and starts to take over. The wisdom of the ruler is lost, the people are duped, and the domain becomes a tyranny and eventually collapses in ruins.

McGilchrist uses the legend to describe the relationship, as he sees it, between the two hemispheres of our brains. It is commonly assumed that the right hemisphere (RH) and the left hemisphere (LH) do different things; indeed we have come to accept an 'entrenched prejudice' that the left brain does all the important serious stuff – like language and processing experience – with the right brain adding a bit of colour to life, but no more; largely the 'silent' part, of no real value. But the latest research has found that both hemispheres attend to all aspects of our experience of the world and what we do with that experience, but in different ways. The LH is extensively dependent on the RH, and we dismiss the significance of the RH at our peril.

He writes:

> I take for granted that the contributions made by the left hemisphere, to language and systematic thought in particular, are invaluable. Our talent for division, for seeing the parts, is of staggering importance, second only to our capacity to transcend it, in order to see the whole. These gifts of the left hemisphere have helped us achieve nothing less than civilisation itself, with all that that means… We need the ability to make fine discriminations, and to use reason appropriately. But these contributions need to be made in the service of something else, that only the right hemisphere can bring. Alone they are destructive. And right now they may be bringing us close to forfeiting the civilisation they helped to create. (McGilchrist 2010, p.93)

With his experience as a psychiatrist, McGilchrist writes convincingly about the pathologies of a society where the LH has the ascendency, losing what the RH knows. He has seen the mental illness caused by excessive control-freakery, the lockdown into anxiety caused by hyper self-reflexivity.

He explores how Western culture has become dominated by a LH approach. Without the whole picture that the RH comprehends, the LH becomes obsessed with analysing, decoding, dissecting, with processes and procedures, strategies and tactics that end up leading in ever-tightening utilitarian and instrumental spirals. Without the RH, the LH fails to see the wood for the trees and gets lost in a forest of regulations and rules that close down the imagination that follows knowledge like a sinking star, far beyond the bound of human thought.

When teaching becomes dominated by an overly-managed and performance-driven ideology, its broader and deeper purposes are lost. Maddy and Craig want to resist the ways in which education has become dominated by LH instrumentality and functionality. They are searching for an education for Emily that will be humane but also wise, holding together both the RH and LH and what each contributes, with their different ways of attending to the world.

E.D. Hirsch

E.D. Hirsch hasn't read McGilchrist (as far as I know), but he'd find a lot to agree with. The two main books of Hirsch's that I refer to are *Cultural Literacy* (1988) and *The Knowledge Deficit* (2006).

Hirsch has argued consistently through his long career – often in the face of controversy and opposition – against the dominance of the LH in learning, against the impoverishment of education by too much focus on the narrow decoding of meaning rather than building the cultural knowledge that gives the comprehension that the RH brings. For him, cultural literacy is fundamental to enable the child to comprehend the wood, so the trees then can be attended to properly in all their differences and details. Broad and deep cultural literacy enables education to engage and attend to what needs to be learned and understood, on the basis of a broad hinterland of background knowledge. Then education is the beginning of wisdom that develops throughout our lives.

For the young child, it begins with being read to, and then learning to read deeply. Reading is absolutely crucial to this way of seeing education. Reading, which takes deliberate practice, and learning good material off by heart, is the best start in life anyone can give a child. This lifelong learning should start in the home, as Maddy and Craig have done. They hope it will continue during Emily's school years, so she receives a rich diet of knowledge in order to understand all the subjects at school, reading with understanding and intelligence. With a rich hinterland of knowledge, accumulated carefully and systematically over the years a child is in school, any new material then makes sense and grows in elaborate meaning. Children can absorb much more, from an early age, than is usually assumed today.

Hirsch and McGilchrist

Hirsch and McGilchrist are the two thinkers who run through this book. Bringing their thought together suggests that educationalists today need be much more concerned than most have been over the last 60 years or so, that children develop a hinterland of cultural literacy that allows them to attend to what the RH honours – beyond the narrow instrumental and utilitarian focus that concerns the LH. The rich analysis of each thinker will offer a hinterland that engages the RH, contributing to human fullness of life.

It's important to remember, throughout what follows, that McGilchrist uses this distinction metaphorically. He's very cautious about it becoming a rigid polarisation that means the brain and its functioning is misunderstood. Both the RH and the LH are essential in their collaboration. The distinction is how each attends to the world around and what each focuses on. Each is lost without the other. His use of the metaphor takes the relationship and applies it to human culture.

The RH is engaged by that which is other to us – or to use a technical word, *heteronomous* to us. Attention to the other – whether it is the world around us, other people, or what can be conceived of as God – is at risk when the LH dominates. The LH will prioritise *autonomy* – convinced, narrowly, that the self has everything within itself to analyse and judge and decide. Unfortunately, as McGilchrist argues, when left to its own autonomous devices, the LH fails to see what the RH perceives; it fails to engage with the other without the prompting of the RH.

Redressing this distortion is badly required – not least in education where the domination of the LH has led to ever more narrow attention, centring on the child as an individualistic, even solipsistic atom that needs to be tested and examined, with oppressive targets and processes. Education then delivers only instrumental ends – the next test to pass, a college or university place, finding a job. Lost entirely is the RH apprehension that education is an end in itself, to be pursued for its own sake and enabling the human person to flourish with a rich hinterland of moral and emotional knowledge, able to live life in all its abundance.

Not a blueprint

Parenting and education go hand in hand. This book outlines where education might go if it is to prepare young people for the future. I do my best to anticipate that future – in all its digital complexity.

There are two sorts of chapters. There are nine essays on thankfulness, self-forgetfulness, carefulness, playfulness, resource-fulness, thoughtfulness, fruitfulness, truthfulness and hopefulness. Each stands alone and can be read separately. The other sort of chapter (including Chapter 3 and Chapter 7) intersperses – like the Preface, which set the scene. Chapter 3 covers current literature on character education; Chapter 7 covers the digital challenges ahead. These chapters bring Maddy and Craig back, so the material is seen through their eyes.

This book does not provide a curriculum, or a blueprint for an educational policy: that's not my job or expertise. It does, though, outline some directions I think we should be travelling in if education is going to do its job of preparing today's digital generation for adulthood.

Maddy and Craig, and their daughter Emily and their friends are loosely based on my own four children, who are in their twenties and thirties, considering many of the issues of this book. I am writing for their generation, and for the teachers who will educate Emily and her digital generation, so we will all think more deeply about how to enrich education so it inspires a humane future for digital generations to come.

Schooled to be risk-averse?

Is Norman Doidge right when he writes this in the foreword of Jordan Peterson's latest book?

> [T]his generation, many of whom were raised in small families by hyper-protective parents, on soft-surface playgrounds, and then taught in universities with 'safe spaces' where they don't have to hear things they don't want to – schooled to be risk-averse – has among it, now, millions who feel stultified by this underestimation of their potential resilience and who have embraced Jordan's message that each individual has ultimate responsibility to bear; that if one wants to live a full life, one first sets one's own house in order; and only then can one sensibly aim to take on bigger responsibilities. (Peterson 2018, p.xxiii)

Jordan Peterson stirs controversy and division as he challenges entrenched ideologies. His views on some matters, like gender and sexuality, are trenchant and, I believe, wrong. However, he does encourage a re-engagement with cultural knowledge, and with values and virtues. He excites an appetite to think more deeply about what it means to be a human being, what flourishing means today, that is worth engaging with, if only to disagree.

Flourishing in a digital age

This is particularly important in a digital age which impacts in all directions. Robots are now learning in deep and sophisticated ways. All the predictions are that automation is going to affect significantly the number of jobs that humans do, and not just repetitive, non-cognitive, predictable work. One of the reasons for education is to prepare young people for work. If the work isn't there anymore, or is changing fast, then what more can education offer that can lead to fruitful and occupied lives for all?

Characterful

In 2013 I wrote a book entitled *Why Rousseau Was Wrong*, which addressed (amongst other things) the impact Jean-Jacques Rousseau has had on educational theory and ideology (Ward 2013). Education to develop character, I argued then, was the best way to counter the excessive individualism that pervades child-centred education.

Since then, I've been interested in human flourishing, what 'fullness of life' or abundance is. The Greek word is *pleroma*. It means an overflowing generosity that goes beyond what's required, taking us to a place of wholeness. If education is an adventure, then wherever someone might travel – in mind, heart, soul or body – there is always more to discover. The RH reaches out to drink life to the lees, always curious, interested, roaming with a hungry heart. Fullness is what it seeks.

The popularity of 'mindfulness' got me thinking about other ways we are '-ful'. Other words started to turn over in my mind. Carefulness. Faithfulness. Playfulness. Fruitfulness. Joyfulness. Truthfulness. Perhaps a book that explored such fullnesses as character virtues might be helpful. The title *Full of Character* presented itself, and here we are.

Character education

There's been a lot written lately about character in education. Nicky Morgan is a good place to start. She was the Secretary of State for Education in the UK from 2014 to 2016 and has written a helpful review of character education in the UK today (Morgan 2017). She draws on others in the field, particularly James Arthur and the Jubilee Centre for Character and Virtue in Birmingham.[1] And three key authors in Canada and the States: David Brooks, Paul Tough and Angela Duckworth.

The central question they are all addressing is 'How can we shape children and young people so they learn character

---

1   www.jubileecentre.ac.uk

traits that sustain them through life?' Character is a lifelong process that begins when we're young. However old or young we are, it's about training ourselves to be more loving, or kinder to others, so that such characteristics become our default behaviour.

For example, the Jubilee Centre in Birmingham has the Knightly Virtues Programme for children. It uses the retelling of classic stories, which provide an attractive and potent source for the development of the following eight character virtues: gratitude, courage, humility, service, justice, honesty, love and self-discipline (Arthur *et al.* 2017).

Those working at the Jubilee Centre look back to the Greek philosopher Aristotle and to his writings on virtue, so the next few sections give a brief introduction to him; then we consider the difference between character and personality, then the idea of *deliberate practice* is explored, followed by some explanation of the term *synaptogenesis*.

We are in Aristotle territory

Aristotle wrote about virtue in ancient Greece in the fourth century before the Christian era (BCE), and he's central to the approach that many character educationalists take.[2] Aristotle believed virtues were learned. Just as you'd train yourself for strength (the Greek word for 'virtue' can be translated into 'strength'), you could train yourself in moral virtue, like training to excel at sport, or to play a musical instrument. He rated self-control very highly, a key virtue that led to the goal of human flourishing in a good life, which he called *eudaimonia*. *Eudaimonia* is stronger than 'happiness'; more like fulfilment. It's often translated as 'flourishing'.

Friendship was extremely important to Aristotle. The acquisition of virtue is never a solitary endeavour. It's always

---

2   See Aristotle's *Nicomachean Ethics* – there are lots of editions and translations. I've got the Oxford University Press edition, published in 2002 and edited by Sarah Broadie and Christopher Rowe, with an introduction and commentary.

developed with others – mentors, parents, friends, colleagues – as we grow as social beings in the world. He thought friendship was foundational to a good society – that people met together to talk and discuss what the good life (*eudaimonia*) was and how to achieve it. In conversation and with the guidance of others, we grow in virtue, strengthening our moral world view and ethical judgement. He also said that an important aspect of a fulfilled life is practical wisdom, or *phronesis*, which is when a person makes good decisions that lead to *eudaimonia*.

This Aristotelian approach lies behind what a number of educationalists are thinking and is central to this book.

Character and personality

Both 'character' and 'personality' have been theorised from classical times. Personality is often considered with five 'ranges' in mind: openness to experience, conscientiousness, extraversion, agreeableness and emotional stability. These components are usually thought to be more weighted by a person's genetics than the environment, so personality is a set of innate traits, with each of us on a spectrum on those five ranges.

The word 'character' comes from a Greek word that means 'stamp', indicating training, habit and formation. The former UK Prime Minister Harold Wilson was once asked if he was born in Yorkshire. 'Not born; forged!' he said. Yorkshire character ran through him like the lettering through a piece of Scarborough Rock.

Say my personality has a propensity to grumpiness, for instance, or laziness when it comes to housework. Or I'm naturally shy and run a mile from performing in public. To have character means I consciously catch myself before I inflict my bad mood on others. Or I establish a routine to clean the loo. With a big presentation coming up, I practise relaxation techniques and rescript the negative internal stuff to be more confident. Such things help me to develop character. I recognise my default personality and deliberately train myself into other habits.

In this scheme of things, personality is primary, and character is a secondary opportunity to nurture and prune the personality we have been given. With self-awareness and discernment, someone with character has developed particular characteristics that enhance, correct and shape the given personality traits.

Deliberate practice

Character is what we have when we train ourselves in particular virtues, or habits of the heart. There will be many habits, or fullnesses, that apply to us – and some that don't, but should. To be full of character is to have trained particular virtues and habits within us, so they become second nature, characteristic of who we are.

That training can be referred to as *deliberate practice*. This is practice that is focused, repetitive and purposeful, building up neural pathways in our brains that strengthen habitual behaviours in us. Playing scales on the piano. Drilling information until it's off by heart. Exercising daily. So we could say that character is the result of deliberate practice that shapes us in particular ways.

Character is built through habit

Character is built through habit, by learning through the repetition of deliberate practice. Whether this is training our bodies until a behaviour becomes second nature, accomplished without thinking about it (like cleaning teeth, riding a bike, driving, touch-typing), or more a matter of our social reaction in a given situation (like smiling when we enter the room, whatever we feel inside, or telling our partner we love them, even when we're irritated by that pernickety thing they've just done), we act or react in habitual ways and there's a predictability about us that becomes characteristic. Others come to recognise that that's what we're like. We are characteristically reliable, or kind, insightful, wise or perspicacious.

Of course, we can be characteristically unpleasant, or cruel, too – some people learn anti-social behaviour so it too is hard-wired. Or, in another direction, some find themselves reacting emotionally to situations because of past trauma that trap them into automatic patterns of behaviour which are hard to escape. Then we can be characteristically anxious, or fearful, with learned behaviours that are not good for us, or for others around us. Learning to develop a different character can help enormously, as Paul Tough shows in his book *How Children Succeed* (Tough 2012).

Education, as a lifelong enterprise, can establish consistent habits of body, heart and mind that enable the human person to grow towards fulfilment and flourishing in life. This may involve a commitment to excellence that entails real cost, even suffering – as many sportspersons, musicians or artists will attest.

Synaptogenesis – human and machine

Learning good habits takes deliberate practice which changes the plasticity of our brains. From our earliest days, we react to our environments, developing synapses and neural pathways, so some are strengthened over others and come to fire in particular ways. The building-up of neural pathways in our brains is technically called *synaptogenesis*.

It's interesting that AI scientists increasingly use this language to describe machine learning. They talk of hard-wiring connections and self-learning algorithms, modelled on synaptogenesis. We'll look further at this in Chapter 7.

In human brains, deep learning is reinforced, engrained, embedded in the neural pathways of our minds. When those neural pathways aren't formed from a baby's earliest days, as happens through parenting that doesn't establish good attachment from babyhood, then it becomes even more important to develop character, to train ourselves to respond differently.

This deep learning is not about writing ourselves in stone; it is not deterministic. That's very clear when we let ourselves down, when we behave, every so often, in ways that are 'out of character'. Sometimes our character, that deep learning, fails us when we're up against adversity. But usually character builds upon our given personality, through the deliberate cultivation of habits that shape our brains and our behaviour over time, in ways that enable us to flourish and aspire to fulfilment.

Character education has seen something of a revival over recent decades, after half a century when education theory was dominated by other ideas. Since the 1960s and 70s, when cognitive psychology came into its ascendancy with the pioneering work of Kohlberg, Piaget and Erikson, the emphasis centred much more on the individual children, and how their innate knowledge and skills could be developed appropriately to their readiness. These decades, according to Arthur and his colleagues, were dominated by psychology, and marked by moral subjectivism, which is when any moral judgement is dismissed as 'just a matter of opinion' (Arthur *et al.* 2017, p.56). We return to this in Chapter 11.

Progressivism

There's another '-ism' that's been dominant since the 1950s. 'Progressivism'[3] is the word E.D. Hirsch uses to describe two key ideas that belong in a long tradition of Romantic ideas dating back to Rousseau. One emphasised the innate goodness and ability of the child, where the job of education is to free the child to express what's within. This Hirsch calls 'naturalism'. Children are best educated, in this view, by allowing them to find out for themselves through hands-on experience, trusting their own innate goodness and nature to teach them what's right and wrong and what to learn. Wordsworth's lines capture this perfectly:

---

3   https://thetraditionalteacher.wordpress.com/what-is-progressivism

One impulse from a vernal wood
Can teach us more of man
Of moral evil and of good
Than all the sages can.

(William Wordsworth 1798, 'The Tables Turned')

In Progressivism, naturalism is coupled with 'formalism', which is what the teacher contributes; the how-to strategies that enable the child to gain transferable skills. As Hirsch writes:

> The various schools of 'progressive' educational thinkers have agreed on this point. A specific, factual curriculum, they hold, is not needed for gaining all-purpose cognitive skills and strategies. Instead of burdening our minds with a lot of dead facts, we should become expert in solving problems, in thinking critically – in reading fluently – and then we will be able to learn anything we need. (Hirsch 2006, p.11)

Hirsch says this sounds plausible, but he says it doesn't work. Instead, 'The only thing that transforms reading skill and critical thinking skill into general all-purpose abilities is a person's possession of general, all-purpose knowledge' (Hirsch 2006, p.12).

'Formalism' is a good example of what McGilchrist calls a LH approach, with all the appeal that the LH has in today's world. The emphasis on 'how-to' strategies, rather than openness to acquiring new knowledge, is so common today that it can be difficult to think differently. But that's what Hirsch (and McGilchrist in his field) are calling for. Something different to the naturalism and formalism that constitute 'progressive' educational ideology.

Educare and *educere*

The distinction between the two approaches – the re-emerging character education, and the child-centred progressivist ideology of recent decades – is caught by the two Latin words:

educare and *educere*. It's a good distinction.[4] *Educare* can be translated as 'to bring up, train, and to mould'. *Educere* means 'to lead and draw out that which lies within'. *Educare* is well illustrated by the African proverb that 'it takes the whole village to raise a child'. *Educere* is captured by Michelangelo's saying about sculpture: 'Every block of stone has a statue inside it and it is the task of the sculptor to discover it.'

The *educere* approach has a long history, going back to Jean-Jacques Rousseau, whose book *Émile* has had an enormous impact on education over the intervening centuries, maturing during the 1960s and 70s.

Rousseau's legacy

Rousseau saw us all as individuals, yearning to be free of the chains that bind us into families and society. Education enabled the child to become what he was, free from constraint, from the responsibilities that tied him to others. Rousseau's story of the education of *Émile* (1762) encouraged a pedagogical approach that turned away from training in traditional wisdom (*phronesis*, in Aristotelian parlance) and knowledge handed on from one generation to the next, towards an understanding of freedom as individualistic self-realisation. Throughout the Romantic Movement, the child became a symbol of the freedom to cast off the encumbrances of tradition and parents, and to follow her own star, a free spirit who should not be shackled by the responsibilities of society or civilisation (Cunningham 2005; Gavin 2012; Ward 2013).

Education today has to be both. The parent and teacher need to enable the child to discover her gifts and flourish; they also need to shape the child to be full of character. Too much of Rousseau's influence continues, however: you see it in the

---

4   A distinction made by the Archbishop of York, John Sentamu, at the launch of the Foundation for Educational Leadership, February 2017. See https://cms.archbishopofyork.org/concerns/education/church-england-foundation-educational-leadership

progressive educational literature that puts 'The Unique Child' in the centre. The progressive Rousseauian approach fails to recognise that a child is born into a family, traditions, the social networks and friendships that together will bring him up. That cultural literacy and knowledge are essential if he is to flourish.

Progressivism since Rousseau has focused on the individual. Autonomy – which sees the self as independent and free, self-governing – is individualistic in a way that can lead to narcissism. Émile was educated alone, with his tutor looking on – the blueprint for a child- and self-centred education. Maddy and Craig want Emily to be educated within a school and family, so she flourishes within different social settings and generations, engaging with what is other to her, culturally literate and thoughtful for others and the world around, wise and hopeful in the communities that surround her. They hope she will learn a rich hinterland, growing to be wise and knowledgeable. They hope her education will give her more than transferable skills and the ability to pass exams.

What this book offers

This book offers nine character 'fullnesses' to enrich education. In each chapter – or essay, really – I hope to inspire a different habit of the heart and provoke thoughtfulness about the hinterland of knowledge, deliberate practice, virtue and character that's needed to meet the challenges of the future. The nine essays will have an accumulative effect, with themes running through them that build a picture, rather than offer a linear argument that develops from one to the other. For example, throughout there will be attention to what the RH stretches for, the wisdom of a wide engagement with current reading and cultural understanding, including knowledge through bodily engagement with real material stuff.

Another theme is the distinction between *autonomy* with *heteronomy*.

Autonomy is attention to self and judges everything by what the self thinks within its own frame of insight. It started with key philosophers of the Enlightenment – Descartes, Kant and Rousseau – in the belief that the human reason had all it needed to work out what it needed to know, without reference to anything other, whether it be God, or other authorities or institutions. Perhaps here is the beginning of the dominance of the LH in Western culture, as McGilchrist understands it. The RH, on the other hand, reaches for the other, and so our humanity grows as we relate with other people around us, developing as a member of social groups, friendships and networks. The RH seeks other writers and ideas that stretch us and inspire us to think differently. The idea of *heteronomy* – the challenge of otherness to the self – is foundational to the approach of this book. To take a heteronomous approach is to understand the self as shaped and constituted by what is other to it. We shall return in greater depth to this.

Otherness, in the ultimate sense, is often called 'God'.

The resources of religion

If you read Jordan Peterson's latest book, *12 Rules for Life* (2018) you might be struck by how positive he is about religion in general and Christianity in particular. References to the Bible and to religious wisdom pervade his writing. He's taken with the importance of order in our lives, rather than chaos – and explains how that's a central theme of all the great religions (Peterson 2018). From a dream he has, suspended at the crossing of a Cathedral where existence meant 'suffering and transformation' (Peterson 2018, p.xxxiii), to the clear statement that 'the Bible is, for better or worse, the foundation document of Western civilisation (of Western values, Western morality, and Western conceptions of good and evil)'

(Peterson 2018, p.104),[5] Peterson is unashamedly positive about the contribution of religion to the good life.

James Arthur and his team in Birmingham are more cautious. For them, Aristotelian virtue and character have the advantage of speaking into a secular, multicultural world, without the baggage of religion. He gives credit, though: 'there's no reason to shy away from the fact, however, that notions of moral character and virtue are a mainstay of all the world's great religions…this should be seen as an advantage rather than a disadvantage' (Arthur *et al.* 2017, p.41).[6]

He's right. Despite the awful damage to the credibility of religion caused by abuse, with so many historic cases currently coming to light,[7] all the ancient religions have much to teach about how to live well. I have learned a little about other religions (not enough!), but the Christian tradition is the one I know best. It has good things to contribute to character education.

Christians affirm that faith gives a different perspective on the world. They see with different eyes. A person – like Steven Pinker – looks at the world with eyes that dismiss faith as irrational, unscientific, even damaging. Others will see truth as a social construct, relative to the values and ethos of any given culture – so the claims of religion to be true

---

5   Peterson goes on to say: 'It's the produce of processes that remain fundamentally beyond our comprehension. The Bible is a library composed of many books, each written and edited by many people. It's a truly emergent document – a selected, sequenced and finally coherent story written by no one and everyone over many thousands of years. The Bible has been thrown up, out of the deep, by the collective human imagination, which is itself a product of unimaginable forces operating over unfathomable spans of time. Its careful, respectful study can reveal things to us about what we believe and how we do and should act that can be discovered in almost no other manner.'

6   Arthur *et al.* go on to say: 'religious schools and individuals typically score higher on measures of moral development and virtue than non-religious ones,' but also notes that 'the difference between religious and non-religious participants seemed to lessen after a fairly short intervention to boost virtue literacy.'

7   I'm writing as the Independent Inquiry into Child Sex Abuse is holding its hearings in March 2018.

are discredited. Or someone might not see meaning beyond what is created in an individual life, which comes to an end in death. Some, like Brian Cox, although having no personal faith, are agnostic about whether a Creator God exists and see no conflict between science and religion.[8] There are many perspectives that describe the world in ways that shape knowledge so faith is rendered incredible, impossible, or simply rather bonkers. Notwithstanding the ease at which Christianity can be dismissed today, I draw on its wisdom.

So too does the 2016 Church of England *Vision for Education*, entitled *Deeply Christian, Serving the Common Good*, which offers an outline for 'Educating for Life in All its Fullness', by emphasising wisdom, hope, community and dignity as core virtues, inspired by a Christian vision.[9] That vision takes seriously the word *pleroma* as it's found often in the Bible – translated as abundance, fullness – and central to the teaching of Jesus, as in John's Gospel, chapter 10, verse 10, where Jesus says: 'I came that they may have life, and have it abundantly.'

If we are full of character, then our 'fullness' can be enhanced if we see ourselves as participating in the fullness of God, receiving the grace of God necessary to change and grow. There's a long history of Christian thought that draws on Plato as well as Aristotle, to understand our ultimate reality as dependent on the reality of God. To be 'full of character', then, is to see our humanity fulfilled as we participate in the fullness and abundance of God, 'in whom we live, and move and have our being' (Acts 17.28).

---

8   https://youtu.be/d9LHRfoIhTE
9   www.churchofengland.org/more/education-and-schools/vision-education

Nine 'fulnesses'

Why nine? I'm restricted by space! I would like to have included joyfulness, cheerfulness, faithfulness – and others. Peacefulness. But there you go.

We start with thankfulness. Cicero called it the parent of the virtues, for good reason. An account of Iris Murdoch's death takes us to the idea of life (and death) as a gift, for which we can give thanks. If we can give thanks for death, we can give thanks for most things (though not all, I know). Thankfulness is contrasted with entitlement.

A chapter on self-forgetfulness comes next, which engages with current preoccupations with the autonomous, entitled self; then a chapter that looks at character education in more depth, through the eyes of Maddy, with Emily about to start school. Three chapters follow that belong together – on carefulness (which explores the need for good, careful attachment between baby and parent), playfulness and resourcefulness (which focus on enabling imagination and resilience in the growing child).

A chapter on the impact of the digital age comes after that – and Maddy and Craig are back, picking up on some of the themes of their New Year's Eve party. Then, after two essays on thoughtfulness and fruitfulness, I look at the idea of 'fullness' in more detail as Maddy attends a lecture at the university where she studied. The last two of the nine, truthfulness and hopefulness follow. Chapter 13 considers the idea of 'fulfilment' in more depth, as the friends gather together for another meal together. The Conclusion draws the themes of the book together.

Chapter 1

Thankfulness

Being grateful: the parent of all virtue

Cicero wrote in a letter to Plancius: 'Being and appearing grateful: this is not only the greatest of the virtues but the parent of all others' (*Pro Plancio*, section 80).

A thankful person will naturally respond to life with gratitude. Practising thankfulness is the best place to start, if only because it enhances well-being. In one study, people were asked to list all the things they were grateful for, once a week for ten weeks. Those who developed the habit of thankfulness reported a greater sense of well-being, enjoyed better health and exercised more. They were more emotionally supportive to others (McCullough, Emmons and Tsang 2002; Watkins *et al.* 2003; see also Twenge and Campbell 2013).

A sense of gift

However, it's not simply that thankfulness enhances well-being that matters here. The habit of thankfulness is the parent of moral and emotional knowledge because it begins with a sense of gift, and a sense of gift immediately has the person looking outwards, away from the self, engaged with the gift and the source of the gift which is other to the self.

We can go through life with one of two approaches. One way is to feel entitled to things, so that we take what happens, and people around us, as ours by right, to be used, turned to our advantage or grumbled about. This puts the autonomous self in charge.

Or we can receive what happens as a gift – including life itself.

Entitlement – or gift. It's hard to do both at the same time. The way we go makes all the difference.

When children receive things – like life, or an education – as a gift rather than as an entitlement, they learn that they are not in the centre of things, but part of something bigger that they can learn about, share, and pass on in turn. The word 'tradition' means to hand on. When we receive our education as something handed on, we receive the best gift on offer. If we think we're entitled to it, then the whole emphasis shifts. Then my education is mine by right. It's mine, to take or leave, depending on how I feel. I'm in control, at the centre of things. Inevitably, this will mean a more instrumental and utilitarian approach.

It's easy to learn entitlement today. But we are happier and more fulfilled if we learn thankfulness. Less likely to end up with mental health issues, too. Learning how to say thank you from the earliest days of a child's life establishes an attitude to life and others that builds sociality and trust, friendship and generosity that helps on the journey to be full of character.

Thankfulness or entitlement?

Thankfulness can seem all rather naïve, though. What is the value of thankfulness when things are really tough? What about stuff that really needs to be changed because it's clearly unfair, unjust? What's the point in thankfulness then?

Humane and civilised societies have the law and human rights in place, a legislative structure to enable everyone, including the poorest and most vulnerable, to get what they need or deserve, and for those who have been harmed, to find justice. The law, what and whom it protects, is essential – and can be easily undermined by practices that blatantly flout trust, like corruption, or inhuman treatment and torture, or institutional abuse or racism. The justice system needs to be trustworthy – along with all civil and political institutions.

Human rights

There's debate about whether human rights actually exist or not. They do exist when they belong within a civilised society, where there's a rule of law to enforce them, and a general acceptance by the people that they are worth protecting. As such, they are a good and necessary thing. They give a sense of the rightness of the things that society holds in common – its understanding of how people should behave towards others and property. Human rights, with this approach, belong organically within a civilised society.

Children – in Western societies – are brought up knowing that they have rights, expecting to be treated in ways that respect their dignity and enhance their well-being and self-esteem.[1]

Entitlement

It can get complicated, though, when a sense of entitlement, or right, extends further and further into life. For example, to a perceived need for safety, including emotional safety. Jean Twenge has researched the attitudes of what she calls the iGen, who are the generation born after 1995. Many iGen'ers have such a sense of entitlement to safety and emotional security that, when they go to college, they can feel traumatised when someone disagrees with them (Twenge 2017). We're right at the heart – already – of just how complicated it can get, morally and legally.

Entitlement brings it back to 'me' all the time, to what I need and want. The LH is there, wanting to control the environment around me, so I don't have to take on stuff that's going to challenge me. If the RH is dominant, on the other hand,

---

1   www.unicef.org.uk/what-we-do/un-convention-child-rights

different opinions are welcomed with a sense of thankfulness for the new possibilities offered.

'I wouldn't mind doing that myself'

I've just finished John Bayley's account of his marriage to Iris Murdoch, who was one of the great twentieth-century novelists. He stayed with her during her last five years as she declined with Alzheimer's (Bayley 2003). He never fell out of love with her, despite her inability to relate to him, and his deep loneliness that prompted all sorts of fantasies and imaginary friends.

It's a story of thankfulness. In 1994 Bayley watched her lose everything. His account is brave and honest.

Iris died in Vale House on February the eighth 1999. The reassurance I and all those other friends could not give her had come at last. This was the best of the friends.

She had grown steadily weaker. Without bother or fuss, as if someone she trusted had helped her to come to a decision, she stopped eating and drinking. Gentle pressure from those kind nurses but no insistence. No horror of being put on a drip.

During the last week she took to opening her blue eyes very wide, as if merrily. Her face was still round and beautiful, although the body I held in my arms was shrunken and light. When she died I closed her eyes and then opened them, as if we could still play together. She had looked and not seen for days, but now she seemed to see me.

Tricia O'Leary, the head of the home, came in. She was crying, rather to my surprise, as she must have seen this happen a great many times before. But they had all come to love Iris very much.

Dying had been so quiet that I found myself saying to Tricia, 'I wouldn't mind doing that myself.' She smiled and took my hand and Maureen brought me a cup of strong tea.

I thought thankfully of those 'few words' no one was going to have to say at a funeral or a Memorial Service. Iris had told me years back that she didn't want either. She had been firm about that. So there would be a Wake instead, a big party for all her friends. (Bayley 2003, pp.437–8)

Thankfulness for death. Death as the last and best friend. 'I wouldn't mind doing that myself.'

Bayley gave Murdoch a good death that was five years in the happening.

Euthanasia: a good death. Today, it's a word used to campaign for the right to die. This is an instance when I don't think the language of entitlement is right. To insist that we have the right to die when we choose (or when someone else chooses for us?) takes us to the heart of the difference between seeing our life and all that happens as a gift, or, conversely, as an entitlement. If we have a right to things, then we will approach our lives in a certain way. If everything is a gift, the chances are we will be against euthanasia.

Not rights but gifts

It's a basic choice – gift or entitlement. It doesn't mean we have to reject the law and human rights. They are a gift too. Without the law to protect human life and property, to control behaviour that is anti-social and dangerous to public safety, society would soon collapse. Without human rights legislation, the vulnerable are even more vulnerable. But to understand ourselves only in terms of rights and entitlement sells humanity short. Humanity is more than that. A society founded on a sense of gratitude, rather than a sense of entitlement, offers a different culture in which to grow up. To use McGilchrist's metaphorical approach: A sense of gift engages the RH and its attention to that which is other to us. Rights and entitlement focus our LH in a forensic direction, drilling down into me and what's owed me. Without a sense of thankfulness for the privilege of the gifts we have received, we end up always wanting more of what we think we should have, and we end up joyless and selfish. We don't learn how to give and take, to reciprocate good will, praise and forgiveness.

Saying grace

One of the most obvious and simple ways to develop a culture of thankfulness is the habit of saying 'grace' before (and after) meals. Rabbi Jonathan Sacks writes this:

> There is one spiritual discipline which religion once gave us and which we still need. It is the simple act of saying 'thank you' to God. There are prayers in which we ask God for the things we do not have, but there are others in which we simply thank God for the things we do have: family, friends, life itself with its counterpoint of pleasure and pain, the sheer exaltation of knowing that we are here when we might not have been. Gratitude, the acknowledgement that what we have is a gift, is one of the most profound religious emotions. It is to the mind what serotonin is to the brain. (Sacks 2000, p.15)

Saying grace can be a good way to begin the habit of thankfulness within a family. It celebrates a sense of blessing in life that acknowledges the other – other people around us with whom we eat, and those who have prepared the food. It is the opportunity to remember people who haven't got food to eat, strengthening the gratitude and the sense of how precious the food is before us. It recognises the otherness of the food we are about to consume – that it belongs to the good, material world that we rely upon in so many ways. Saying grace, blessing the food and the meal, takes us out of ourselves and a utilitarian view of food, and into the sociality that makes us human, part of the whole of the natural order so we remember our stewardship of the gifts we are given and use them wisely. If we deliberately practise saying grace, we will grow in thankful character, and so will the children around us.

The Church of England (CofE) *Vision for Education* of 2016 locates thankfulness firmly within a sense of God's blessing:

Blessing is a central biblical activity, forming what might be called a dynamic ecology of blessing: God blesses human beings and creation; creation and human beings can bless God; humans can bless each other; and the dynamic crosses generations and peoples. Like other ecologies, it can go terribly wrong, but the vision is of God-given fullness of life in which each person is both blessed and a blessing. Education can be one of the greatest blessings in anyone's life. (Church of England 2016, p.19)

Learning how to say 'thank you' and 'please', to receive thankfully rather than to expect with a sense of entitlement can start early in a child's life. It can be part of the culture of a school as well. Michaela Community School has appreciation sessions at every meal, as part of their overall culture of hard work, kindness and gratitude. The children are thankful, and happier as a result, says the school's founder, Katharine Birbalsingh.[2]

Cultural hinterland as gift

The quality of mercy is not strained.
It droppeth as the gentle rain from heaven,
Upon the place beneath.
It is twice blessed.
It blesseth him that gives and him that takes.

(Shakespeare, *The Merchant of Venice*, Act IV, Scene I)

Our cultural heritage – including such poetry as this – is a gift. It allows us to open our hearts and minds, to grow our souls and imaginations in directions we don't anticipate. A cultural hinterland waters and blesses us with images and metaphors, giving us rich language, well-known words, prayers and poems that, when learned by heart, form us in the habit of giving thanks for knowledge as a gift. We are given words which are there when needed, with emotional resilience and wisdom,

2   http://mcsbrent.co.uk

that frame life in ways that nourish the soul. One of the ways to practise thankfulness is to learn poetry off by heart, giving thanks for the cultural literacy we receive.

Dorothy L. Sayers wrote an essay in 1948, *The Lost Tools of Learning*, in which she described three stages of child development:

> Looking back upon myself (since I am the child I know best and the only child I can pretend to know from the inside) I recognise in myself three stages of development. These, in a rough-and-ready fashion, I will call the Poll-parrot, the Pert and the Poetic – the latter, coinciding, approximately, with the onset of puberty. The Poll-parrot stage is the one in which learning by heart is easy and, on the whole, pleasurable; whereas reasoning is difficult and, on the whole, little relished. At this age, one readily memorises the shapes and appearances of things; one likes to recite the number-plates of cars; one rejoices in the chanting of rhymes and the rumble and thunder of unintelligible polysyllables; one enjoys the mere accumulation of things. (Sayers 1948, p.15)

Learning things off by heart from the very beginning of a child's life, starting with nursery rhymes and songs, helps the development of language. More than anything, though, it gives a child the beginnings of a hinterland of music, literature, poetry and prose that is a gift for life.

Something similar happens when people go to church and experience what is called 'the liturgy', which is the set words that have been developed over the centuries. Good liturgy has its own pace and rhythms, words and actions and musical beauty, which carries the worshippers along as if in a deep river where familiar, rich images wash over them and soak deeply in. The main prayer at a service of communion, when the bread and wine are blessed, is called the Eucharist – which means 'Thanksgiving' in Greek. At the heart of the religious sensibility – and not just Christian – is a sense of thanksgiving.

To cultivate the habit of thankfulness is to know there are things that aren't ours by right or entitlement. We don't deserve them. They are ours only as gift. Saying 'thank you' instils the best possible beginning to lifelong education: the habit of thankfulness.

But what of suffering and pain?

What of stuff that's bad and abusive?

Abusive behaviour from others should not be received at all, let alone as a gift. If someone is cruel, or causes pain or harm, there is no gift there. And when we inflict pain or suffering on someone else, we should take responsibility for the damage we've done, and seek to say sorry. Sometimes the pain caused is unbearable. Sometimes the abuse requires the law; reporting it is absolutely the right thing to do. When it falls short of a crime, though, we should try as hard as we can to forgive and be forgiven.

In the older version of the Christian Lord's Prayer it says: 'Forgive us our trespasses as we forgive them that trespass against us.' The word 'trespass' reminds me that I shouldn't go where I'm not welcome. I shouldn't trespass on the sacred ground that is someone else without their permission. When I have done that and caused pain, I have felt deep shame and guilt – awful negative feelings that cry out for forgiveness. Learning to forgive, and be forgiven, belongs within the frame of thanksgiving.

Two wolves

Forgiveness. We're back with 'give', or gift. To forgive is to re-establish the sense of givenness to life and relationship. It's different when we have the 'entitlement' approach; then, when a wrong's been done, talk of forgiveness will often cause offence. It's satisfaction that's required; the wrongdoer needs to be

punished. The LH drills down, in a transactional way, to what
is owed. When satisfaction doesn't come, the wronged person
often continues to carry the weight of wrong, festering away.
There's a popular story about two wolves, which describes two
wolves inside us: one benign and good; the other full of anger,
regret and bitterness. The one that wins is the one that's fed.[3]

Sometimes, though, the only way the hurt and pain can be
resolved is through proper legal processes. All organisations
today have a duty to ensure that children and vulnerable adults
are safe, and to report if harm is done, or has been done in the
past.[4] There's no excuse at all. Talk of forgiveness is inappropriate
when criminal abuse has occurred.[5]

When we live with pain or suffering, caused by circumstances
that don't involve criminal abuse, then, sometimes, it's
appropriate to see the experience with a thankful heart. It
brings us back to John Bayley and how he received Iris's illness
and death. Pain and suffering that is ours simply because that's
life, which has to be endured, will test us to the limit and often
beyond. It's easy to blame others, to be angry, to become bitter.
To live through pain and suffering, often we don't know how
we manage it. There's a story that Christians often tell, entitled
Footprints in the Sand.[6] Sometimes only afterwards can we find
a sense of thankfulness.

The opportunity to give thanks

When we cultivate a sense of thankfulness, our character grows.
We stop feeling entitled to things and begin to see everything
as a gift. This day – even with any pain or suffering that might
happen (and who knows what's in store?) – this life, is the
opportunity to give thanks.

---

3   www.firstpeople.us/FP-Html-Legends/TwoWolves-Cherokee.html
4   www.nspcc.org.uk/preventing-abuse/safeguarding
5   For more on forgiveness, see https://www.theforgivenessproject.com
6   www.onlythebible.com/Poems/Footprints-in-the-Sand-Poem.html

Malcolm Guite, a contemporary UK poet,[7] found himself at a bus stop one morning, with the words of an old prayer going around in his mind.[8]

> One of the pleasures of familiar texts, often repeated, known by heart without there ever having been a time when you consciously memorised them, is that they are richly available whenever you summon them, and they sometimes come unbidden to your mind in idle moments: while waiting for trains or buses, or on some short familiar walk. So it was that I found the words of the General Thanksgiving praying themselves through me as I waited for an early morning bus to Cambridge – a bus that, I hoped, would get me to college in time for breakfast. (*Church Times*, 2 March 2018, p.56)

He goes on to think about the words of the prayer which offer 'most humble and hearty thanks' – and is led to contemplate what sort of breakfast comes to mind. Not muesli, but a full English, he thinks, because the prayer is a generous prayer, full of 'alls': *all* mercies, *all* thy goodness and loving kindness, *all* the blessings of this life, *all* honour and glory.

The General Thanksgiving is a 'both/and' prayer – with lots of things on the plate. He comments:

> the difference, of course, is that when it comes to breakfast you can, I regret to say, have too much of a good thing, but you can never have too much thanksgiving. A hearty breakfast might leave you a little weighted and ponderous, but a hearty

---

7 www.malcolmguite.com

8 'Almighty God, Father of all mercies, we thine unworthy servants do give thee most humble and hearty thanks for all thy goodness and loving-kindness to us and to all men. We bless thee for our creation, preservation, and all the blessings of this life; but above all for thine inestimable love in the redemption of the world by our Lord Jesus Christ, for the means of grace, and for the hope of glory. And, we beseech thee, give us that due sense of all thy mercies, that our hearts may be unfeignedly thankful; and that we show forth thy praise, not only with our lips, but in our lives, by giving up our selves to thy service, and by walking before thee in holiness and righteousness all our days; through Jesus Christ our Lord, to whom, with thee and the Holy Spirit, be all honour and glory, world without end. Amen.'

thanksgiving tends to lighten your step, and give you edge and appetite for all that the day might bring. (*Church Times*, 2 March 2018, p.56)

Conclusion

This chapter begins the fullnesses with the habit of thankfulness to emphasise the importance of the attitude that parent, teacher and child bring to education. If the attitude is one of thankfulness, children are likely to grow with a greater sense of fulfilment and mental well-being and appreciate their education as a gift to be enjoyed, nourished and continued through life.

Developing habits of thankfulness starts early, as soon as the child can speak. Learning to say 'please' and 'thank you', and then learning words, songs, poems and rhymes off by heart, increases the sense of a gift received that endures through life, beginning the development of moral and emotional knowledge that enhances resourcefulness to face the future.

Thankfulness turns the self away from *autonomy* towards *heteronomy* – the engagement with the other that stirs the self out of the need to control the environment with a sense of entitlement and into an appreciation of gift and blessing.

Thankfulness:
from conscious incompetence to unconscious competence

How might a school culture reflect the character of thankfulness and challenge a culture of entitlement?

Culture: What literature, music, art best express thankfulness? How might children engage and respond with appreciation?

Character: What habits could children practise deliberately to be thankful, expressing appreciation when appropriate?

Call: As a way of understanding the profession of teaching as a vocation, what more could the headteacher and staff do to model thankfulness?

Go to the website https://gratefulness.org

- Say 'thank you' for one thing every day and make a note of what it was.

- Encourage, even insist, that children you know say 'please' and 'thank you' appropriately.

- Say grace before meals.

- Thank someone else for something good he has done that hasn't been noticed.

- As Professor John Rodwell[9] said:

   When water arrives in your sink or springs from your shower, give thanks for its presence and purity. Send it on its way as little dirtied as you can, mindful of the marks you yourself leave on Creation. And while the water is with you, remember that you have it on loan.

---

9   From a talk he gave at The College of the Resurrection during Holy Week, 2018.

Chapter 2

Self-Forgetfulness

There's an ancient myth of Narcissus, as true now as ever.

A sixteen-year-old youth, and very beautiful, Narcissus aroused great love in all who met him, including the nymph Echo. He rejected her, as he rejected all advances, and she wasted away to the haunting voice we hear in rocks and cliffs. One day, Narcissus lay down to drink at a quiet pool in the woods and for the first time he saw his own reflection. Immediately he was entranced, besotted. He fell in love for the first time. Whenever he reached out to touch, though, the image rippled away. He could not draw himself away from the beauty before him. He wasted away, as Echo had done. His body was never found, only the white and gold flower that nods in the wind in the springtime of the year, the narcissus flower.

Charlie Brooker uses the image of a black phone, cracked across. The impact is simple and immediate, with powerful resonances in a culture that many think is increasingly narcissistic and over-preoccupied with the self. And broken.

This chapter covers a lot of ground, to capture the narcissism that puts the self at the centre of things, with a forensic LH attention to me, myself, I, and seeming inability to empathise, or engage with otherness around. Not everyone, of course, is narcissistic, or even self-absorbed – many, many people and young people are not. The rising rates of mental illness, though, suggest something is wrong, and it might be that McGilchrist's metaphorical distinction between the LH and the RH helps: that we find it difficult today to access the wider and deeper hinterland of emotional and moral knowledge that keeps us sane.

Will Storr's book *Selfie* offers a credible history of the growth of self-preoccupation through the twentieth century, tracing its progress from a key figure, Ayn Rand, who was a fanatical individualist and influenced many people in a large number of walks of life, from economics to education (Storr 2017). The whole idea of 'self-esteem', which seems so natural to us today, has its own story, and it's worth hearing, as Storr researched it.

Storr illustrates what he calls a self-obsessed age by telling the story of a young person called CJ. McGilchrist's description of the madness of a LH dominated world could be this.

CJ's parents are anxious, even to the extent that they move house to protect her. They give her everything she asks for, and constantly affirm and praise her, parenting on the principle that her happiness is paramount.

CJ grows up with no boundaries, and with an intense anger has no outlet, except when she starts to self-harm. Storr's graphic description of the power she feels as she slashes herself with a razor takes us to the heart of why so many young people self-harm today. He captures the sense of power that results. CJ has been brought up to put herself first. Storr describes how obsessed she is by her selfie habit (Storr 2017, pp.281ff).

The gamified individualist economy

CJ isn't every young person, by any means. Most young people aren't brought up with so much indulgence, for one thing. But, Storr says, she is a product of a neoliberal humanist culture where our humanity has become a product in a game. He calls it a 'gamified individualist economy' (Storr 2017, p.284). The self is a pawn that plays competitively on digital platforms for likes, feedback and friends – the approval of the tribe (Storr 2017). When we win the game, we can become extremely wealthy celebrities. When we are rejected, there can be appalling consequences, contributing to the already terrible statistics on suicide, self-harm and eating disorder (Storr 2017).

The narcissistic culture that creates someone like CJ is identifiable throughout the Western world and its cultures, wherever neoliberalism is the dominant economic system. Neoliberalism turns 'the self' into a product, and so we commodify our appearance and life to feed the market forces that have infiltrated our shallowest desires. We are seduced by our identity, which is then intensified into tribal belonging that is re-enforced and perpetuated by the echo chambers of social media, trapping us as effectively as CJ was trapped in her parent's luxurious mansion.

The habit of self-forgetfulness, alongside that of thankfulness, are two basic character fullnesses that are worth practising, particularly with children, if the 'self' isn't to become a commodity like this, in a hyper-individualised society. As Narcissus showed, there are deeply destructive impulses at play, and the old truth holds good, that we will find ourselves more, the less attention we give 'me, myself, I'. Practising self-forgetfulness is to focus away from the black mirror and seek humane relationships with others. We know ourselves best as we are known in love by others.

Individualism/individuality

It's really important to understand the roots of individualism, so we can think 'the individual' differently.

Individualism is not the same as individuality – there's a crucial distinction.

Individualism creates the solipsistic, atomised 'self' who is conceived as separate, divided off from others – it's this that can be commodified so easily. Individuality, on the other hand, sees us as indivisible from the whole. A good example is the member of a choir, or an orchestra, or sports team, where each individual has their part to play, contributing to the body. Without their gifts, the whole is diminished. If someone plays the prima donna part, with an inflated sense of self, she damages the performance by throwing everyone else out.

McGilchrist's metaphorical approach would explain it like this: the LH sees the individual as an atomised item, to be compartmentalised; the RH sees the whole as greater than the sum of its parts. Western society has been seduced by the LH attention, so the individual is where we start in our understanding of what it means to be human. Much better to see our individuality as that which belongs to others, to the team, the community, the school, the orchestra – whatever the social body is that we belong to.

When we are individualistic, we become vulnerable to economic forces that will shrewdly market our 'selves' to ourselves.[1]

Hyper-individualism: economic roots

The *economic* roots of the neoliberalism that has turned the 'self' into a marketable commodity are short, extending only to the 1980s when Friedrich Hayek[2] influenced Margaret Thatcher and Ronald Reagan with his dream of a market economy free from state regulation. Neoliberalism provided the economic soil for new markets to emerge with the 'self' centre stage. Storr notes:

> Free markets become the engines of a new kind of society in which everything possible would be reconfigured around the principle of competition. The human world [became] a kind of game in which we'd all compete with each other... All this would put individualism back, where it belonged, at the heart of Western Society. (Storr 2017, pp.179–80)

Hayek's neoliberalism took root in the USA in the 1940s with the help of the Mont Pelerin Society and flourished in the 1970s through a network of well-funded 'think tanks', to

---

1   Simon Blackburn is good on this in *Mirror, Mirror: The Uses and Abuses of Self-Love*, Princeton University Press, 2014, chapter 3.

2   Friedrich Hayek, born Vienna, Austria (1899–1992).

bear fruit as the guiding principle behind the governments of Reagan and Thatcher.

When Thatcher said, 'Economics is the method. The object is to change the soul,' she meant that British people had to rediscover the virtue of traditional values such as hard work and thrift.[3] The deregulation of the banks in 1986 didn't lead to this, though, but rather to atomised individuals (there is no such thing as society, remember) competing in supposedly self-correcting, wealth-creating free markets whose 'invisible hand' could be relied upon to raise everyone into a stable and wealthy future. In this new neoliberal world, you had to be fitter, smarter and faster than your neighbours. As Storr puts it, 'it meant doubling and then tripling down on the fabulous power of Me' (Storr 2017, p.182).

Hyper-individualism: cultural roots

The *cultural* roots of hyper-individualism go back further and deeper.

Rousseau's Émile was taught to disdain the social connections that humanity previously knew to be essential to a healthy society and individual life (read John Donne's 'No Man is an Island', for example, for contrast).[4] Émile's fictional upbringing became the blueprint for individualistic, child-centred education, nurtured by the Romantic Movement, and developed by the pedagogy of John Dewey, and the psychology of Jean Piaget. You could say that CJ is Émile's direct descendant.

The cultural story of twentieth-century hyper-individualism took a significant turn when the idea of 'self-esteem' took hold

---

3   See Gideon Rachman's opinion piece in *The Financial Times*, 'The End of the Thatcher Era', 27 April 2009.

4   'No man is an Iland, intire of itselfe; every man is a peece of the Continent, a part of the maine; if a Clod bee washed away by the Sea, Europe is the lesse, as well as if a Promontorie were, as well as if a Manor of thy friends or of thine owne were; any mans death diminishes me, because I am involved in Mankinde; And therefore never send to know for whom the bell tolls; It tolls for thee.' From John Donne's 'Meditation XVII' from *Devotions upon Emergent Occasions*, 1624.

of the steering wheel. Storr (2017) tells the story of Ayn Rand's excessive individualism, and how one of her followers, John Vasconcellos, brought 'self-esteem' to the world.

Self-esteem

Manipulating uncertain research from the University of California, Vasconcellos argued that poor self-esteem was linked with alcoholism, drug abuse, crime and violence, child abuse, teenage pregnancy, prostitution, chronic welfare dependency and failure of children to learn (Storr 2017), and he managed, by 1990, with a good public relations and media campaign, to convince the government to make it policy. California soaked it up, and the world followed, teaching students from the youngest age how special they were, how much their self-esteem mattered (Storr 2017).

The great problem with self-esteem is it plays directly into a narcissistic culture and teaches the child entitlement (Twenge and Campbell 2013). What are the signs? Firstly, the parenting will tend to be permissive, and the education will be focused on self-esteem. Then the child will have bought into a media culture that peddles ideas of shallow celebrity as the goal for life. The child will have been brought up with fantasies that construct the perfect self, full of self-esteem, with little concern for relationships, or responsibility and self-control (Twenge and Campbell 2013).

The age of narcissism

There is convincing research that Western culture has shifted in a narcissistic direction. The original myth of Narcissus says it all, with its nihilistic and morbid account of the tragedy of self-admiration. People with narcissistic personality disorder see themselves as fundamentally superior (special, entitled and unique). They lack emotional warmth or caring and loving relationships with other people, and the result is a grandiose, inflated self-image and lack of deep connection to others. When the culture is narcissistic it looks like this.

Parents are more likely to be overindulgent and over-praise, putting children in charge, dressing them in clothes that declare 'I'm the Boss'. Such parenting conveys a discomfort with authority, preferring instead to befriend their children, and treat them as equals (Twenge and Campbell 2013). This is the age of the weak parent, who gives too 'much power to children [and] teaches an entitled view of life, with all of the fun and choices but none of the responsibility'.

Instead, to promote success, it's much better to give praise for working hard, rather than telling a child she is special and smart (Twenge and Campbell 2013, pp.82–4). Teaching self-esteem takes the child and his parents into a narcissistic 'I am special' loop, based on the mistaken premise that children who feel good about themselves will be more likely to follow the rules and not cheat or lie. The evidence points in the opposite direction. Special people don't need to follow the rules, and narcissistic people are more, not less, likely to cheat, just as they are more likely to be aggressive (Twenge and Campbell 2013).[5]

Entitlement

We looked at entitlement in the essay on thankfulness. It's one of the key components of narcissism.

Entitled people don't see the world through another person's eyes or empathise with another's misfortunes; instead they focus on their own experience, outcomes and

5   Evidence that parental overpraise is a cause of narcissism was presented in 2015, at the Proceedings of the National Academy of Sciences. The aim was to test two long-competing theories: the idea that children become narcissistic when their parents are cold and rejecting, or that children become more narcissistic when parents over-praise them. Dr Eddie Brummelman and colleagues found 'very strong support…that the more parents overvalued their kids, the more narcissistic their kids had become six months later. There was no evidence that lack of parental warmth or affection predicted narcissism' (see www.pnas.org/content/112/12/3659).

needs (Twenge and Campbell 2013). Entitlement has a far-reaching and corrosive effect on society, destroying practices of reciprocity and obligation, which are the glue that binds society together. Entitlement dissolves that glue (Twenge and Campbell 2013).

Where is religion in all this?

Religion and volunteering to help others should, in theory, counteract this sort of cultural narcissism. That's not been the case. Churches have withered when they have not aligned themselves with The Individual; whereas when they have adapted to the narcissistic culture, they have thrived. It's bad news for more traditional religious organisations that have little to offer the individual up front, but challenge narcissism by teaching belief in an other larger than the self, rules that apply to everyone, and the value of community, forgiveness, self-sacrifice and humility.

In the USA this has led to some interesting religious phenomena. Twenge and Campbell describe the Lakewood Church in Houston, Texas, where religion fundamentally aligns with narcissistic culture. Joel Osteen, the pastor, taught that 'God didn't create you to be average'; 'God would not have put the dream in your head if He had not already given you everything you need to fulfil it', with a clear endorsement of a prosperity Christianity.

That's the USA. It's true, though, across the Western world – the religions that don't buy into the individualistic/narcissistic culture are dying. Many church congregations attempt to appeal by offering what they think the world wants – worship and music in cultural forms that resonate, emotivist preaching and marketing holiness in a world that demands branding. Such a response will always be reactive and shallow, as it doesn't offer a proper counter-cultural critique of hyper-individualism.

To promote instead a different understanding of what it means to be a human person, living a deep and fulfilled life, is to draw on resources that are there within Christianity, and within good religions the world over, where religion builds on thankfulness rather than entitlement. Where loving one's neighbour and fostering social cohesion enable the individual to flourish, not at the expense of one's neighbours, but building the trust and reciprocity that all societies need to survive and grow. Good religion offers the opportunity for the individual to find themselves and personal fulfilment in relationship and community.

Unless the religions of the Western world can recommend this in today's societies and culture, their essential gift to humanity is lost and humanity is much the poorer. Indeed, is at danger of self-destructing, as Narcissus did, in a nihilistic vortex of Me.

What's needed is a healthy dose of self-forgetfulness

Storr says that the story of our culture about 'the self' is starting to fail, 'to creak and crack as the actual truth of what it is to be a living human presses in on it' (Storr 2017, p.328). Charlie Brooker's black mirror image again. Storr advocates psychological tests to find out who we really are and learn to accept ourselves and others as the flawed human beings we are. I don't think this goes deep enough. Ultimately, this threatens to remain within a loop of self-regard.[6] To go deeper is to draw on the wisdom of religions that have been wrestling with the problem of the self for millennia.

According to Matthew's gospel: 'Those who find their life will lose it, and those who lose their life for my sake will find

---

6   Simon Blackburn expresses some concern about therapy. He says about Polonius' speech 'To thine own self be true': 'What if Laertes' own self is insincere and insecure, irresolute and unknowing, all the way down?... Even worse, Laertes' own self might be steeped in sin. "Get in touch with your inner self," urges the therapist, perhaps unconscious that the inner self may be a pretty nasty piece of work' (Blackburn 2014, p.181).

it' (Matthew 10.39). This enigmatic saying is worth exploring further. The 'self', as contemporary Western culture promotes it, is living out the first part, 'losing' its life in excessive 'finding', without any attention to the latter part.

Losing self to find it

Many will go in a Buddhist direction, taking us to self-forgetfulness by way of mindfulness. The popularity of mindfulness has grown significantly since the beginning of the twenty-first century and now has a widespread appeal and effectiveness in coping with anxiety, chronic pain, insomnia and all sorts of other medical conditions. Children, adolescents – people of all ages – are finding benefit from the practice. It's a way of inner stillness and peace, enabling change to the way you think and feel, and helping to cope with difficult situations and make wise decisions.

Anything that helps people cope with life better has to be a good thing. But I am left cautious, not only because mindfulness is lucrative business, feeding the neoliberal culture with its offer of stress-relief and personalised peace. As long ago as 2013, Purser and Loy wrote 'beyond McMindfulness', suspicious that the 'universal panacea for resolving almost every area of daily concern' was a 'lucrative cottage industry'.[7] Mindfulness can also become a self-absorbed process, dependent on human effort, where there is no ultimate other to guide the inner journey. Some have reported how nightmarish the experience can be.[8]

---

7   They write: 'Business savvy consultants pushing mindfulness training promise that it will improve work efficiency, reduce absenteeism, and enhance the "soft skills" that are crucial to career success. Some even assert that mindfulness training can act as a "disruptive technology," reforming even the most dysfunctional companies into kinder, more compassionate and sustainable organizations. So far, however, no empirical studies have been published that support these claims.' www.huffingtonpost.com/ron-purser/beyond-mcmindfulness_b_3519289.html

8   www.theguardian.com/lifeandstyle/2016/jan/23/is-mindfulness-making-us-ill

Matthew's gospel captures something else: the self gained not by human effort, but by losing the self in order to find it. This is to embrace *heteronomy* rather than *autonomy*. It's to turn away from the belief that the self is sufficient to itself, and to understand that the self only really finds itself in relation with 'the other'. It's to reject the narcissism of the neoliberal gamified culture, in order to find the human self, to seek self-forgetfulness, to remember who we truly are. This is unlikely to flood ever-greedy markets, but it could undermine their power by refusing to see the 'self' as a commodity. It is to offer what Christianity and other religions should be offering, which is a bold critique of narcissistic culture wherever it is found, for the sake of the human self. It is to promote a different anthropology, one where the self is found and fulfilled within the fullness of God.

Practices of self-forgetfulness will include voluntary commitments to others in need, and anything that focuses the attention away from the self, towards other activities and people. It is to close down the constant monologue inside your head that is absorbed with self, and instead think about other, fruitful activities, and other people – which is what prayer does. It is to look to the world beyond your head.

The world beyond your head

Matthew Crawford's book about attention to the world beyond our heads offers rich resources for self-forgetfulness (Crawford 2015).

He is concerned by the amount of attention that's given to the virtual world stimulated in our heads by digital engagement. He speaks of a cultural iceberg in which our mental lives are fractured, with diminished attention spans and a widespread sense of distraction, our brains rewired by new habits of information grazing and electronic stimulation. We lack time and space for serious, concentrated engagement. We also lack 'the sort of guidance that once would have been supplied by tradition, religion, or the kinds of communities that make deep demands on us' (Crawford 2015, pp.4–5). We have allowed our attention to be monetized by advertisements, by hassle, by information, such that 'if you want your [attention] back you're going to have to pay for it' (Crawford 2015, p.12).

This is a book about attention. He refers to Simone Weil to make the point that 'to attend to anything in a sustained way requires actively *excluding* all the other things that grab at our attention. It requires, if not ruthlessness toward oneself, a capacity for self-regulation' (Crawford 2015, p.15). Without such self-control, we become open to manipulation. With self-control we can allow ourselves to submit to 'things that have their own intractable ways, whether the thing be a musical instrument, a garden, or the building of a bridge' (Crawford 2015, p.24). We can forget the autonomy of our sense of self and attend to the reality of the world around us.

Autonomy and heteronomy

Crawford knows that the terms 'submission' and 'authority' jar the modern ear. He uses the distinction of *autonomy* with *heteronomy* and, as we've seen, it's an important distinction. To recap: *Autonomy* is attention to self and judges everything by what the self thinks, within its own frame of insight. It started with key philosophers of the Enlightenment – Descartes, Kant, and Rousseau – in the belief that the human reason had all it needed to work out what it needed to know, without reference to any other, whether it be God, or other authorities or institutions. Perhaps here is the beginning of the dominance of the LH in Western culture, as McGilchrist (2010) understands it. Crawford writes:

> In a culture predicated on this autonomy-heteronomy distinction, it is difficult to think clearly about attention – the faculty that joins us to the world – because everything located outside your head is regarded as a potential source of unfreedom, and therefore a threat to the self. This makes education a tricky matter. (Crawford 2015, p.131)

Heteronomy, on the other hand, has the humility to accept the authority of that which is other to the self. As such, it isn't easily understood today.

Crawford commends embracing the otherness of what is around us, attending to it, and giving it authority to change us. Instead of fearing that the other might compromise me, I need to be open to allow it to *constitute* the self – change and form me differently.

This is to encourage the self to attend to what it isn't – other people, the world around, objects and things. Material stuff. God. This is to allow what we do – the skills we might acquire, the training and expertise we gain – to shape our being, who we are. Doing becomes being. This can be best understood if we think about becoming competent as a cook, or as a gardener, by practising the skills deliberately. Disciplined by this or that practice, we become a cook, or a gardener. The activity is more than just skills: I become what I do. Through the exercise of a skill, the self that acts in the world takes on a definite shape. It comes to be in a relation of *fit* to a world it has *grasped*.

This is different to the autonomous self which stays in a relation of mastery in the world. It stays in control of the self, accruing transferable skills to itself, but refusing to see the self as changed by them.

When we operate as autonomous selves, we are dealing with a world essentially of our own creation and projection. This is, Crawford says, to accept the invitation to narcissism, and makes us more easily manipulated.

> As atomized individuals called to create meaning for ourselves, we find ourselves the recipients of all manner of solicitude and guidance. We are offered forms of unfreedom that come slyly wrapped in autonomy talk: NO LIMITS! as the credit card offer says. YOU'RE IN CHARGE. Autonomy talk speaks the consumerist language of maximizing the number of choices you face… It suggests that freedom is something we

are entitled to, and it consists in liberation from constraints imposed by one's circumstances. (Crawford 2015, p.26)

Instead of the false freedom offered by this rhetoric of choice, Crawford offers the freedom of disciplined attention that accepts the otherness of the real world and its constraints, working with what's given. Anything that takes practice, that we drill ourselves at until we become more and more expert, has the capacity to change us. You're working with the stuff of the world around and it shapes you, your hands. This is the opportunity to forget yourself in the discipline of practice, engaging in the acquisition of skills and working within the constraints of the real world.

The task, then, is one of losing the autonomous self by paying attention to the world around, learning skills and changing by submission to the other, in order to find myself as a cook, or a gardener, or an engineer, or a teacher. Then I am constituted by the knowledge and expertise I have, which is other to me and shapes me.

Crawford's argument is deeply interesting, and important as we consider self-forgetfulness. He commends the discipline of skilled practices to engage with the world, as heteronomous rather than autonomous beings, in ways that change me and my core understanding of myself.

Embodied knowledge

Here we can return, if we want, to religion and the Christian understanding of incarnation (which is the theological word for embodiment). This takes seriously the idea that we are most human when we live in our bodies in a world that is valuable for itself, as matter, as body, as stuff, shaped by that which is other to me, a reality that constitutes me throughout my being, and enables me to describe myself differently to the autonomous me that never loses control, is never lost in wonder, love and praise. This real world is the one we should seek. Crawford calls it the world beyond our heads. Others see it as taken into the world and further into the fullness and abundance of life.

And it's all real

Something of what this means is beautifully expressed here, as Francis Spufford describes the experience of sitting in a Church:

> The silence has no tune. It doesn't sing... Which is welcome, because it's the unending song of my self that I've come in here to get a break from. I breathe in, I breathe out. I breathe in, I breathe out. I breathe in, I breathe out: noticing the action of my lungs swelling and compressing, swelling and compressing, much more than I usually do, and so far as I have to have something to concentrate on I concentrate on that, just that, the in and out of my breath, trying to think of nothing else but the air moving... I'm deliberately abandoning the enterprise of making sense of myself. I breathe in, I breathe out... And it's all real... The real immensities of time and of space merge; are – always were – the same real immensity.
>
> But now it gets indescribable. Now I register something that precedes all this manifold immensity that is not-me and yet is real; something makes itself felt from beyond or behind or beneath it all. What can 'beyond' or 'behind' or 'beneath' mean, when all possible directions or dimensions are already included in the sum of what is so? I don't know. I've only got metaphors to work with, and this is where metaphor, which compares one existing thing to another thing, is being asked to reach beyond its competence.
>
> ...Beyond, behind, beneath all solid things there seems to be solidity. Behind, beneath, beyond all changes, all wheeling and whirring processes, all flows, there seems to be flow itself. And though I'm in the dark behind my closed eyelids, and light is part of the everything it feels as if I'm feeling beyond, so can only be a metaphor here, it seems to shine, this universal backing to things, with lightless light, or dark light;

choose your paradox. It feels as if everything is backed with light, everything floats on a sea of light, everything is just a surface feature of the light. And that includes me. Every tricky thing I am, my sprawling piles of memories and secrets and misunderstandings, float on the sea; are local corrugations and whorls with the limitless light just behind.

And now I've forgotten to breathe, because the shining something, an infinitesimal distance away out of the universe, is breathing in me and through me, and though the experience is grand beyond my power to convey, it's not impersonal. Someone, not something, is here... I am being known; known in some wholly accurate and complete way that is only possible when the point of view is not another local self in the world but glows in the whole medium in which I live and move. I am being seen from inside, but without any of my own illusions. I am being seen from behind, beneath, beyond. I am being read by what I am made of. (Spufford 2014, pp.57ff.)

Conclusion

This chapter has taken us to the heart of the preoccupation with the self that pervades and threatens Western culture. We have traced the history of hyper-individualism through the twentieth century and seen how self-absorption tends to narcissism and makes the individual vulnerable to neoliberal economic forces that turn the self into a commodity.

We have seen how religions, which should challenge this 'gamified individualist economy', fail to thrive unless they follow suit, by appealing to the success ethic, and aligning with contemporary culture. Yet religion also holds the way out, by developing deliberate practices that enable the self to focus attention away from self into voluntary work for others, or into prayer, and so be constituted into a different identity or character.

Self-forgetfulness:
from conscious incompetence to unconscious competence

How might a school culture reflect the character of self-forgetfulness and challenge a culture of narcissism?

Culture: What literature, music, art best express self-forgetfulness? How might children engage and respond with appreciation?

Character: What habits could children practise deliberately to be self-forgetful?

Call: As a way of understanding the profession of teaching as a vocation, what more could the headteacher and staff do to model self-forgetfulness?

-   Consider the difference between what Spufford experienced and 'mindfulness'.

-   Find an activity in which you can lose yourself by attending wholly to what you're doing. Join a choir, or a civic association that needs you and your gifts.

-   Read a book and become absorbed in the plot or characters. Iris Murdoch's book *The Sea, The Sea* is a great exploration of narcissism.

Chapter 3

Character Education

Emily starts school in September

Emily starts school in September. The local primary school, St Michael's, has consistently done well in Ofsted reports, despite being in the North of England where children can face a double whammy of poor schools and poverty.[1] Maddy's questions still circulate in her mind. Principally, how the next 12–14 formative years, and they hope three more at college or university, are going to prepare their daughter for the world of the future.

Maddy works in a legal office, and she can see how automation is creeping in, with programmes and algorithms doing more and more of the routine stuff. She's read about how the research she does, scanning through countless documents to find material to support the cases in hand, could soon be done by clever machines that can read it all far more quickly. Emily's going to need to be very versatile to cope in the workplace of the future. Maddy believes it will help if she has emotional and moral resources from her cultural heritage to help her to cope with an uncertain future.

Craig and Maddy are very much in favour of free education for all and want Emily to learn alongside other children from different backgrounds and cultures. They worry about the

---

1   www.childrenscommissioner.gov.uk/publication/growing-up-north-time-to-leave-the-north-south-divide-behind

pressures that teachers cope with, to measure outcomes and monitor attainment levels. It all seems so soulless, somehow – like it misses the point completely of what education should be about. So controlled and procedural – LH dominated, as McGilchrist (2010) would say.

Maddy asked to see Mrs Jenkins, the head, who looked sympathetic and harassed. She explained that the school was becoming part of a bigger Multi-Academy Trust, or MAT as she called it, and that was taking up a lot of time.

She too hated the instrumentalism of it all. She said she knew how tired and demoralised the teachers were over the excessive quantification and measurement they had to fulfil. So much marking! That they longed just to teach, and not to have to take such notice of the administrators, policymakers and inspectors who always seemed to be there, and even if not in real presence, then in your mind as you imagined them watching your every move. Gone was the discretion and wise judgement of past eras, when teachers had freedom to go with the mood of the class or take off on some really interesting avenue of knowledge that wasn't ever going to be tested. Or focus on what sort of person this child was going to grow up to be. She quoted Geoff Barton who had just given a speech that she'd heard at the Annual Conference of the Association of School and College Leaders (ASCL):

> We know that the biggest and most immediate issue is funding – we also know that this isn't a matter of money. Because as education leaders we know that you can only significantly reduce costs by cutting courses, increasing class sizes, and limiting the breadth of provision.
>
> And as we've seen over the past year, that is leading to a worrying reduction in creative arts subjects such as dance and music and drama. It's leading to the marginalisation of these important subjects. As developments in artificial intelligence and automation gather momentum, if our young people are to

outpace the robots, then this is precisely the time when we need to celebrate creativity, empathy, a deeper sense of being human.[2]

Wisdom, dignity, hope and community

Maddy picked up on this, and asked Mrs Jenkins what the school did when it came to that 'deeper sense of being human' – moral and character education. Mrs Jenkins emphasised how the school was Church of England, and took that seriously, with assemblies on different values each term, with wisdom, dignity, hope and community as core values throughout the school. They used the excellent *Understanding Christianity* material that the Church of England had recently produced.[3]

She also said she was aware of the work that the Jubilee Centre for Character and Virtue was doing in Birmingham, and how she'd love to do more to bring their stuff into the school. Emily said she'd go away and Google it.[4] Mrs Jenkins said she'd welcome further conversation. Emily left the school wondering where this would end, and how she'd find the capacity to get more involved. But then, it would be worth it, particularly if Emily was going to benefit.

The Church of England's 2016 *Vision for Education*

Mrs Jenkins emailed the next day with a link to the Church of England's 2016 *Vision for Education*. She said she thought it was good, though she was struggling to find the time to think through how it might make a difference.[5]

---

2   Geoff Barton is the General Secretary of the Association of School and College Leaders. www.ascl.org.uk/professional-development/conferences/ascl-annual-conference/geoff-barton-annual-conference-2018-speech.html
3   www.understandingchristianity.org.uk
4   www.jubileecentre.ac.uk
5   www.churchofengland.org/more/education-and-schools/vision-education

It was good, the Vision. Maddy wasn't a church goer but saw what they were getting at. How religion helps a child develop a sense of what's right and wrong, and moral virtues. *The Vision* had four basic elements: Wisdom, Hope, Community and Dignity – that's where Mrs Jenkins had got the school values from!

She understood more about what the Church of England (CofE) hoped to do in its church schools – which had been going for over 200 years. She hadn't realised that. She hadn't realised, either that you didn't have to be Christian to go to a CofE school. That some CofE schools are 100 per cent Asian heritage, and the Muslim parents much prefer the school to be Christian than secularist. Maddy liked the way the Vision document emphasised hospitality of diversity, respect for freedom of religion and belief – and how different traditions were encouraged to contribute. The whole emphasis on academic rigour combined with a rounded approach to personal development, with worship at the heart, sounded good. The big questions were good too:

- Who am I?

- Why am I here?

- What do I desire?

- How then shall I live?

The questions were framed within an idea of fullness of life and wisdom.

'Wisdom' suggested depth – alongside the other concepts of information, skills, critical thinking, measurement and assessment, appraisal, outcomes, etc., etc. Maddy agreed with the report when it said 'the present regimes of measurement and assessment are often too limited, leaving much scope for wise improvement...' (Church of England Education Office 2016, p.14, n.6) It was what the report said about reading that really inspired her, though:

Other forms of reading – for pleasure, information, knowledge, know-how, assessment, and so on – are valuable, but reading for depth of meaning and wisdom is also something well worth learning. Learning this at school can give a habit whose value increases over the years. (Church of England Education Office 2016, p.14, n.7)

The report also outlined what 'fullness of life' meant, besides the dignity, wisdom, hope and community. Maddy thought it neat that 'Fullness of Life' came from the Bible, at John 10.10, where Jesus says, 'I came that they may have fullness of life.' 10:10 schools: that worked as a strapline! The report also talked of blessing, creativity, joy, reconciling and glory – all words that intrigued her. Not words often heard where education is involved these days.

Mrs Jenkins said that a leading school that had first used the 10:10 strapline as its own was in London. Set up as one of the first academies by Dr Priscilla Chadwick, Twyford Church of England Academies Trust[6] included three outstanding schools, with Dame Alice Hudson as the executive head teacher, all flourishing with a bold Christian ethos, where the curriculum was integrated well with proper attention to the development of the moral character of each child. She found the website and showed it to Maddy.[7] Before coming north, Mrs Jenkins had been head teacher of one of the primary schools that fed Twyford and said how much she'd gained from the experience of working with the school, learning from its ethos.

Next, Maddy Googled the Jubilee Centre website. Immediately her eye was caught by resources for new parents.[8] Plenty of books to read with Emily that reflected compassion, gratitude and honesty – for ages 0–12. Really helpful. And it was a great website. Lots going on.

---

6   https://twyford.ealing.sch.uk
7   https://twyfordacademies.org.uk/assets/documents/Curriculum_Policy.pdf
8   www.jubileecentre.ac.uk/1764/character-education/parent-resources

When she next talked with Mrs Jenkins, another couple of books were recommended. Mrs Jenkins hadn't had a chance to read Angela Duckworth's new book *Grit* (Duckworth 2017), but someone else had said it was good. She also mentioned an American called David Brooks who had written an acclaimed book *The Social Animal*, which came out in 2011 and got the ball rolling in terms of popularising the idea of character to offer something different to overly instrumental educational processes.

Résumé virtues and eulogy virtues

Mrs Jenkins had read another book by Brooks, though, *The Road to Character*. She read this passage aloud to Maddy:

> Character is a set of dispositions, desires, and habits that are slowly engraved during the struggle against your own weakness. You become more disciplined, considerate, and loving through a thousand small acts of self-control, sharing, service, friendship and refined enjoyment. If you make disciplined, caring choices, you are slowly engraving certain tendencies into your mind. (Brooks 2015, pp.263–4)

She explained how he distinguishes between what he calls *résumé virtues* and *eulogy virtues*. Résumé virtues are those you list on your CV; eulogy virtues are what people say about you at your funeral. He argued that 'our education system is certainly oriented around the résumé virtues more than the eulogy ones' (Brooks 2015, p.ix.). He talked of Adam I and Adam II.

Adam I is the career-oriented, ambitious side of our nature – the external, résumé Adam. He wants to build, create, produce and discover things; high status and success. Adam II is more internal. He wants to embody moral qualities, with a serene inner character, a quiet but solid sense of right and wrong – to do, and be, good: 'Adam II wants to love intimately, to sacrifice self in the service of others, to live in obedience to some transcendent truth, to have a cohesive inner soul that honors creation and one's own possibilities' (Brooks 2015, p.x). Mrs Jenkins said it was a thoughtful read, with a good undergirding of philosophy, though there's a great deal of anecdotal illustration to plough through. She mentioned a humility code that he ends with, which she said she tried to put into practice herself. She had the headlines pinned to her fridge. Maddy thought Adam I sounded like the personification of McGilchrist's emissary – the LH dominated, functional and instrumental self that is in such ascendancy today. Adam II sounded like the RH 'master' – thoughtful, concerned with the bigger, moral picture – who had been usurped by the more aggressive Adam I.

The Jubilee Centre for Character and Virtues

Maddy had lots to think about. Mrs Jenkins lent her a book about the Jubilee Centre for Character and Virtues.[9] It offered a robust and rigorous research- and evidence-based approach, both objective and non-political. It took the line that virtues can be learned and taught; that education is an intrinsically moral enterprise; that character education should be intentional, organised and reflective. It maintained the importance of character virtues as the basis of individual and societal flourishing. Taught and caught, they should permeate all subject teaching and learning, within a school that bases its ethos and culture on them, and indeed extends character and virtue learning to the whole school, involving community learning, service and volunteering as well.

The Jubilee Centre says there are four areas of virtue: moral, performance, intellectual and civic (Arthur *et al.* 2017).

- Moral virtues are those that enable sound ethical response, such as courage, self-discipline, compassion, gratitude, justice, humility and honesty.

---

9 Founded in 2012 by James Arthur with funding by the John Templeton Foundation.

- Performance virtues can be used to good and bad ends. They are the qualities that enable us to manage our lives effectively, such as resilience, determination, confidence, teamwork.

- Civic virtues are necessary for engaged and responsible citizenship, like service, citizenship, volunteering. They assist the flourishing of each person and promote the common good of society.

- Intellectual virtues are the rational prerequisites for right action and correct thinking and include reasoning, curiosity and perseverance.

Who the teacher is matters in this scheme of things. Teaching is a self-giving vocation, fundamentally a moral enterprise, that can easily lose its appeal, the more professionalised it becomes and is dominated by:

> policies [that] are counterproductive for both teaching and teachers. They reduce teaching to skill, efficiency and instrumental purposes, in which *explicit* values disappear... Wisdom is subverted by bureaucratic measures that focus on compliance with instrumental ends. Unfortunately, teacher training has suffered also and is increasingly lacking any clear moral compass. (Arthur *et al.* 2017, p.7)

The dominance of a LH world view couldn't be clearer.

Essentially, good teachers must have the following qualities: They must know and like their subject and continue to learn it; they must like their pupils, know their faces and names and treat them as individuals; they must have good characters, and be kind, caring and patient so that their pupils will pick this up in their teaching. Teachers should also be determined, have a sense of humour and speak with authority – including moral authority. Students will respect and trust such teachers but will easily detect the teacher who does not display these qualities and virtues.

However, the down-side of a LH approach was only too apparent from passages like this:

> Teachers are increasingly given rules and standards to follow by those who are not teachers; and incentives, such as performance pay, are used to encourage them to help students perform better in exams. Many schools have become completely compliant to these external standards, and in the process have become rigid and narrow in their expectations for teachers and pupils. With too many exams, targets and assessments, teaching has become more like a business and in the process the power of education as transformation, rather than mere transmission of information, has been lost. The focus on league tables and exams has changed the way students learn and are taught. (Arthur *et al.* 2017, p.9)

As Maddy read on, she began to feel the stirrings of real excitement that here was hope for the future. This was the sort of stuff she wanted for Emily – a real education that would encourage a rich and wise character to develop, based on a hinterland of cultural literacy and a thought-through process of accumulative knowledge acquisition. She wanted to get more involved and thought she'd ask Mrs Jenkins how best to do that, once Emily had settled into school.

Music

The one thing that was missing was any real musical education offered at the school. Maddy had grown up in a Cathedral city and had been a chorister there. She'd been lucky to join the choir which was one of the few, then, that accepted girls (many more Cathedrals had girls' choirs now). For free she'd received a musical education second to none, with a great repertoire of music that she'd never forgotten. The experience had been brilliant, and Maddy knew how many choristers go on to perform in internationally renowned choirs, such that the UK is perceived to be a powerhouse of musical training.

It was more than that though. Maddy had experienced the musical training as an education that was significantly different to that of mainstream schooling. There was lots of learning music and words by heart in order to perform to a standard of excellence, rather than passing exams, or other benchmarks of progress. Maddy learned to be part of a choir. She learned self-discipline, self-confidence, and her character had blossomed. She knew that her experience as a chorister had been noted by her employer and had helped to get her the job.

Maddy had been formed by the experience – by the repetitive, deliberate practice, day in, day out. It was hard work, but real fun, and had given her a distinctive cultural and moral formation. She thought of the long hours of disciplined practice, singing, and then also training her fingers to know and play the flute and piano, hearing the sounds in her head, obedient to the mechanical reality of the instrument, to the music before her. She'd learned to respect the musical traditions she'd learned about, from the past, but which were also alive today. To learn a piece of music, or a song, was to attend to other traditions, and to accept external realities not as a threat to her, but essential if she was to acquire proficiency and knowledge that enables her to contribute to the cultural enrichment of the community of the Cathedral. She had gone on to develop a love of jazz and all the more because she understood its cultural heritage, embedded in her own history.

Sometimes, people would dismiss her chorister experience as 'elitist', but she knew differently. She herself had come from a really poor home and had known what it was like to be at the receiving end of racism, just as her mum and grandma had before her. She'd been lucky that her mother loved singing and had encouraged her to respond when the Cathedral Director of Music had come to her school to listen to the children, even though she was the only black girl to step forward. Maddy had really grown in confidence and knew her social mobility had increased because she'd been in the choir. She liked the fact that she had belonged to an ancient tradition too – one that went right back to the sixth century and Benedict, with the wisdom of centuries of reflection on what it means to be a human person and to flourish in community.

The Benedictine way

Maddy described to Craig what she understood as the Benedictine way, and then to Mrs Jenkins, too, when she next met with her. Their conversations were really good.[10] She said that it continued formative practices that shape people to be corporate rather than individualistic – encouraging a 'we' identity rather than a 'me' identity. The Benedictine way of life lent itself to character formation, valuing the deliberate practice of habits and virtues that take discipline and time to acquire.

The Benedictine way took seriously the importance of doing things for their own sake – like play, friendship, worship, beauty and education too – rather than for any instrumental or utilitarian reason. It prized highly the pursuit of excellence for its own sake.

Benedictine monks and sisters – and other religious orders too – lay great store by prayer, reading and intellectual study and physical work. The psalms and scriptures are learned by heart.

The Benedictine way of life has often been at the forefront of education, with a civilising effect on the communities and population around the abbey, wherever it was, over the centuries. The tradition was handed on, from the past, through the present and into the future, transcending present time and space, holding the memory of what has gone before,

---

10   Further information can be gained by watching www.youtube.com/watch?v =tDnY9oQ3Esg where a leading contemporary interpreter, Esther de Waal, speaks about the Benedictine Way; or visit the website of convents and monasteries, such as the sisters at West Malling in Kent: www.mallingabbey. org/our-life.html, or at Worth Abbey in West Sussex: www.worthabbey.net/ Monastic-Spirituality

and bearing hope for what the future brings. That continuity, and sense of the long term, creates stability, and is Benedictine in spirit.

An education based on this does not begin with child-centredness and the individual, but with the tradition of the choir, or the ethos of the school, or the way of life within a religious community that shapes the individual.

Maddy quickly learned as a child that the purpose of singing is to learn and perform to the best of her ability, to enhance the worship that is offered to God. This made learning different to school. As a chorister she was nurtured, and her abilities were drawn out appropriately to her maturity. She was never at the centre of her learning, though. This was not a child-centred education. The needs of the choir as it fulfils its end of singing to the glory of God were more important than her or any other individual.

A deep and broad hinterland

Maddy had once read something David Lammy MP had written as he wrote of his training as a chorister at Peterborough Cathedral. She had immediately identified with it:

> I was given the opportunity to sing some of the greatest music ever produced, standing in surroundings I could once not have dreamed of… It was not for a prize, a record contract or a financial reward, but simply for what I was doing. I experienced, for perhaps the first time, the transcendence of applying myself completely to something. This was what I understood aspiration to mean: the urge to learn a craft, to do something brilliantly, to fulfil a talent through hard work. (Lammy 2011, p.132)

She wanted this for Emily. The wide range of music learned – some of it very difficult – off by heart. A deep and broad hinterland that was there for the rest of life.

She didn't care about utilitarian skills for the workforce, transferable competencies that can be ticked off. She knew how formulaic tests and exams were. She didn't agree with how the education system encouraged tasting different topics, and then moving on to the next, in the belief that learning 'how-to' was better than learning something in depth. That wasn't what she wanted for Emily. She wanted her to encounter difficult and challenging material and come to know it intimately, over a number of years. She remembered the director of music at the Cathedral. He knew that children were capable of more than is usually assumed. How they could give the level of commitment and discipline that formed their character as choristers. How they rose to the challenge of the intensity of learning. Much was expected of her as a young child. She'd been trained to perform, with excellence; to do justice to the living tradition that she and the others had inherited and which was their responsibility to pass on to future generations. The individuality of each child was crucial, for each brought something unique; but this education is not individualistic, but corporate.

Maddy knocked on Mrs Jenkins' door and managed to find her with some time to talk. They had a really interesting conversation. Mrs Jenkins said how good it was to step back and think more deeply about it all. In 2015, when it came out, she had read a report entitled *The Power of Music*.[11] By Susan Hallam MBE, it argued that music education should be more highly valued than it is.

Mrs Jenkins was a church-goer and was left thinking about the choir at church. She thought she might have a conversation with the priest about whether the school could help in building up the choir. It would need to start small, because there was

---

11   Susan Hallam, MBE, *The Power of Music: A research synthesis of the impact of actively making music on the intellectual, social and personal development of children and young people*, published in Great Britain in 2015 on behalf of the Music Education Council by the International Music Education Research Centre (iMerc), Department of Culture, Communication and Media, UCL Institute of Education, University College London.

so little capacity amongst the staff. But there might be some possibilities there. Maddy said she'd help.

Paul Tough: *How Children Succeed*

The next thing Mrs Jenkins suggested reading was Paul Tough's book *How Children Succeed* (Tough 2012). Maddy found it particularly interesting, given the challenges of her own childhood. Tough focused on children in poverty and asked questions such as: Which skills and traits lead to success? How do they develop in childhood? And what kind of interventions might help children do better? He concluded that the psychological traits that really helped children through school were an inclination to persist at boring and unrewarding tasks, the ability to delay gratification, the tendency to follow through on a plan – all things Maddy had learned as a chorister. Her chorister training had also been valuable when she went to university, and then to work.

Cultural literacy

The conversations with Mrs Jenkins continued. The next thing she recommended was rather old-fashioned. Mrs Jenkins wasn't sure Maddy would warm to it, especially as E.D. Hirsch had influenced Michael Gove.[12] Hirsch had argued that the best way to counter poverty in children is to provide an education that offers cultural literacy and enrichment (Hirsch 1988, 1996).

Hirsch said that 'knowledge' should not be contrasted with 'thinking skills' – they were not mutually exclusive alternatives – but instead thinking skills could be 'knowledge-rich' or 'knowledge-lite'. The purpose of a good education is to teach children how to think clearly – to see through dubious reasoning, to avoid being conned, to learn how to question their own assumptions, to discover how to be objective or to

---

12 UK Secretary of State for Education 2010–14.

argue a case with clarity. That was best accomplished on a good knowledge base. Mrs Jenkins said that there was an interesting school in London, called Michaela Community School, where Hirsch's ideas were being put into practice. Maddy remembered that Benji had mentioned it. There the emphasis was on an education that wasn't just learning how to find things out, to be critical, sceptical, but was a lifelong possession of knowledge. Mrs Jenkins had just bought *Battle Hymn of the Tiger Teachers*, which was edited by the headmistress, Katharine Birbalsingh (2016). She said she'd pass it on when she'd finished it.

Hirsch, in his book *The Knowledge Deficit* (2007), argued that in order to read with understanding, a child needs to develop, accumulatively, a rich background knowledge that fills in the gaps. It's not enough to know the rules of language, to be able to dissect the sentence, or to comprehend the main idea. Unless that hinterland is there, the child will fall further and further behind. It's called 'The Matthew Effect', described by Hirsch like this:

> In order to learn how to read with understanding, you already have to be able to read with understanding. Long before Joseph Heller's *Catch-22*, his idea was implied in the Gospel of Matthew, which stated that those who already have shall gain more, while from those who have not shall be taken away even what they have. Alluding to this biblical passage, reading researchers have spoken of the 'Matthew effect' in reading. Those who already have good language understanding will gain still more language proficiency, while those who lack initial understanding will fall further and further behind. (Hirsch 2006, p.25)

There's a real knowledge deficit, he said, in today's children, between what can be taken for granted and what needs to be explained.

> Reading proficiency, listening proficiency, speaking proficiency, and writing proficiency all require possession of the

broad knowledge that the general readers is assumed to have and also the understanding that others can be expected to possess that knowledge. (Hirsch 2006, pp.71–2)

Not to have a good cultural literacy disadvantages children, particularly children from minority communities, who will struggle to understand the codes that are used unconsciously within a culture, unless they grow up learning a coherent introduction to the taken-for-granted meanings that lie behind the language used.

Maddy recognised this. The culture of her home, where her mum and grandma still carried on the Barbadian customs that her grandma had been brought up with, was very different to school. It had been hard to understand a lot of stuff that was just assumed amongst the white kids and staff. Again, the chorister experience had really helped, because it gave her a repertoire of poetry and literature, and constant exposure to the Bible, that helped her make sense of lessons at school. The more times she heard a passage or sang a psalm, she unconsciously reorganised the words in her brain. Different aspects emerged, and what seemed important the last time she sang that psalm now wasn't so fascinating. She found she inhabited the knowledge differently and saw it in a new way as she developed expertise.[13]

Maddy was having an influence on Mrs Jenkins, too. She found herself reappraising her sense of vocation as a head. She had listened and read more about what the Benedictine tradition offers, and had taken on board what Paul Tough and others were saying about the advantages of a pedagogy that takes formation seriously, and the acquisition of cultural literacy.

Education in a digital future

When Maddy told Mrs Jenkins about her own anxieties about automation and the digital future, she responded that she

---

13   David Brooks in *The Social Animal* (2012) describes this of one of his characters, Harold, who's told to read a passage again and again.

thought it was going to be inevitable that children of the digital generation would stay abreast of digital advances. She thought the best thing a school could do today was sustain what makes the child humane and creative – with a rich cultural hinterland, and moral character. Her conversations with Maddy had reminded her of the importance of learning stuff off by heart to ensure cultural literacy and developing a sense of character. Of course, it would be important to reflect the cultural diversity of the different children at St Michael's, but that would help all children understand each other better, if they learned Rumi and Attar of Nishapur alongside Shakespeare, Alice Oswald with Benjamin Zephaniah. Alongside acquiring the obvious computer skills, they would also gain the resources to seek out imaginative, creative and fruitful occupations that would ensure education continues as a lifelong pursuit, for a world where work might not be on the cards.

Maddy was left determined she was going to continue to read with Emily, often stuff that challenged her beyond her capabilities. Mrs Jenkins drew her attention to work done by the think-tank *Civitas* that had developed Hirsch's ideas of a core knowledge foundation in the UK.[14] They provided activities, stories and lesson plans, and a series of books, *What Your Child Needs to Know*, for ages 4–11, in English, Maths, Science, History, Geography, Music and Art. On Mrs Jenkins' book shelf was also the book *Character Toolkit for Teachers: 100+ Classroom and Whole School Character Education Activities for 5- to 11-Year-Olds* by Frederika Roberts and Elizabeth Wright (2018).

Conclusion

This chapter has reviewed the main literature on character education, showing a move away from a 'progressive' approach, with its emphasis on naturalism and formalism, towards one which values cultural literacy and the knowledge that enables

---

14   www.coreknowledge.org.uk

the understanding to make reading the gateway to other bodies of knowledge and disciplines. E.D. Hirsch has influenced a growing number of educationalists.

The focus on character has also been covered, including the latest contribution from the Church of England, both in terms of its 2016 *Vision*, and also the flagship Academies Trust at Twyford, in Ealing, London.

The questions that Maddy is pondering are real. What does education need to offer, as we look to the digital future? Other contributions – for example, by Paul Tough (in greater depth) and Angela Duckworth – are explored in subsequent chapters.

We leave Maddy, Craig and Emily, and go to the third character-fullness – carefulness – which examines the attachment that's required for new babies and infants to ensure they develop emotionally and psychologically. Essays on playfulness and resourcefulness follow. In each of these, how the brain functions and learns will be highlighted, leading into the next more theoretical chapter about machine learning in a digital age.

Chapter 4

Carefulness

A baby cries. It's difficult to ignore. The sound is designed to get on the nerves. If there's no response from anyone, eventually the baby will exhaust himself and sleep. This might work occasionally, but if it happens too often and the lack of response becomes normal, then serious damage is done.

The carefulness with which a baby is nurtured in her early years is crucial.

To be careful with other people, with property and things, with cultures around us, is an important aspect of our humanity. What we care for and take responsibility for indicates where our loyalties lie. To care beyond our own kin takes carefulness from the personal into social action, volunteering, charity work and into a characterful habit that makes us humane. To be careful in a delicate situation, with someone who has particular needs or fragility, or to care for the stranger in our midst, the refugee, or homeless person, begins, most often, with the experience of someone else's carefulness and attention towards us in our early years.

Attachment

John Bowlby (1907–90) was the first to research the significance of the relationship between child and mother (or prime caregiver) in the 1940s, publishing *Maternal Care and Mental Health* (Bowlby and WHO 1952). His lifelong work on

'attachment' has had a profound effect on the understanding
of child development. He showed how babies whose parents
responded readily and fully to their cries in the first months
of life were, at one year, more independent and intrepid than
babies whose parents had ignored their cries.

For many years Bowlby worked closely with Donald
Winnicott, whose writings on play are covered in the next
chapter. A significant follower was Mary Ainsworth, who
in turn influenced one of the leading experts on attachment
today, Patricia McKinsey Crittenden (Crittenden *et al.* 2014).
Crittenden is notable for the way in which she embeds the
child/mother dyad within family and social networks, in what
she terms the 'Dynamic Maturational Model' of attachment and
adaptation. I also draw on Sue Gerhardt's *Why Love Matters*,
where she gives a clear explanation of how the brain develops
neurologically as the child grows (Gerhardt 2015).

Care

The UK state is taking more children from their parents than at
any time since the 1980s.[1] For a number of reasons, increasing
poverty being one, some children are in such need or danger that
they have to be removed from the parental home. They become
'cared-for' children, but the 'care' they receive can be mixed:
Some care is excellent, but many suffer a lack of institutional
carefulness. They do not receive a continuity of care that is vital if
they are to learn to trust. If reliable and consistent relationships
are missing, it becomes difficult to work through the disruption
they experience. A society's carefulness with cared-for children
is a sign of how mature and civilised that society is.

---

1   *The Economist*, 24 March 2018, p.25.

Pre-school foundation years

In normal circumstances, a child's education builds on the care that initial caregivers, usually parents, provide. The pre-school foundation years provide the security and stability that enable the child to benefit from the opportunities and challenges of school. In 2010 the UK politician Frank Field MP produced a report entitled *The Foundation Years* (Field 2010). He recognised that children struggle when they are emotionally impoverished through poor attachment. When attachment is not securely formed, the results can be devastating: the child can fail to flourish at school, in relationships, and later at work, with poor attachment leading to impaired physical, psychological and emotional health, which can result in offending behaviour, and involvement with the criminal justice system.

Field spoke of the 'rupturing of a good parenting tradition' and argued that it should be a priority to reverse this social trend, for the good of society, including the quality of care received by cared-for children. He described the impact on schools of children who had experienced emotionally disorganised foundation years, leaving teachers struggling with a range of behaviours that were hard to contain and address.

Why Love Matters

Careful, attentive attachment that shapes the primary bond between child and mother starts before birth. Susan Gerhardt in *Why Love Matters* draws on research that indicates that a pregnant woman's own stress will impact on the baby's future outcome: for instance, a depressed mother is more likely to have a child predisposed to depression. Stress is transmitted across the placenta (Gerhardt 2015, p.26). However, more important is the establishment of good attachment in the post-natal period. Love matters; carefulness is its expression. Gerhardt writes:

> For example positive bonding and secure attachment during the first year can enable a small hippocampus affected by

[pre-natal] stress to be restored to normal volume. New growth also takes place in the pre-frontal cortex in response to positive social experiences. This can offer different ways of managing and regulating emotion. In other words, if love can be found, it still has the power to shape a new reality. (Gerhardt 2015, p.27)

So the baby cries; exhausts herself and sleeps. Mother, next time, is preoccupied and again leaves her to cry herself to sleep. Gerhardt explains how, in the baby's brain, the hormone cortisol is particularly important to the way the baby responds. Cortisol stimulates the sympathetic and parasympathetic neural systems that trigger conscious and unconscious reactions, depending on the stimulus. As the baby receives positive facial expressions within secure and safe careful relationships, cortisol enables the brain to develop normally. However, disapproval or rejection can cause an overdose of cortisol, which can produce a sudden lurch from sympathetic arousal to parasympathetic arousal, creating the physical effects of a sudden drop in blood pressure and shallow breathing (Gerhardt 2015). With reassurance, a child can recover quickly from this state; however, if that reassurance doesn't come, the baby will overdose on cortisol, stuck in a state of negative arousal which does permanent damage.

Fight, flight, freeze

Excessive levels of cortisol overstimulate the amygdala that triggers adrenaline, which in turn stimulates more cortisol, which leads to more primitive reactions, such as the well-recognised 'flight', 'fight' or 'freeze' responses (Gerhardt 2015). Toxic levels of cortisol can result in a persistent sense of powerlessness and unrelieved, chronic stress, causing many emotional dysfunctions such as depression, anxiety and suicidal tendencies in adulthood, as well as eating disorders, alcoholism, obesity and sexual abuse, with physical as well as psychological damage to the body's systems (Gerhardt 2015).

This has an impact on the baby neurologically. From before birth as the child's neurological system develops, there are primitive neural pathways that enable survival behaviours, the most significant being the *vagal nerve*. The branches of the vagal nerve serve different evolutionary stress responses, for example, its more primitive branches stimulate fighting or flight, or freezing (FFF). The more evolved branches are linked to social communication and stress reduction behaviours. When these more evolved responses fail, the child will revert to the more primitive FFF reactions. So these neural pathways regulate emotional and social behaviour, and determine how a growing infant copes when aroused or distressed.

The *vagal brake* kicks into action when a distressed child is calmed, enabling the automatic regulation of stress levels. Later in life it can be triggered consciously, as when we breathe deeply when anxious, or close our eyes in prayer or mindfulness. Such conscious behaviours are most effective if we have experienced careful attention when a baby, allowing the vagal brake to operate normally. If there is a lack of reassurance from the mother, the vagal brake is not going to work to disengage the vagal nerve, so the child will be left with the FFF response. He may develop difficulties sucking, swallowing, digesting – all physiological functions which depend on relaxing. Future anxiety states often begin here.

When the reassurance is forthcoming and the vagal brake works well, the baby will learn different states of arousal, from being calm and restful, to giving focused attention, to play, eating, exercise and exhibiting distress, confident it will elicit an appropriate response (Crittenden *et al.* 2014). So when things go well, the mother will respond to the baby's cry with warmth and affection. Within days, the baby – Crittenden calls her 'Mary' – will recognise a sequence:

> As soon as her mother's hands touch her, the neural circuits for down-regulating stress-response systems are triggered into action and Mary begins to calm… By some months later,

Mary knows, just *knows* when she hears her mother's voice call out from another room, that mother and comfort and milk and all things good are on the way – and Mary begins to calm herself. This is the momentous power of her mother's contingent responsiveness offered in the context of Mary's own biological maturation. (Crittenden *et al.* 2014, p.15)

As the baby begins to predict and trust the response, she is enabled to regulate her arousal. This is a skill that involves activation of higher-order brain circuits that enable emotional self-regulation. As her brain matures, 'by the middle of the first year of life, Mary gives a brief cry – and listens. Her mother calls back – and Mary settles, knowing she was understood and her mother is coming' (Crittenden *et al.* 2014, p.15). The child makes the gradual transition from automatic neural responses, triggered by cortisol, towards self-regulation which will become the ability to override emotional states with self-control.

Crittenden explains how easily it can be interrupted, though. If the crying time is too long, allowing the baby to become seriously distressed, and the mother is anxious, then a different sequence can occur. She writes:

[The mother] reaches down to pick Mary up, but Mary is squirming; she's somatically aroused and hard to calm. Mary's mother is rushed, her hands are too tight on Mary, her voice too fast and high-pitched, her rocking too frantic…a struggle begins and Mary's mother feels a bit frantic and helpless against such howling and activity in her 'difficult' baby. (Crittenden *et al.* 2014, p.16)

If this is the usual sequence, then the baby will be fed, changed and cared for physically, but it will be hard for her to read the signs in a predictable way and process the links between her own behaviour and her mother's response. Crittenden says that in the long term such babies are less skilled at regulating the vagal brake in adulthood, engaging and disengaging with others and the daily challenges of life.

Crittenden's great insight is that this mother/baby attachment doesn't happen in isolation (indeed, when it does, it can be a particularly vulnerable dyad). It happens inter-generationally, and within social and familial contexts that shape and influence the beginning of the child's life (Crittenden *et al.* 2014). Attachment, she says, happens when the knowledge of one generation is passed to the next, interaction by repeated interaction, in a context where adaptation is always required. Behaviours learned when the mother was a child herself are passed on, for good or ill, when she becomes a parent, adapting (or not) to meet different circumstances.

Bodily knowing

One of the key arguments of this book is for an education that takes seriously embodied knowledge embedded in the real world, engaging with what is other to us – *heteronomy*, rather than *autonomy*. It begins, as Crittenden explains, with the knowledge between child and mother, self and other, which is a bodily knowledge. It's where the child first learns about 'otherness', and it's a bodily knowing:

> Babies feel in their bodies what they know about their safety: this is why a mother's sensory input – her voice, her face, her smell, her touch, her rocking – is so powerful. We too can discern a baby's emotional state through the baby's body. When we hold a baby, we feel as she relaxes, stiffens, or hangs limp like an object not a living creature. Babies express intense somatic discomfort through their inability to eat, sleep, or retain food. Their bodies know what they cannot say. (Crittenden *et al.* 2014, p.16)

The engagement with the material world – the world beyond our heads – is fundamental to what it means to be human, and it begins here, in the embodied knowing of baby with mother. It comes into play as the baby grows older, when certain objects have powerful associations – a blanket, or a toy – with the warmth of mother, comforting him into toddlerhood.[2] Crittenden describes such things as 'dispositional representations', and explains that they can have either a positive or negative impact. Negatively, for example, if the baby has been exposed to domestic violence – perhaps her parents have shouted loudly at each other, or her mother has been hit while the baby was in her arms – then the sound of a raised human voice may activate a 'dispositional representation' that causes the child to freeze, exhibiting an innate fear response as the primitive vagal neural system kicks in, triggering vigilance, body stillness, decreased vocalisations, slow heart rate and sensitivity to pain. Long before the baby understands language, already sound, touch, sight, and taste can provoke learned behaviours that cause the baby to regulate his arousal or activate defensive body states (Crittenden *et al.* 2014).

Insecure attachment

There's a spectrum that is used to identify the range of attachment. When a child cannot trust her mother or the caregivers around, she will exhibit avoidance, or resistance, indicating the insecurity of her attachment. When the child has little or no experience of security, Gerhardt describes it as 'disorganised' attachment, and says this has the strongest links with serious future emotional difficulties. It happens in families where the child struggles to find a coherent defensive strategy, like avoidance or resistance. 'Very often,' writes Gerhardt, 'the parents themselves have been overwhelmed by traumatic experiences in their own lives that have not been processed effectively, such as bereavement or some kind of important loss, or some form of abuse' (Gerhardt 2015, p.42).

---

2   This is similar to what Winnicott called 'transitional objects', which enable the negotiation with the real world beyond the comfort of the initial caregiver, as we see in Chapter 5 on playfulness, though Winnicott's focus was more on the relation between the child and the reality of the world around, than the internal psychological dynamic that is the focus of those interested in attachment.

When parents themselves find it difficult to regulate their stress levels and establish emotional self-control, they are likely to respond inappropriately to a baby when he gets on their nerves, and in turn, the baby will not develop his own steady responses as he grows into a toddler (Gerhardt 2015).

With disorganised attachment, the child then lives with levels of stress that cause dysfunction in relationship, and during her education. This has a profound impact on the growing sense of self.

> In families which neglect or criticise their children too much, there can be a fundamental uncertainty about the worth of the self. The internal working model will be one of inner worthlessness or even badness in anticipating a critical or neglectful other. These expectations inform behaviour and often draw others into confirming the expectations, setting up a vicious cycle which is hard to break. (Gerhardt 2015, p.173)

When attachment has been disorganised, and the family or care systems do little or nothing to alleviate the vicious cycle, then education becomes even more important, potentially providing an institutional carefulness that can change the fortunes of the stressed child. For further exploration, this video is well worth watching.[3]

The rupturing of a good parenting tradition

What Frank Field called the rupturing of a good parenting tradition has its roots in cultural changes in parenting. Jean Twenge's work on *Generation Me* (2014) and the *iGen* (2017) indicate how parental authority is often confused today, with real difficulties in establishing what good authority looks like. The story of CJ (see Chapter 2) illustrated parenting that offered her no friction or challenge. The experts on attachment believe

---

3   https://developingchild.harvard.edu/resources/inbrief-the-impact-of-early-adversity-on-childrens-development-video

that good parenting requires the ability to say 'No!' and establish boundaries that enable the child to locate herself within the real world. Boundaries become particularly important in a digital age where, as Matthew Crawford (2015) has described, people of all ages can lose a sense of themselves in the frictionless world of virtual reality.

Normally, during toddlerhood, there will be the beginning of awareness and intention. By 18 months the child will recognise himself in a mirror, with a developing self-consciousness. By this time, he will check if he is watched before doing something naughty. Crittenden *et al.* (2014) note that the developmental changes in toddlerhood enable the growing ability to deal with a complexity of psychological processes and manage multiple, interconnected relationships. She describes how a child becomes ready to learn, and how competent parents let children do for themselves what they can do for themselves. A key aspect of that learning is the acquisition of habitual responses, which happen as the child engages with different experiences. How things go from this point onwards is crucial.

When self-awareness becomes social

The child's growing self-awareness can easily become self-absorption, within a culture and society that stresses the Rousseauian emphasis on freedom from the constraint of authority figures. Called 'freedom', this can bring with it a great weight of existential responsibility for the individual. Crawford explains how Western culture often promotes the Nietzschean strong, self-reliant hero, who '[has] to be ready to reinvent yourself at any time, like a good democratic *Übermensch*' (Crawford 2015, p.163). The pressure is on young people to be self-determining and flexible; to demonstrate personal initiative and take nothing for granted; to succeed in a culture of performance and heightened competition. Such a culture infects our education systems, setting young people up to seek individual success. In this world, failure carries stigma, rather than being viewed positively as necessary to growing up and learning from experience (Crawford 2015).

The beginning of hyper-individualism is here, when the child develops in a culture that has forgotten the social nature of society. How children grow socially requires renewed attention.

In a world that tends to excessive individualism, even solipsism, we have to remember that our experiences are not simply our own. Individuality (rather than individualism) is based on our experience of other people, from the word go. It begins not solipsistically but sociably, in co-operation with others. There's continuity from a child's initial relationships of attachment towards growing individuality that is shaped by connectedness. That connectedness between the growing sense of self and other people offers the rough with the smooth, the heteronomous encounter – the friction of otherness – that forms the self. When the child is brought up to be *autonomous*, this essential growth into human personhood, which is primarily social, is undermined.

The Pert and Poetic Ages

With the onset of language and self-awareness, everything needs to be negotiated. How parents manage this will have implications for how their children relate with teachers in school, with friends, girlfriends/boyfriends and spouse, and, eventually, with their own children. Dorothy L. Sayers – from a different era – reflected on three stages, as we saw in Chapter 1. Here are the next two stages, which illuminate the process a child goes through:

> The Pert Age, only too familiar to all who have to do with children: it is characterised by contradicting, answering-back, liking to 'catch people out' (especially one's elders) and in the propounding of conundrums (especially the kind with a nasty verbal catch in them). Its nuisance-value is extremely high. The Poetic Age is popularly known as the 'difficult' age. It is self-centred; it yearns to express itself; it rather specialises

in being misunderstood; it is restless and tries to achieve independence; and, with good luck and good guidance, it should show the beginnings of creativeness, a reaching-out towards a synthesis of what it already knows, and a deliberate eagerness to know and do some one thing in preference to all others. (Sayers 1948, p.15)

The issue of authority is really important to enable this development through the usual vicissitudes of childhood and teenage years.

Authoritative parenting

Crittenden writes well about authoritative parenting. In balanced family systems, she says parents adopt a clear decision-making position with regard to their child but include the child's expressed preferences in their decision. An important feature of this process is that the parents consider safety and danger first; when there is danger, the parent's priorities prevail and discussion is secondary to respectful compliance. Where there is no danger, children's preferences become more important. However:

children who are raised too permissively show poor emotion regulation and use more non-verbal communication than other children, are contrary and oppositional, give up easily when things don't work out, and, in cases of substantial threat to the child may show antisocial behaviour. On the other hand, they can be engagingly disarming, funny, and fierce; for sure, you want them on your side and not against you. (Crittenden *et al.* 2014, p.55)[4]

---

4   A good website to explore further, particularly about different parenting styles – and the four styles are usually identified as neglectful, permissive, authoritarian and authoritative – can be found here: https://my.vanderbilt.edu/ developmentalpsychologyblog/?s=Types+of +Parenting+Styles

Narrative self

As the child grows, the development of the social self who has a sense of narrative autobiography is crucial to emotional security as an adult. If the childhood attachment has been disorganised, then it will be difficult to establish a sense of self that is resourceful in coping with danger and difficulty. If such a person then suffers trauma, it will be intensified and Post Traumatic Stress Disorder can result – the ongoing experience of stress and anxiety that does not let up (Crittenden *et al.* 2014).

In less extreme situations, Gerhardt points to research that indicates that it doesn't matter so much whether someone had a 'happy childhood' or not. The person's current emotional security will depend much more on having an internally coherent and consistent narrative (Gerhardt 2015, p.71). Memory is crucial as good events remembered from the past can reinforce positivity in facing and anticipating the future. The development of language and story is fundamental to shape the emotional life within. Gerhardt explains how the hippocampus works with its central role of selecting significant memories from current experience to store in long-term memory. It brings information together from various sources in the brain, situating it in time and place. Gerhardt writes:

> There is a before, during and after. This enables the child to start to create a narrative self, not just a self that lives in the moment. Parents can now talk to their child about the future – 'Cheer up, we're going to the park to see the ducks later this morning' – and they can refer to the past – 'Remember when you took off all your clothes at Uncle Bob's wedding!' (Gerhardt 2015, p.70)

Learning off by heart

Play can greatly enhance the child's ability to make sense of her world by engaging the child's attention with emotionally significant stuff from nursery rhymes to books, art, poetry, plays and film. These challenge the child appropriately with worlds different to her own. Learning material off by heart from the earliest days of a child's life (even if it is not understood entirely as understanding will come later, and if the material is good, will never be exhausted) provide an ever-expanding map of words and images that shape the emotional and cultural hinterland from then on. I remember nursing someone who had severe memory loss, and as I bathed her, I sang the words of an old, familiar hymn to the tune of 'Crimond'. Her face lit up as she joined in, recalling the words and tune from her childhood. Momentarily, she was back, experiencing her humanity, within emotional and social range again.

Children who learn even the simplest rhymes and words off by heart encourage neural pathways that strengthen memory and develop emotional intelligence. In a digital world where we rely increasingly on data storage and algorithms to remember for us, our memory and emotional intelligence begin to suffer. In order for our humanity to survive – indeed, for the digital world itself to benefit from our humanity – it is important that we apply great carefulness over how babies, infants and young children are introduced to the world around them – the materiality of books and cultural objects – that enable them to grow emotionally into human maturity.

Conclusion

This chapter has examined the foundation years, when a child and infant lay down the ability to respond with others, principally the parent, and so enable stress to be managed and learning to happen within a secure and challenging environment. When a child is treated with carefulness, the groundwork is in place to develop as a self who can engage with the world, benefitting from the heteronomy that shapes someone to be full of character.

Carefulness:
from conscious incompetence to unconscious competence

Watch https://my.vanderbilt.edu/developmental psychology
blog/?s=Types+of+Parenting+Styles.

1. Decide what parenting style best characterises the
   way you were brought up.

2. Identify amongst the parents around you the four
   types.

3. Reflect on your ideal parenting type, and why.

Consider your interactions (if any) with infants. Has this
chapter caused you to change your behaviour at all? If so,
how?

Chapter 5

Playfulness

If you Google 'play', guess what? You get Google Play. (This is the Wikipedia entry):

> **Google Play** (formerly **Android Market**) is a digital distribution service operated and developed by Google. It serves as the official app store for the Android operating system, allowing users to browse and download applications developed with the Android software development kit (SDK) and published through Google. Google Play also serves as a digital media store, offering music, magazines, books, movies, and television programs. It previously offered Google hardware devices for purchase until the introduction of a separate online hardware retailer, Google Store, on March 11, 2015.

A little further on, there's the Oxford Dictionary definition:

play | Definition of play in English by Oxford Dictionaries

https://en.oxforddictionaries.com/definition/play

Definition of *play* – engage in activity for enjoyment and recreation rather than a serious or practical purpose, take part in (a sport), be cooperative.

Then, a little further on again, there is the Play England website:[1]

PLAY IS IMPORTANT

---

1   www.playengland.org.uk

Play is an essential part of every child's life. It is vital for the enjoyment of childhood as well as for social, emotional, intellectual and physical development. When children are asked about what they think is important in their lives, playing and friends are usually at the top of the list. (Play England 2018)

Homo sapiens depends on Homo ludens

As we consider what makes for fullness of character, the human capacity for play is fundamental: *Homo sapiens* depends on Homo ludens, as Winnicott's spirit would agree.

We shall explore the impact of video and online gaming has on the brain, drawing on Susan Greenfield's (2014) work. We shall consider what prohibits a child from playing, which will take us to Tim Gill's (2009) research on the risk-averse society, including the latest reports on making urban areas more child-friendly, and to Sue Palmer's (2006) campaign against toxic childhood, and the growing concern that children are increasingly disengaged from the natural world.

Given the importance of safety to the iGeneration (born after 1995, researched by Jean Twenge (2017)), is an overriding concern with emotional security closing down openness to challenge?

Playfulness is crucial to the child, and also to the adult who is full of character. The more deeply the play engages *heteronomously* with the other, the more imaginative and full will be the life experience of the person – this is the opportunity for the RH to be part of all that it meets, to encounter new adventure, to seek a newer world. Play is absolutely essential to a sense of fulfilment, and the worship of God can contribute a great deal to shape a playful character throughout one's life towards abundance of life.

Lost in play

It was Donald Winnicott who wrote so powerfully, in *The Child, the Family and the Outside World* and *Playing and Reality*, of the importance of play in a child's life. In order for children to develop as human beings and grow into adult life, they need to play, taking risks emotionally and physically to find the resources within.

At any age, Winnicott thought play was crucial to allow the person to come alive internally, with motivation to discover more. The child – or adult – at play is, he thought, most truly themselves. His practice as a psychiatrist and psychoanalyst revolved around encouraging children to play, watching as they used string or squiggled patterns.

Winnicott lectured widely, urging those who cared for children to play with them with warmth and engagement, instilling confidence for the encounter with the world around. He explained how, when there was no response to their playfulness, the child would stop trying to engage and withdraw. Winnicott wrote about how playing took place in the space, which was full of potentiality, between the baby and the mother-figure, in the safe, facilitating environment in which the child could take risks, opening up to others, exploring the boundaries and horizons around (Winnicott 1969).

Within this space, toys could help children to explore reality by making up stories and using their imagination. Winnicott called such objects 'transitional' between the child's imagination and the reality of the world. Transitional objects enabled the negotiation of security and separation from the parent, and a developing sense of self in relation to others in the world around. Playing with transitional objects enables the child to develop with a creative imagination the capacity to be genuine and loving in their relations with others.

With adults, Winnicott argued, the playfulness continues in art and culture, enabling further exploration in greater emotional and moral depth. He wrote that 'the abstractions of politics and economics and philosophy and culture [are a] "third area" of cultural experience which is a derivative of play' (Winnicott 1971, p.163 and p.120). We talk of a child becoming 'lost in play'. The adult too can become lost in play as she contemplates beauty and finds her mind inspired by art or nature, or in worship.

Online play

Play for many today means online. Contemporary research into online gaming highlights many of the advantages of computer games; but points out serious downsides too.

In *Mind Change*, Susan Greenfield devotes three chapters to video games and online gaming. She notes that 'since 1970, the radius of activity for a child, namely the amount of space in which they freely wander around the area surrounding the home, has shrunk by an astonishing 90 per cent' (Greenfield 2014, p.19). Most children now play indoors, onscreen. She comments that the content of a screen-based lifestyle is unprecedented in how it shapes thoughts and feelings, and through the corollary effects of *not* exercising by playing and learning outside (Greenfield 2014). She reflects that in earlier decades, play meant that the story came from inside your head and arose from interaction with your friends. It was '*your* game, *your* story, *your* internally driven scenario above all for *your* imagination – *you* were the driver and *you* were in control of your own inner private world, your own inner reality. But now the screen is the driver' (Greenfield 2014, pp.21–2). She explains why video games are so addictive, what they do to attention, and their impact on aggression and recklessness.

There is evidence that video games can have a beneficial, remedial effect over a wide range of impairments, including a reversal of cognitive decline in the elderly. They can reduce delusional symptoms in schizophrenic patients. Although they can lead to increased aggression and lower pro-social behaviour, they can help some adolescents with autistic spectrum disorders, enabling social development and psychological well-being (Greenfield 2014). Traditional games that involve personal interaction, however, help much more in the interpretation of body language – how to employ eye contact, learning to empathise and developing cognitive skills such as reasoning and memory. Greenfield concludes that 'video games, could, for the first time, be dissociating fun from any of the survival-value requisites that traditional games have met' (Greenfield 2014, p.158).

Online gaming enables players to create their own avatars – much larger in scope than the first-person shooter games.[2] Thousands of human players are able to interact in the same virtual world simultaneously and 'this global game is persistent, in that regardless of whether or not a gamer is logged in, the world continues to turn in the cyber sphere, updating and evolving (Greenfield 2014, p.160).

The impact of engagement on sites such as Second Life can have real-life consequences, even destroying relationships.[3] Games involving avatars are very addictive, requiring high levels of personal attachment and emotional investment, such that addiction is common. Greenfield describes how excessive levels of dopamine in the brain, caused by gaming, change the size of brain structures, particularly enlarging the ventral striatum where dopamine is released (Greenfield 2014).

This has serious consequences. Chamath Palihapitiya, who was vice-president for user growth at Facebook before he left the company in 2011, said: 'The short-term, dopamine-driven feedback loops that we have created are destroying how society works. No civil discourse, no cooperation, misinformation, mistruth.'[4] Greenfield cites a professor of English who played *World of Warcraft* for 60 hours a week:

---

2   First-person shooter games are typically made up of purely 'instance' scenarios, in which the plot only exists for the duration of the fame and can be restarted at the original point an infinite number of times (Greenfield 2014).

3   www.theguardian.com/technology/2008/nov/13/second-life-divorce

4   Chamath Palihapitiya, at a Stanford Business School event in November 2017, reported in Julia Carrie Wong 'Former Facebook executive: social media is ripping society apart', *The Guardian*, 11 December 2017.

'[It] made me feel god like… I have ultimate control and can do what I want with few real repercussions. The real world makes me feel impotent…a computer malfunction, a sobbing child, a suddenly dead cell phone battery, the littlest hitch in daily living feels profoundly disempowering.' (Greenfield 2014, p.170)

This player is now not just playing a game, but rather an idealised life that is simultaneously exciting and safe, physically and mentally. From a real world that is messy and ambiguous, or dull and difficult, online gaming with your avatar, to whom you become as attached as to real-world people, draws you in: 'They are literally exploring a new identity for themselves in this game world that is better, faster, fitter, stronger, thinner, taller, prettier, smarter than they are or probably *can ever be*' (Greenfield 2014, pp.172–3).

Whereas Winnicott's transitional objects enabled children – and adults as they use paintings, sculptures, *objets d'art*, religious icons or the sacraments – to engage with the real world and grow in understanding of self in relationship, playing online, particularly those games that involve an avatar, result in a confused understanding of self. Is the avatar operating as a transitional identity? Or does the identity of the avatar and the player become one? Either way, there is something essentially different to Winnicott's understanding of transference onto the transitional object, allowing the imagination to extend and flourish where the heteronomy is truly with the other and not with just another projection of self.

Greenfield suspects that avatar players have a 'sneaky feeling' that what they are doing lacks any real significance or meaning.

Gamers become extremely emotionally dependent on their avatars. They are as attached to their avatars, their guild, their team as someone in the real world may be attached to their real-world relationships or objects. In these instances, the momentary context has shifted online into an artificial world. And what if so much of your life story isn't a story at all, not a sequence of events but, as is the case with first-person shooter games, an atomised, fragmented set of experiences that have no consequences in the real world? In either case, you might start to feel uncertain about who you actually are. (Greenfield 2014, pp.173-4)

Attention

Greenfield also has concerns about what video games do to attention. She acknowledges that *selective* visual attention might be improved in the short term with video gaming, but fears that this could be to the detriment of *sustained* attention over the longer term, the kind of attention needed to reflect and to understand something in depth (Greenfield 2014).

One of the most remarkable things about children – or adults – playing, led by their own imagination, either by themselves or with others, is the absorption that gives rise to the expression 'lost in play'. A playful character never loses the ability to concentrate with deep attention. It could be asserted that playing a video game obsessively exhibits the same deep attention (Parkin 2017), but there is an obvious difference: Compare the obsessive, addictive attention to an online game with the quiet, still attention of a father and child watching a kingfisher on a riverbank. One of the ways in which we can tell the difference is by the fruitfulness of the attention.

Greenfield's research points to an increase of aggression and recklessness, which, she suggests, means we are living in an unprecedented era where an increasing number of people are rehearsing and learning a new default mindset for negotiating the world: 'one of low-grade aggression, short attention span and a reckless obsession with the here and now' (Greenfield 2014, p.211).

Greenfield's assessment is thorough and worrying. She argues that digital technologies are leaving their mark on our brains to the detriment of our humanity. Such concerns need to be heard, particularly as we move more deeply into the digital age.[5]

Taking risks

Winnicott's work focused on creating a healthy facilitating environment where children play with reality, taking risks and exploring themselves in relation to the frictions of the world and people around. His thinking has influenced subsequent advocates of play like Tim Gill.[6]

Gill's great concern is that we now live in an increasingly risk-averse society, where children's safety is higher on the agenda than ever, despite the fact that children have never been more physically safe (see Twenge 2017). He thinks society has become so risk-averse that the learning and playfulness of childhood is compromised.

In December 2017 the report *Cities Alive: Designing for Urban Childhoods* was released, in order to promote 'cities where children of all ages are active and visible in the public realm… able to play outdoors and…get around independently', including engaging with nature.[7] The report catalogues cities around the world that are now taking seriously the need for adventurous places for children to play, where they learn to deal with risk in responsible ways. The report criticises the preoccupation with safety that has dominated since public playgrounds were first built over 100 years ago – a preoccupation driven by worries about liability and litigation. Today's designers are working with safety and public health agencies to do a risk/benefit assessment, and as a result, British playgrounds have become notably more challenging and adventurous, which is spreading to other countries. Playgrounds are one thing…

---

5   See also James Williams (2018).
6   See Tim Gill's blog: https://rethinkingchildhood.com
7   www.arup.com/publications/research/section/cities-alive-designing-for-urban-childhoods

Engagement with wild nature is another

The replacement of age-old play activities (running, climbing, pretending, making, sharing) by a solitary, sedentary, screen-based lifestyle can be attributed to parental and school anxiety, restricting children's physical activity, play and freedom to roam.[8] Partly those fears are rational – there are more cars on the roads, and terrorist attacks do happen – but mainly they are irrational. For most in the developed world, life is generally safer than it's ever been.

Sue Palmer (2006) points out that there is a huge market in safety. She offers a range of very helpful suggestions for parents on how to spend time with children outside, to enable them to acquire, amongst other things, reliable pedestrian skills. Mainly, though, she says parents have much more work to do to banish their own irrational anxiety, and to spend time with their children, providing them with the life skills necessary to assume greater independence, to grow in self-control and self-confidence, so they can cope in a relatively unsupervised environment.

Teachers, too, have become more risk-averse. NASUWT, the Teachers' Union, advises its members to consider carefully whether or not to participate in non-contractual educational visits and journeys (Gill 2009). Risk aversion is fuelled by the media, with stories that give priority to trauma, particularly if children are involved. A culture of risk aversion that has encroached into every aspect of children's lives – in school, in

---

8   Greenfield says the same (2014, p.19). She quotes Dr Joe Frost's book *A History of Children's Play and Play Environments*, which traces the history of children's play from their early records in ancient Greece and Rome to the present time and concludes: 'Children in America have become less and less active, abandoning traditional outdoor play, work and other physical activity for sedentary, indoor virtual play, technology play or cyber playgrounds, coupled with diets of junk food.' This, Greenfield says, leads to the consequences of play deprivation, which may well become a fundamental issue in the welfare of children. For example, they may no longer develop a realistic sense of risk, nor an imagination that allows them to suggest to their friends, as all previous generations have done, 'Let's make up a game...'

social play, in children's clubs and 'adventure' trips and in the wider public realm.

A different imagination is required, before we forget how important risk and adventure are to being human. There's a growing literature and movement – see the further reading section at the end of this chapter. The debate about childhood safety and the need for resilience in today's world is continued in Chapter 6 on resourcefulness. Here, it's important to think about how playfulness and play engage the imagination, enabling engagement with the heteronomy of nature, transitional objects, other people, and the world at large. This engagement enables the child to grow in confidence.

Play at the boundaries

One of the things that playfulness enables is the deep connections between the self and other people and things, whether that other is person or thing. *Heteronomy* rather than *autonomy* belongs here, at the boundary where play engages the self with the realities of life and the world.

Elizabeth Spiegel is the chess teacher at a public middle school in Brooklyn, who trains children to have the mental resourcefulness to win at chess. To do this, they need to learn how to fail. Spiegel's blog has this entry describing her experience at a girls' national tournament:

> The first day and a half was pretty bad. I was on a complete rampage, going over every game and being a huge bitch all the time: saying things like 'THAT IS COMPLETELY UNACCEPTABLE!!!' to 11-year-olds for hanging pieces or not having a reason for a move. I said some amazing things to kids, including 'You can count to two, right? Then you should have seen that!' and 'If you are not going to pay more attention, you should quit chess, because you are wasting everyone's time.'
>
> By the end of round three I was starting to feel like an abusive jerk and was about to give up and be fake nice instead.

But then in round four everyone took more than an hour and started playing well. And I really believe that's why we seem to win girls' national sections pretty easily every year: most people won't tell teenage girls (especially the together, articulate ones) that they are lazy and the quality of their work is unacceptable. And sometimes kids need to hear that, or they have no reason to step up. (Tough 2012, p.120)[9]

Real play, as opposed to online gaming, is challenging, and pushes the child (and adult) to engage at the boundaries of self and world, of what is safe and what is adventurous, where things become meaningful.

The divinely ordained game

This can help face into the fear of nothingness, of death, of waste. Often we shield ourselves from the fear that our lives are meaningless, or we are helpless, by becoming ever more caught up in functional and instrumental activity that is driven by the need to meet measurable targets. Our RH attention to the bigger questions of meaning becomes blocked by LH focus on goals, strategies and processes, as we find systems in life to block out fear. We measure ourselves by success. Then the greatest fear we face is the fear of failure. Which is easy to manage, for we work harder; we make sure we succeed. It's a pattern very familiar in today's society, beset as it is with instrumental rationality that enables us, very effectively, to close down the deeper questions of the purpose of life.

The early twentieth-century Roman Catholic theologian, Romano Guardini, wrote this about worship:

It teach[es] the soul not to see purposes everywhere, not to be conscious of the end it wishes to attain, not to be desirous of being over clever and grown-up, but to understand simplicity in life. The soul must learn to abandon, at least in prayer,

---

9   See her blog at http://lizzyknowsall.blogspot.co.uk

the restlessness of purposeful activity; it must learn to waste time for the sake of God, and to be prepared for the sacred game with sayings and thoughts and gestures, without always immediately asking 'why?' and 'wherefore?' It must learn not to be continually yearning to do something, to attack something, to accomplish something useful, but to play the divinely ordained game of the liturgy in liberty and beauty and holy joy before God. (Guardini 1997, p.72)

Such an approach encourages humanity to attend to that which is other, to develop our RH attention. Herbert McCabe has said something very similar: that prayer is about wasting time in God. Both writers are keen to commend worship as place and time when children and adults can lay aside the need to be purposeful, useful, functional and instrumental, and instead engage in deep playfulness that allows an encounter with the heteronomy that is God. Worship is a sacred game, full of sayings and thoughts and gestures, of profound significance. It enables all, of whatever age, to become again like a small child, playing, caught up in the all-embracing significance of play, absorbed by the rules and actions of the game. The play of worship is for its own sake. It takes us out of ourselves in a way that enables us to participate in the fullness of God.

Conclusion

This chapter has considered how play enables engagement with otherness – through toys, with people, and ultimately with God – so the child and adult find self when lost in play, and are therefore able to explore and grow a sense of self, shaped by the heteronomy of the other. This deep significance of play is in contrast to the seductions of online gaming, and how virtuality traps the imagination, rather than allowing sociality to develop through real encounter with real people and things.

We've looked at the work of Tim Gill and others to challenge risk aversion in Western society, and how playing in the natural world – rewilding the child, as Monbiot (2013a, 2013b) coins it – is to be commended. The work of the Forest Schools Association is worth exploring in this context, and reference is provided in the next section on further reading.

Further reading and information

St Cuthbert's Wild School for Boys is a heartening read for any parent concerned about a risk-averse culture (Skeels 2013).

Robert Macfarlane and Jackie Morris's *The Lost Words: A Spell Book* is a lament for the lack of childhood engagement with the natural world (Macfarlane and Morris 2017).

The Forest School Association[10] and Forest Schools first appeared in the UK in the mid-1990s. While they are still less widespread than in Denmark or Sweden, their growing number is a sign that risk aversion can be challenged. Its ethos includes an appreciation of the value of woodland settings as challenging, stimulating environments, and a holistic approach to learning in which children enjoy relative freedom to explore the setting and develop confidence and competence.

George Monbiot is a passionate contemporary advocate of rewilding the child (Monbiot 2013a). He drew on research from King's College London to find that children who spend time learning in natural environments 'perform better in reading, mathematics, science and social studies'. He accompanied the adventure learning charity WideHorizons with a group of ten-year-olds from a deprived borough in London to Wales. Many had never been to the countryside before or seen the sea. He writes: 'I discovered that none of them knew what happens if you touch a nettle' (Monbiot 2013b). Children who have never visited the countryside – 50 per cent in the UK, according to WideHorizons – live under constant restraint.

---

10   www.forestschoolassociation.org

The National Trust in the UK has an excellent report on nature deficit disorder (Moss 2012). Also worth reading is Richard Louv's *Last Child in the Woods* (Louv 2010).

Playfulness:
from conscious incompetence to unconscious competence

Culture: What literature, music, art best express playfulness? How might children engage and respond with appreciation?

Character: What habits could children practise deliberately to be playful, in ways that will continue into adulthood?

Call: As a way of understanding the profession of teaching as a vocation, what more could the Headteacher and staff do to model playfulness?

- Consider the ways you play, and what the fruits of that play are.

- When did you last climb a tree, or build a sandcastle, or dam a stream? Teach a child you know these things.

- If you are a teacher or a parent, what team sports or games are offered at the school? How might sport and games be developed?

- Follow up ideas at www.nationaltrust.org.uk/50-things-to-do.

Chapter 6

Resourcefulness

Post-Traumatic Stress Disorder and Adverse Childhood Experience

When early attachment has not been secure, children can live, sometimes for the rest of their lives, in a perpetual state of anxiety. In Chapter 4, we saw how the vagal nerve is involved in various stress responses such as fight, flight, freeze (FFF) and also how the vagal brake is activated when we are calmed. When there is a lack of reassurance to calm a distressed child, the vagal brake does not engage the vagal nerve and so the child is left with the FFF response.

Future anxiety states often begin here and can lead to the severe experience of Post-Traumatic Stress Disorder (PTSD). The trauma may be caused by intense one-off or sustained negative experiences such as constant chaotic parenting, where the child lives with high levels of uncertainty, even violence and abuse. These are called *Adverse Childhood Experiences*, where there is a neurological reaction to stress, and the anxiety becomes hard-wired. There's a huge research base exploring Adverse Childhood Experience that can be followed up here.[1]

So what happens? The normal response to trauma is to be afraid, and the amygdala triggers a freeze, fight or flight response.

---

1   www.cdc.gov/violenceprevention/acestudy/index.html

The sympathetic nervous system releases adrenalin, which causes the hypothalamus to set off a chain reaction that produces cortisol to enable that response, which, in normal situations, dies down within a few hours. When the trauma is extreme or chronic, it can take years to recover, if ever. But when really terrible things happen to people, it can prove too difficult to integrate the awful experience. Then the person continues to have distressing dreams, insomnia, irritability and anxiety, and will struggle to talk about the trauma. Sufferers may experience flashbacks, panic or depression. They relive the experience over and over, vulnerable to reminders of the experience, hyper-vigilant and watchful for signs that something bad will happen again. According to Gerhardt, 'PTSD is the diagnosis for people who don't recover' (Gerhardt 2015, p.159).

When you're overwhelmed by uncontrollable impulses and distracted by negative feelings, it's hard to learn the alphabet. Paul Tough's book *How Children Succeed* gives lots of examples and evidence of the effectiveness of developing what he calls 'performance character', where children learn how to improve the self-control that enables them to live with PTSD by developing executive functions that make it possible to get through the day (Tough 2012, pp.18–19).

Poverty in childhood

Tough describes the effectiveness of helping children develop character strengths that enable them to respond to intervention. He shows a way out of the usual disadvantages that poverty causes.

> The teenage years are difficult for almost every child, and for children growing up in adversity, adolescence can often mark a terrible turning point, the moment when early wounds produce bad decisions, and bad decisions produce devastating results. But teenagers also have the ability – or at

least the potential – to rethink and remake their lives in a way
that younger children do not. (Tough 2012, p.48)

All of Tough's examples are from the education system in
the USA.

In the UK, a disciplined approach is being pioneered at
Michaela Community School in Wembley, London. There
a conscious policy is in place to reassert traditional forms of
authority, in the belief that children benefit from unambiguous
discipline. Children who have a disruptive upbringing are not
excused because of their disruptive background. Instead, the
expectation is that they can and will change, if they are treated
with a 'no excuses' discipline. With constant reinforcement
and encouragement (carrot and stick), and reminders of why
the rules are in place, most children change their behaviour
(Birbalsingh, 2016).

This takes us to the heart of this chapter on resourcefulness.
What enables children and young people from any background
to develop the character to be challenged and work with it? So
that in turn they give and take such challenge, encouraging
others, in a way that reveals an emotional and psychological
resourcefulness that shows they are ready for adulthood?

Resilient, or resourceful?

I'm using the word 'resourcefulness' instead of the more
current 'resilience', because I think it brings different things to
the table. Resilience training is widespread today – in schools
and in the military – seeking to enable young people and adults
to cope or survive in adverse circumstances. Resourcefulness,
though, suggests more than the reactive ability to cope. The
resourceful person will bring resources to the situation, not
only to cope with challenge and failure but also to turn things
around for the benefit of all concerned. Resilience enables
survival; resourcefulness brings more: self-control, and the
emotional and psychological strength to give of self to enable

others to survive and flourish. Resilience is a survival mode; resourcefulness, a flourishing mode. You're saying something quite different when you say 'I'm a resourceful person', rather than 'I'm resilient'. A resourceful person is resilient, and more.

Resourcefulness offers a holistic approach. Resourceful people are good to have around, because whatever the situation, they know how to dig deep within for what will enhance what's going on, in good directions: whether it's the emotional resourcefulness to sit down and listen, drawing on their own awareness of the seriousness of the content of what's being said to them, or the practical resourcefulness to change a flat tyre, or check the oil. Resourceful people will bring creative ideas that are appropriate to the project – ideas that won't just be about expressing their own 'creativity', but which will be thought through for the project itself, giving something extra, without regard for whether they get credit or not. Resourceful people will be able to be in the background, knowing that their sense of ego, or self, isn't lessened if they are not in the limelight. They also have the confidence to step forward when it's required. They can lead, and follow.

Resourcefulness belongs with the *performance* character that Paul Tough describes, that enables the teenager to develop executive functions that override the instinctive, limbic reactions they feel through the day, and to learn to manage their emotions, including varying levels of anxiety. Tough is great on *performance* character. He dismisses too quickly, to my mind, the value of *moral* character. He dismisses it for the usual reasons and prejudices, that morality is rule-based and imposed. Both are required, though, to enable people to respond in adversity from an integrated set of values and well-rounded moral ground. Moral character enables them not only to succeed in life as an individual, but to see their whole life as an opportunity to enhance the lives of others; indeed, to build a better world through their care and passion.

Underestimating young people

Often we underestimate young people. Gill believes growing adult intervention in childhood has minimised risk at the expense of childhood experience (Gill 2009).

It takes time and dedication to develop the hard-wiring of moral character that makes someone resourceful and able to respond reliably in any circumstance. It takes the sort of habit-learning and formation that an athlete undertakes when she trains; repeating actions and routines until they are beyond boring. Moral training requires the same practice to be kind, courageous, or to notice what needs to be done. It can be learned at any time of life, though.

Grit

Paul Tough collaborated with Angela Duckworth, who went on to write *Grit* (Duckworth 2017). This is well worth reading, particularly for those embarking on parenthood.[2] Duckworth writes:

> The perseverance that contributes to grit comes with deliberate practice – the daily discipline of trying to do things better than we did yesterday. This is focused, full-hearted, challenge-exceeding-skill practice that leads to mastery, where the person zeros in on weaknesses. To be gritty is to resist complacency; it is to say 'Whatever it takes, I want to improve!' (Duckworth 2017, p.91)

We've seen how the acquisition of habit – of moving from conscious incompetence to unconscious competence – is important to character. Duckworth spells this out for parents, in the recognition that wise parenting is hard work. She recommends extra-curricular activities (and particularly those led by adults other than parents, as parents are too inclined to

---

2   Duckworth's TED talk is available here: www.ted.com/talks/angela_lee_
     duckworth_grit_the_power_of_passion_and_perseverance

praise their children, which doesn't promote grit). Coaches and teachers, and other volunteer adults are more likely to hold children to task, encouraging them to do hard things that interest and challenge them, at the same time as having fun. She says this is much better than the three hours a day watching television and playing video games that American kids spend, as well as the additional time drained away 'checking social media feeds, texting friends links to cat videos and tracking the Kardashians as they figure out which outfit to wear' (Duckworth 2017, p.225). Research shows that those who do extra-curricular activities, and for more than two years, are more likely to get a job and earn more money (Duckworth 2017). The appeal of performance character is here – that character will bring success – but there's more with Duckworth: she's more concerned about moral character than Tough is.

Grit includes doing hard things, and not giving up. Duckworth recommends that young people should choose their hard things to do, and pick up an extra hard thing every year in high school. This happens best within a culture in which there are shared norms and values: 'If you want to be grittier, find a gritty culture and join it. If you're a leader, and you want the people in your organisation to be grittier, create a gritty culture' (Duckworth 2017, p.245).

'*Sisu*' is Finnish for perseverance, and in that culture the reasoning goes:

> It sometimes feels like we have nothing left to give, and yet, in those dark and desperate moments, we find that if we just keep putting one foot in front of the other, there is a way to accomplish what all reason seems to argue against. (Duckworth 2017, p.252)

Failures are going to happen; it's how we face into them that's more important than succeeding. Grit is about having the (sometimes fierce) resolve to take responsibility for failing and working away at weakness. It's about developing habits that mean we challenge ourselves and exceed through practice.

Grittier people are *dramatically* more motivated than others to seek a meaningful, other-centred life (Aristotle's *eudaimonia*) (Duckworth 2017, p.147), which will often include a sense of wanting to benefit other people. Duckworth tells this little parable:

> Consider the parable of the bricklayers. Three bricklayers are asked: 'What are you doing?'
> The first says, 'I am laying bricks.'
> The second says, 'I am building a church.'
> And the third says, 'I am building the house of God.'
> The first bricklayer has a job. The second bricklayer has a career. The third bricklayer has a calling. (Duckworth 2017, p.149)

Fortunate people who see their work as a calling – as opposed to a job or a career – reliably say that their work makes the world a better place, and it's these people who seem most satisfied with their jobs and their lives overall, with a sense of purpose that comes from outside the self (Duckworth 2017).

We shall return to this in Chapter 9 on fruitfulness.

Intrapersonal, interpersonal and intellectual

Duckworth identifies three clusters to describe character: intrapersonal, interpersonal and intellectual; or strengths of will, heart and mind (Duckworth 2017). She groups them like this:

- *Intrapersonal* includes traits like self-control (resisting temptations like texting and video games), and what contributes to performance character – the virtues that are likely to land us a job.

- *Interpersonal* are the social virtues, like gratitude, kindness, thoughtfulness, which give us social intelligence. These are virtues that help you get along with and provide assistance to other people, and mean we have moral character. They are the sort of things people say about us in the eulogy when we die.

- *Intellectual* characteristics include virtues such as curiosity and zest, the virtues that keep us active and open engagement with the world of ideas.

She says that character will include all these three types of virtue. Duckworth's book is good. Hers is the latest in a number of character education approaches, signalling a welcome emergence of viewing education as formative of the person.

Risk adversity

Jean Twenge has researched what she calls the 'iGen'. She suggests that they have been cocooned at home in security, such that when they leave home, they are overly concerned with their own emotional safety (Twenge 2017). She writes:

> iGen'ers' interest in safety may be at least partially rooted in their long childhoods... As 10-year-olds are treated like 6-year-olds, 14-year-olds like 10-year-olds, and 18-year-olds like 14-year-olds, children and teens spend more years fully aware that they are safe and protected in the cocoon of childhood. When they go to college, they suddenly feel unprotected and vulnerable and go about trying to recreate the feeling of home and safety that they were in just a few months before. (Twenge 2017, pp.163–4)

Physically, they are safer than ever before, but are not encountering the world out there, for fear of the risks. Frank Furedi, author of *Paranoid Parenting*, wrote in a 2004 article:[3]

> Parents are almost forced to fall in line... The minority of parents who try to resist it are stigmatised as irresponsible.

---

3   Furedi, F. (2004) 'Do we worry too much about the safety of our children?' *Independent on Sunday*, 24 October 2004, available at www.frankfuredi.com/ inthenews/do_we_worry_too_much_about_the_safety_of_our_children, accessed on 12 July 2018.

When your own kid is the only one allowed to go shopping, to go to the swimming pool by himself, it looks very strange.

Snowflakes

They have been called the 'Snowflake Generation'. 'Poor little Snowflake' became the defining insult of 2016, describing young adults who are viewed as less resilient and more prone to taking offence than previous generations.[4] As Claire Fox uses it, it often infers a sense of entitlement, coupled with an identity politics that closes down free speech. She uses it of young people whom she calls easily offended and thin-skinned.[5] Fox has reason to challenge. She was due to appear at a school in Hertfordshire, but reported:

> Several of the students said, 'How dare you invite this terrible woman to speak?' and said to me that I'd come there and upset them. They were giving a literal demonstration of my very speech, she says.[6]

Fox is concerned about the way controversial speakers have been disinvited on university and college campuses,[7] closing down free speech and debate, for the sake of the emotional safety of the students, but depriving them of the opportunity to hear and engage with views they find challenging. Fox

4   Rebecca Nicholson in *The Guardian*, Monday 28 November 2016, modified on Saturday 25 November 2017, see www.theguardian.com/science/2016/nov/28/snowflake-insult-disdain-young-people

5   Claire Fox (2006) *I Find That Offensive*; London: Biteback Publishing. Claire is the Director of the Academy of Ideas, which she established to create a public space where ideas can be contested without constraint. She has written about generation snowflake in articles for *The Spectator* ('How We Train Our Kids to Be Censorious Cry-Babies', 4 June 2016) and for the *Daily Mail* ('Why Today's Young Women Are Just So Feeble', 9 June 2016). Her website is at http://academyofideas.org.uk

6   Quoted by Nicholson in www.theguardian.com/science/2016/nov/28/snowflake-insult-disdain-young-people

7   Notably, Germaine Greer from Cardiff University in 2015.

argues that the Snowflake generation has been raised as 'cotton-wool kids'.

It's disputed.[8] Liv Little has set up gal-dem, which is a collective of more than 70 women of colour who argue that there is a lot of offence in the world and it's important for it to be named and resisted. Carving out safe space is necessary.

The 2014 film *Whiplash*, directed by Damien Chazelle, gives a provocative perspective on all this.

A key question is about space and who hosts it. What happens when the liberal notion of universities as places that host the space so all views can be aired and argued, disputed and debated, becomes itself contested? When the liberal 'hosting' of the space to learn is no longer trusted as somewhere that will hold people free of harm and offence? The question is open wide about who hosts instead.

Hannah Arendt, the Jewish-American political theorist (1906–95), wrote that when an adult is not in a position of authority, peer group authority will rule.[9] Without any consensus – for when anyone can call 'offence', what results is a libertarian free-for-all relativism – the public space for debate very quickly closes down into a moral vacuum where my truth is as good as your truth. Such moral vacuums usually attract the most powerful, or the most 'entitled', who then dominates. Totalitarianism can result.

There's a great deal to be said for the liberal traditions that host our places of learning, where 'entitlement' is neutralised.

To benefit from education requires not just resilience, but a resourcefulness that can take challenge – whether intellectual,

---

8   See Angus Harrison's article in *Vice* at www.vice.com/en_uk/article/3bwjeb/
     were-either-generation-snowflake-or-the-new-young-fogey; also Liv Little,
     22-year-old Editor-in-Chief of the magazine *gal-dem*, recently selected as one of
     the BBC's 100 most influential and inspirational women of 2016, who finds the
     idea that she and her peers are self-obsessed and unable to cope with the world
     absurd. 'I don't get what they want to happen. Do they want people to be quiet
     and suck it up? Do they want people to have breakdowns and be really unhappy
     and accept a political system that doesn't represent them?'; see www.gal-dem.com
9   Arendt's essay 'The Crisis in Education' can be found here: www.digital
     counterrevolution.co.uk/2016/hannah-arendt-the-crisis-in-education-full-text

emotional, personal, or political – and respond without the instinctive feeling of offence. The character strength of self-control is needed more often if the conversation is to continue within education systems that hold onto the necessity of embracing material that is challenging.

For those who suffer serious and diagnosed PTSD, trigger warnings are important and should be in place with proper pastoral support for students who require it, to enable them to develop as much resilience as they need to realise their potential.[10] Safe spaces, with mutual support and resources, are not an end in themselves, though, but places that enable engagement in the wider world to continue, heteronomous learning that shapes the self.

Trustworthy institutions

There is a deeper question behind the debates about trigger warnings and snowflakes. No longer are educational institutions trusted, as once they were, to offer an implicit moral foundation to enable the flourishing of students in a community to which all belong, transcending the tribal allegiances of identity politics. To be a resourceful person in today's world is to seek to find a deeper morality than that of tribal belonging, or individual libertarianism, or utilitarian instrumentalism, rooting oneself into a desire for the common good, and seeking to serve that common good through the resources that one brings to the wider world. Institutions that are part of society – even when flawed – are really important in which to learn that deeper morality. The fact they are flawed is a lesson in itself, for institutions fail as well, and need to repent when they betray the

---

10   See 'Academic Ethics: The Legal Tangle of "Trigger Warnings"' by Brian Leiter (November, 2016) at www.chronicle.com/article/Academic-Ethics-The-Legal/238356; 'A Quick Lesson on What Trigger Warnings Actually Do' by Lindsay Holmes at www.huffingtonpost.co.uk/entry/university-of-chicago-trigger-warning_us_57bf16d9e4b085c1ff28176d; 'Too many academics are now censoring themselves' by Frank Furedi at www.theguardian.com/education/2016/oct/11/censor-lecturers-trigger-warnings-students-distressed

trust invested in them. But that's not to say that they shouldn't continue to exist, wiser and more careful, with good regulation in place, to nurture the children and young people in their care towards adulthood.

Lifelong learning

Resourcefulness concerns lifelong learning. It is an ongoing seeking after wisdom, in a world which often prohibits children from developing the resources to cope with risk or danger, not least by the anxieties and expectations of the parents and adults around them.

Horace encouraged people to grow in knowledge and understanding, to dare to be wise. Some people – the wiser ones – never stop: They go on interested and curious in the world around them until they die. They carry on reading, and listening, discussing, debating, open to others across the generations, open to expanding their horizons. They walk up mountains because there's more to see from the summit. They understand that education never ends, that it is a lifelong journey. It takes resourcefulness to continue to seek out new adventures.

It takes resourcefulness, too, to seek to teach in turn. To respond to the sense of vocation that teaching should have at its heart, and train to give of oneself, to give resources to others, particularly children, so they can learn in turn.

Conclusion

Resourcefulness is stronger than resilience in enabling a more creative engagement with what challenges people of all ages, and particularly young people. Given the trauma of PTSD and Adverse Childhood Experience, which can seriously debilitate young people for the rest of their lives, we've looked at the idea of grit, of developing habits of deliberate practice that build moral and performance character in interpersonal, intrapersonal and intellectual areas, better to cope with negative experience, and also the inevitable failure that is part of life. A strong sense of authority and discipline can be a real benefit, within an environment of tough love and trust.

We've considered the defensiveness that seeks to protect the self against offence, and the way this can close down free debate and exposure to uncomfortable, heteronomous opinions and learning that challenge the autonomous self. Resourcefulness is the developed habit of the heart that seeks out that which challenges, and engages with it, on a lifelong journey that sees learning as an adventure.

Resourcefulness:
from conscious incompetence to unconscious competence

Culture: What literature, music, art best express resourcefulness? How might children engage and respond with appreciation?

Character: What habits could children practise deliberately to be resourceful?

Call: As a way of understanding the profession of teaching as a vocation, what more could the headteacher and staff do to model resourcefulness?

- Consider times when you have felt offended by someone's opinions or views. How did you respond? How might you have responded more fruitfully?

- Spend a day doing something that tests your limits (like just drinking water). What do you learn about your resourcefulness?

- Watch the 2014 film *Whiplash*. Do you think Andrew's personality was destroyed by Fletcher, or did he gain character?

- Jordan Peterson has polarised opinion as he challenges the political correctness of what he calls 'neo-Marxist ideologues'. Watch his lecture 'Professor against Political Correctness' on YouTube. What is your response?

- Duckworth talks about taking up hard things to do. If you are a parent or teacher, how might you encourage children or teenagers around you to do this?

Chapter 7

The Digital Age

Maddy works as a legal researcher. Her undergraduate degree was in theology. When she graduated, she didn't have a clue what to do, so drifted a bit, off and on with Craig. When he found work as a landscape gardener, they decided to settle down. That was five years ago. Maddy found work at the large legal firm in the town. Emily came along, and between them they managed work and childcare, so Maddy could continue to work.

Jobs at risk of automation

It was a colleague at work that put her onto Robert Peston's latest book *WTF* (Peston 2017). The chapter 'We Are Terminated' on the impact of automation on work rattled her. Maddy realised that the work she did was vulnerable in a way she had never thought possible. The Bank of England, according to Peston, is predicting a 'staggering 15 million British jobs at risk of automation' (Peston 2017, p.222), including the sort of research Maddy does. Maddy bought the little book *Will Robots Take Your Job?* It was disconcerting to read that:

> Sophisticated algorithms are gradually taking on a number of tasks performed by paralegal, contract and patent lawyers. More specifically, law firms can now rely on computers that can scan thousands of legal briefs and precedents to assist

in pre-trial research. As an example, one system proved able to analyse and sort 570,000 documents within two days. (Cameron 2017, p.30)

Exactly what Maddy does – but there's no way she can manage this work load. Not in a month of Sundays.

She decided to read more. To understand more about robots. In a bookshop she found a book that had won awards and looked like it might give her something to chew on. She took a deep breath and bought *Life 3.0* by Max Tegmark (2017).

It seemed that the Western world was in the midst of a brain storm – literally. Maddy quickly picked up on the great excitement around in the world of digital research scientists. A significant amount of anxiety too.

Machine learning

Leading professors are predicting that machine learning – which increasingly is modelled on how human beings learn – is likely to take off and outstrip human intelligence (though no one is very sure how or when).[1] Tegmark, a professor at Massachusettts Insititute of Technology (MIT), anticipates a future when humans have been surpassed by artificial intelligence. He argues that humanity needs to be asking some fundamental questions now – now! – to ensure we are ready for a digital future. This chapter is going to engage with his book, as Maddy read it and discussed it with Craig.

Tegmark calls for an open and informed debate about the issues that he outlines in the book. In 2015, he convened a group of scientists and researchers in Puerto Rico. They arrived at a surprising (to him, at least) unanimity about the need for caution and concern about artificial intelligence (AI) safety, to anticipate as many of the dangers as possible, but not so much

---

1   Tegmark says, having outlined the different possibilities and time frames, 'I think it's wise to be humble at this stage and acknowledge how little we know, because for each scenario discussed, I know at least one well-respected AI researcher who views it as a real possibility' (2017, p.157).

so that research becomes risk-averse. Dangers concerning the use of automated weapons systems, for instance, which are a serious threat in the hands of someone who doesn't like you (like a drone programmed to recognise your face, attack you, and then self-destruct).

The most dangerous scenario for humanity, however, is if AI acquires human-level Artificial General Intelligence, and then upgrades itself to Superintelligence, and its goals are not aligned with human ones. In which case, humanity might end up extinct, replaced by AI, or by nothing, in a self-destruction scenario.[2]

Superintelligence

Maddy was gripped. She got hold of *Superintelligence* by Nick Bostrom, a professor at Oxford University (Bostrom 2014). That was rather heavy going. As was Ray Kurzweil's stuff about Singularity (Kurzweil 2014, 2016). But they all seemed to be saying the same sort of thing. Kurzweil cautions:

> Artificial Intelligence is all around us – we no longer have our hand on the plug. The simple act of connecting with someone via a text message, e-mail, or cell phone call uses intelligent algorithms to route the information. Almost every product we touch is originally designed in a collaboration between human and artificial intelligence and then built in automated factories. If all the AI systems decided to go on strike tomorrow, our civilization would be crippled: we couldn't get money from our bank, and indeed, our money would disappear; communication, transportation, and manufacturing would all grind to a halt. Fortunately our intelligent machines are not yet intelligent enough to organise such a conspiracy. (Kurzweil 2014, p.158)

---

2   Tegmark tabulates 12 AI Aftermath Scenarios, which include 'libertarian utopia', 'benevolent dictator', 'egalitarian utopia', 'gatekeeper', 'protector god', 'enslaved god', 'conquerors', 'descendents', 'zookeeper', '1984', 'reversion', and 'self-destruction' (Tegmark 2017, p.162).

Maddy thought it all seemed rather fantastical. Tegmark, Bostrom and others, however, argue that it's important to take the possibility of an intelligence explosion seriously. It's now a 'non-silly topic', according to Bostrom, who adds: 'Away from the popular cacophony, it is now also possible – if one perks up one's ear and angles them correctly – to hear the low-key murmur of a more grownup conversation' (Bostrom 2014, p.321). The scenarios they outline deserve proper consideration and thought – across the board of different disciplines – taking on board the projections of leading AI experts that we might build technology powerful enough permanently to end poverty, disease and war – or end humanity itself. 'We might,' says Tegmark, 'create societies that flourish like never before, on Earth and perhaps beyond, or a Kafkaesque global surveillance state so powerful that it could never be toppled' (Tegmark 2017, p.37).

Others are more sanguine. Will Storr, for instance, in his book *Selfie*:

> It's basically that we're going to keep making more intelligent, faster and faster machines and all of a sudden, there's going to be this exponential, just like brrccccchhhhhxxxssszzzzz, and we don't know what happens. Some people say the Singularity is like the world's end, some people say we're going to evolve into another species. It's meant to represent acceleration, change, and then a moment of complete transformation of the universe. (Storr 2017, pp.269–70)

Maddy was left with a lot of questions. She was struck by what 'intelligence' seemed to mean, and how narrow it was. She liked the fact that a computer can't work out the answer to 'The large ball crashed right through the table because it was made of Styrofoam. What was made of Styrofoam, the large ball or the table?' (Carr 2015, p.121). She was intrigued by Bostrom's questions about how important it was to ensure that Artificial Superintelligence is able to reason morally – and if so, with what sort of morality, given that human beings can't seem to decide.

Deep learning

More than anything, Maddy was fascinated by the language that was used. 'Deep learning' was the term used, and it had real resonances with what she'd read about how Emily learned; as her brain developed through repetitive practice, learning by heart, so the nerves and synapses became 'hard-wired'. Ray Kurzweil's book *How to Create a Mind* (2014) described the human biological brain, seeking to emulate it.[3] It seemed that AI researchers saw direct parallels to human learning.

Bostrom (2014, p.27) quoted Alan Turing, who wrote this in 1950:

> Instead of trying to produce a programme to simulate the adult mind, why not rather try to produce one which simulates the child's? If this were then subjected to an appropriate course of education one would obtain the adult brain.

Maddy knew how a child learns from the carefulness shown to her from her earliest days. She and Craig had encouraged Emily to play at the repetitive games she loved, the habit-forming practice of play and learning that developed her brain. They planned to delay as long as possible giving her a phone and instead play games that helped her focus her attention and concentration, bit by bit, as she grew. Maddy was really struck by Turing's suggestion, that if we want machines to develop in humane ways, with a broad intelligence that works alongside human partners, the same pedagogy might be appropriate for machines as well as humans. As Turing suggested, the machine can be programmed in a similar way to how a child learns.

---

3   'The question,' Kurzweil (2014, pp.181–2) says, 'is whether or not we can find an algorithm that would turn a computer into an entity that is equivalent to a human brain. A computer, after all, can run any algorithm that we might define because of its innate universality (subject only to its capacity). The human brain, on the other hand, is running a specific set of algorithms. Its methods are clever in that it allows for significant plasticity and the restructuring of its own connection based on experience, but these functions can be emulated in software.'

Humane education?

The key questions that played around in Maddy's mind during this time of intense reading were: What is human nature? If we want our computers in the digital age to be humane, how do we educate them to be so? Given that human nature itself can't be counted on to be universally humane, how do we educate our children to be humane? How do we bring up our children and grandchildren so they do not live in the world imagined by Charlie Brooker, whose series *Black Mirror* had so captured Maddy's and Craig's imaginations at New Year?

Maddy had studied different theories of what it means to be a human being, or person, when she was at university. She remembered a particular philosophical framework that suggested that our human nature reaches its fullest expression or fulfilment when the human person is shaped by the reality of God. It needs to be a sophisticated understanding of God (not like that dismissed by Steven Pinker and other humanists) – and for Maddy, that seemed best expressed in Neo-Platonism. As far as Maddy understood, that was to say that God is never knowable by the human mind; that God will always surpass human understanding and imagination. The human person needs a degree of humility to say:

> I accept that human knowledge and intelligence is limited, in that it can't grasp or control that which is experienced as God. However, I believe my sense of self, my thinking and knowing, my imagination, my embodied cognition, is richer when all I am is held within the God who is other to me; when the best of me is found in God, and participates in God's fullness.

It was clear that most AI researchers and scientists dismiss belief in God for a variety of reasons. Maddy had read how computers now absorb and process whole disciplines of knowledge. Maddy wondered what would happen if a computer was programmed to read and digest the philosophy of St Thomas Aquinas. Why not programme a computer to believe in God? A computer thus programmed might become more humane than the best human being and lead the way in AI – or 'wisdom', perhaps, as 'intelligence' would prove to be too narrow a description of the mind that would emerge.

Tegmark asks for contributions to the debate in his book *Life 3.0* (2017, p.335). 'There's mine!' Maddy thought.

Maddy warmed to those writers who wanted to ensure a future of increased co-operation between humanity and computer, characterised by the best human traits.

Hard-wired

Next, Maddy read Susan Greenfield's *Mind Change*. Repetitive actions, including learning material off by heart, means our brains become 'hard-wired', which helps us behave in predictable, characteristic ways, with a body of knowledge memorised and the skills of embodied knowledge that show unconscious competence (which means, when we're in the flow, we don't have to think about what we're doing). As Greenfield explains, the brain's plasticity is moulded in different ways depending on the learning it undergoes – a musician, for example, or a taxicab driver, a basketball player – all will have different brain structures (Greenfield 2014). It seemed sensible to Maddy that Emily needed an education that ensured she was able to do best what AI is least capable of doing, her intelligence broadened by knowledge. Emily's education should develop her creativity and emotional intelligence to engage and work with other people, in the arts, or best of all, as a teacher herself.

Maddy was really struck that the language used to describe how computers learn draws on what is known of how the brain works. The terminology of neural pathways and synapses, of the neocortex and the hippocampus, were all used to describe the deep learning of computers, just as if it described a human's brain function and behaviour. Then she reflected on how people talk of reprogramming themselves, giving themselves a reboot; of their hardware and software. She saw an interesting flow in both directions in the talk of human and artificial intelligence. She wondered about a humane future with all sorts of intelligence informed by humane principles, ethics and morality. About a future in which not only humans but also Superintelligence are full of humane character.

Deep reinforcement learning

According to Nick Bostrom:

> Deep learning methods – essentially many-layered neural networks – have, thanks to a combination of faster computers, larger data sets, and algorithmic refinements, begun to approach (and in some cases exceed) human performance on many perceptual tasks, including handwriting recognition, image recognition and image captioning, speech recognition, and facial recognition. (Bostrom 2014, p.321)

Deep learning, or *deep reinforcement learning*, was developed by DeepMind[4] on the basis that a positive reward increases the tendency to do something again and again. Deep learning enabled a computer to learn to play and excel at games, and now, as Tegmark points out, 'there's no reason why a robot can't ultimately use some variant of deep reinforcement learning to teach itself to walk without help from human programmers' (Tegmark 2017, p.86). Deep learning methods are like human learning, which works by repeating information and actions until they become second nature.

---

4   DeepMind Technologies Limited is a British artificial intelligence company founded in September 2010. The company is based in London, but has research centres in California and Canada. In 2014 it was acquired by Google. Its AlphaZero programme has demonstrated the power of reinforcement learning by excelling at games such as Go and chess.

Life 3.0

Maddy understood why the growing community of philosophers and physicists were excited about the possibilities ahead. She was reassured that many were also deeply anxious about the dangers of automation. Tegmark gave a good overview, with his evolutionary approach.

He mapped out three stages of life in developing levels of sophistication: Life 1.0, 2.0 and 3.0 (Tegmark 2017). Life 1.0 is simple biological life – the level of bacteria, or simple organisms. Humanity today belongs in Life 2.0. Tegmark differentiates between human hardware (biological, material bodies) and human software. He writes:

> By your software, I mean all the algorithms and knowledge that you use to process the information from your senses and decide what to do – everything from the ability to recognize your friends when you see them to your ability to walk, read, write, calculate, sing and tell jokes. (Tegmark 2017, p.27)

Maddy was fascinated by how he continued by using language imported from the computer world to describe human intelligence. She read various passages out to Craig, to see what he thought.

She explained that Tegmark believed that Life 2.0 has evolved sophisticated means of using language and communication that will survive the death of the original brain, and now with computerisation, much of the world's information is available in a few clicks. Flexibility has enabled Life 2.0 to dominate Earth, by freeing human life from its genetic shackles. Each breakthrough enabled the next: language – writing, the printing press, modern science, computers, the internet, etc. – until this ever-faster cultural evolution of our shared software emerged as the dominant force shaping our human future, rendering our glacially slow biological evolution almost irrelevant.

But we're still dependent on our biology, and if we are to progress to the next stage, argues Tegmark, we need to upgrade from what he called 'our largely lifeless cosmos', into a life where the Universe would fulfill its potential, and Life 3.0 would be 'the master of its own destiny, finally fully free from its evolutionary shackles' (Tegmark 2017, p.30).

Craig wanted to hear more; to check out if what he was hearing was right: that Tegmark seemed to dismiss life on Earth so easily. Maddy explained further. Tegmark thought that humanity was now at 2.1, as we perform minor hardware upgrades such as implanting artificial teeth, knees and pacemakers, but more is to come. Tegmark claims that AI researchers think Life 3.0 may arrive during the coming century, perhaps even during our lifetime, spawned by the progress of AI.

Anxieties

Tegmark expresses anxieties about AI safety, but on the whole he locates himself as belonging to the 'Beneficial-AI movement' – on a spectrum of researchers from those he calls 'Confident Digital Utopians' to 'Techno-Skeptics' and 'Neo-Luddites' (Tegmark 2017, p.30ff). He outlines some of the myths and counter-myths that are around, and although there is much that AI experts disagree about, most researchers agree, however, that a digital future is a cause of worry.

It's perhaps a mythical worry that AI will 'turn evil', or become conscious – worries that are clearly explored in such series as Charlie Brooker's *Black Mirror*. Tegmark fears that the goals of AI might become misaligned with human ones (2017, p.44). He argues that it's dangerous to believe that machines can't control humans, or don't have goals. It's important to ask the question: 'What does it mean to say an object can remember, compute and learn?' (Tegmark 2017, p.49). Superintelligence is not likely soon, but it is on the cards, and it's important to plan ahead properly to make sure it is safe.

Dumb and lifeless matter?

Craig cares deeply about the environment. He understands the natural world to have its own deep wisdom, and gets angry when he thinks human beings are exploiting the rich resources of the earth. He wanted to take issue with the way Tegmark referred to 'dumb and lifeless matter', or our 'largely lifeless cosmos'. For him 'matter' was alive, vigorous and full of energy.

Like Maddy, he wondered about the use of the word, or concept, 'intelligence'. It was too narrow a word to describe how we know and understand (not only with our minds but with our bodies), how we judge between right and wrong and make moral decisions, how we seek the truth and pursue wisdom. He thought the rich biosphere of the earth had its own creative wisdom that needed more respect, not less. It certainly didn't need the sort of talk of upgrading, leaving behind planet earth, having exploited it into a fragile, polluted world. Craig was frustrated when he heard of those who expressed their lack of hope by seeking to escape this world. People like the entrepreneur Elon Musk who was projecting, in all seriousness, to establish a colony on Mars, for people who can afford a $200,000 ticket price. Musk plans a colony of a million people to make it self-sustaining, and reckons it could take 100 years, abandoning planet earth to go and destroy another. Craig had no time for this, and suspected Tegmark was friends with Musk.

To be human, too, requires so much more than intelligence, especially when there's no agreement 'on what intelligence is even among intelligent intelligence researchers!', as Tegmark himself said, with competing definitions which include all sorts of aspects, like capacity for logic, understanding, planning, emotional knowledge, self-awareness, creativity, problem-solving and learning (Tegmark 2017, p.49). Tegmark's own definition of intelligence is '*the ability to accomplish complex goals*' (2017, p.50, [my emphasis]). Craig wasn't sure that captures adequately the breadth of the human capacity to do and be beyond the purposeful and utilitarian. So much of his own work, as a landscape gardener, was creating something beautiful – and Craig thought that was the best realisation of our humanity. He believed that meaningfulness is found when we stop striving for the most complex of goals, and consider the lilies of the field.

Broad, rather than narrow

As Craig and Maddy both thought about what they wanted for Emily, they decided that the main advantage that humans have over computers is broad wisdom rather than narrow intelligence. Humanity might now lose to computers at *Go*, or *Jeopardy!* or chess, but having broad general intelligence enabled someone, with training, to develop expertise across a vast range of skills, languages or vocations. They were impressed, though, at the depth of knowledge that Watson had gained through reading 200 million pages of Wikipedia and encyclopaedias, taking only three seconds to respond to unexpected and convoluted questions to win *Jeopardy!* (Kurzweil 2014).

Maddy read more.

Artificial General Intelligence

Artificial General Intelligence (AGI) has been likened (by Hans Moravec[5]) to an ocean that gradually rises against the shore. Chess-playing is now well submerged; driverless cars are at the tideline. As advances in AGI are made, with exponential speed, Ray Kurzweil's idea of *Singularity* begins to take hold. Then all the land is submerged in one vast general intelligence that supersedes all previous life, including human and biological.

AI researchers understand matter – which can be either biological or silicon – as the basic substrate in which intelligence, and memory, can be embodied. A machine learns by laying

---

5   Moravec, H.' (1998) 'When will computer hardware match the human brain?' *Journal of Evolution and Technology 1.*

down changes in the substrate as a result of the repetition of data and function, so intelligence emerges independent of that substrate.[6] Substrate independence is crucial to computer memory, which can now out-remember any biological system. The algorithms are increasingly auto-associative, so search engines are able to learn from human interaction and to remember human preferences.

The name that's given to the substrate that performs computations is 'Computronium'. The neural networks in our brains act as a Computronium, for example, and just as our thinking, imagining and knowing emerge from our neural networks and are therefore substrate-independent, so the computation of a machine is substrate-independent. It can take on a life of its own, independent of its physical substrate, a bit like how waves operate independently of the water, or air that bears them.

Maddy explained to Craig that the substrate independence of computation implies that intelligence doesn't require flesh, blood or carbon atoms. When a computer starts to compute, it rearranges itself to learn. She read out loud:

> When we humans first created pocket calculators and chess programs, *we* did the arranging. For matter to learn, it must instead rearrange *itself* to get better and better at computing the desired function – simply by obeying the laws of physics. (Tegmark 2017, p.71)

Brains learn by hard-wiring, through repetition, the same information or action until it becomes second nature, and now, according to Tegmark and other AI researchers the same processes are now being mimicked by machines, as they learn to learn:

---

6   To explore further, Douglas Hofstadter's 2007 book, *I Am a Strange Loop* (Cambridge, MA: Basic Books), is a good read. See also Tegmark's TED talk 'Consciousness is a mathematical pattern' at www.youtube.com/watch?v=GzCvlFRISIM

Neural networks have now transformed both biological and artificial intelligence, and have recently started dominating the AI subfield known as *machine learning* (the study of algorithms that improve through experience). Before delving deeper into how such networks can learn, let's first understand how they compute. A neural network is simply a group of interconnected neurons that are able to influence each other's behaviour. Your brain contains about as many neurons as there are stars in our Galaxy: in the ballpark of a hundred billion. On average, each of these neurons is connected to about a thousand others via junctions called *synapses*, and it's the strengths of these roughly hundred trillion synapse connections that encode most of the information in your brain. (Tegmark 2017, p.72)

Artificial neural networks

AI researchers now are creating *artificial neural networks* which replicate the way neural networks function in our brains. This draws on research done in 1949 by Donald Hebb, who noticed that if two nearby neurons were frequently active (firing) together in our brains, their synaptic coupling meant that they learned to help trigger each other on a 'fire together, wire together' principle. This understanding of Hebbian learning has led to researchers exposing Computronium in computers to data on a repetitive basis, and so machines now are learning through the repetition and reinforcement.

For Tegmark the physicist, the laws of physics are his baseline. Machines are now learning by being programmed to mimic the way a brain works, and as they develop in sophistication, in accordance with the laws of physics, so, Tegmark says, the brain too must behave likewise, obeying the same laws.

Craig thought a sleight of hand was happening here! He voiced the same concern that he found was shared by Nicholas Carr:

The use of terms like *neural network* and *neuromorphic processing* may give the impression that computers operate the way brains operate (or vice versa). But the terms shouldn't be taken literally; they're figures of speech. Since we don't yet know how brains operate, how thought and consciousness arise from the interplay of neurons, we can't build computers that work as brains do. (Carr 2015, p.119)

Just because a computer can be programmed to learn, modelled on a brain, it doesn't mean that the brain will follow a computer's rules or be reduced in complexity to fit the laws that human researchers devise. There needs to be care about the language used. Craig wasn't happy with how easily the human brain could be explained using computer language.

Maddy and Craig concluded that it seemed likely that human and artificial intelligence will continue to develop in parallel, with mutual learning between the two. But both Maddy and Craig resisted language that reduces the complexity of the human brain, by modelling on a computer. 'Analogously' was important here, but was easily overlooked. The danger of such reductionism is captured by Carr again, quoting Donald Norman: "'the machine-centered viewpoint compares people to machines and finds us wanting, incapable of precise, repetitive, accurate actions." Although it now "pervades society," this view warps our sense of ourselves' (Carr, 2015, p.161).

Moral learning for computers?

For Maddy, the key question was this: If character is formed by deliberate practice into good moral habits, as humans are 'hardwired' when we practise certain behaviours, can computers start to learn to be morally good? What and how machines learn is crucially important if the future is to be as Tegmark (2017) and others, hope.

Maddy and Craig thought the big question was not 'How long will it take until machines can out-compete us at *all* cognitive tasks?' but 'Can machines learn more than intelligence? Can they learn wisdom?'

They were reading Nicholas Carr alongside Tegmark. Carr was more cautious:

> That doesn't mean that computers now have tacit knowledge, or that they've started to think the way we think, or that they'll soon be able to do everything people can do. They don't, they haven't, and they won't. Artificial intelligence is not human intelligence. People are mindful; computers are mindless. But when it comes to performing demanding tasks, whether with the brain or the body, computers are able to replicate our ends without replicating our means. (Carr 2015, p.11)

Leaps of logic and imagination

Craig read this aloud from Carr's book:

> What really makes us smart is not our ability to pull facts from documents or decipher statistical patterns in arrays of data. It's our ability to make sense of things, to weave the knowledge we draw from observation and experience, from *living*, into a rich and fluid understanding of the world that we can then apply to any task or challenge. It's this supple quality of mind, spanning conscious and unconscious cognition, reason and inspiration, that allows human beings to think conceptually, critically, metaphorically, speculatively, wittily – to take leaps of logic and imagination. (Carr 2015, p.121)

Maddy saw the value of friction in life, acting as a catalyst, pushing us to a fuller awareness and deeper understanding of the situation. It seemed important to encourage Emily out into the world, with Craig, in his gardens. And she could read more with her, so she was into books, to build a good, complex cognitive map, and to strengthen her memory and sense of morality and emotional knowledge.

She wanted Emily to think, not only with her brain, but also with her body – to have the sort of intelligence that used tools as part of her. Watching Craig, and the unconscious competence he had when making his designs a reality, she wanted the same knowledge for Emily.

Her reading of McGilchrist suggested that this was to keep RH attention alive in the world, open to the otherness of people, gardens and things. It was to resist the LH focus that Tegmark and others were seduced by, where intelligence meant merely *the ability to accomplish complex goals*. Human beings and their intelligence couldn't be reduced just to this, surely?

Embodied cognition

Maddy and Craig knew that today's world called for human beings to be able to mix the biological with the technical. They were sure that matter did matter – *pace* Tegmark. Maddy liked what Carr had to say about human-centred automation, about collaboration between human and computer: 'Computers do a superior job of sorting through lots of data quickly, but human experts remain subtler and wiser thinkers than their digital partners' (Carr 2015, p.167). She agreed when he questioned the prevailing technology-first attitude. She knew Emily would be computer literate in a way she would never achieve. She thought, as a parent, her best contribution would be to enable Emily to know the joy of using tools well, the delight of being at home in the world where things and stuff were real.

Next, Maddy read Matthew Crawford's book *The World Beyond Your Head*. She was impressed by his analysis of attention, and how distracted we can be today, within what is called the attention economy. Crawford bemoaned the lack of 'authoritative guidance of the sort that was once supplied by tradition, religion, or the kind of communities that make deep demands on us' (Crawford 2015, p.5). That was her role – to encourage Emily to learn about culture – the sort of knowledge that computers wouldn't give her. She liked how Crawford talked about '*submission* to things that have their own intractable ways, whether the thing be a musical instrument, a garden, or the building of a bridge' (Crawford 2015, p.24 [my emphasis]). The idea of heteronomy appealed to her, of attending to stuff that takes you out of yourself to engage with the intractable, the hard and difficult. That's what develops independence of mind and shapes us in particular roles and expertise. According to Crawford (2015, p.26): 'Such independence is won through disciplined attention, in the kind of action that joins us to the world. And – this is important – it is precisely those constraining circumstances that provide the discipline.'

Maddy knew that Emily would have digital know-how at her fingertips from the word go. More important was the knowledge that was in danger of being forgotten. Unconscious competence, not only in cognitive and intellectual knowledge, but also social, emotional, physical, psychological, spiritual and moral learning, was crucial to life skills being secured in a well-rounded way.

Conclusion: moral and cultural knowledge

Maddy wanted for Emily an education that equipped her not only with literacy and numeracy, but also in other directions, towards art and culture, culinary skill, physical dexterity, also the habits that develop a moral compass, and social and life skills that enable psychological health and well-being. It really helped to talk with Craig about her hopes that Emily would be someone with unconscious competence across a range of skills and behaviours, having learned a sense of character that would lead not only to self-fulfilment but also contribute to the common good of the culture and society around. Maddy concluded from her reading, that if we are going to face a future in which AI will play an increasingly important part, the strength of our human character is essential to ensure that the world grows in humane directions.

Emily's moral compass was crucial, if only because it will take a humanity full of moral character to develop computers with moral reasoning. A humane AI future depends on human programmers, after all. Maddy liked the way Carr quotes the political scientist, Charles Rubin, before going on with his own reflection:

> 'In an age of robots', observes the political scientist Charles Rubin, 'we will be as ever before – or perhaps as never before – stuck with morality'. The algorithms will need to be written. The idea we can calculate our way out of moral dilemmas may be simplistic, or even repellent, but that doesn't change the fact that robots and software agents are going to have to calculate their way out of moral dilemmas. Unless and until artificial intelligence attains some semblance of consciousness and is able to feel or at least simulate emotions like affection and regret, no other course will be open to our calculating kin. We may rue the fact that we've succeeded in giving automatons the ability to take moral action before we've figured out how to give them moral sense, but regret doesn't let us off the hook. The age of ethical systems is upon us. If autonomous machines are to be set loose in the world, moral codes will have to be translated, however imperfectly, into software codes. (Carr 2015, p.187)

The worst thing that could happen would be that education reduced human intelligence to model clever (but narrow) artificial intelligence. Humanity needs an education that trains the mind, body, soul and heart to develop moral, emotional and embodied know-how to complement the analytical and conceptual knowledge that has become increasingly dominant.

Crawford was good on this. He argues for a more holistic understanding of how we know – not just as rational, abstracting beings, but also thinking through our bodies – like dogs catching Frisbees on windy days – which is to 'put the mind back in the world, where it belongs, after several centuries of being locked within our heads' (Crawford 2015, p.51).

In a digital age Maddy didn't want to see Emily going in the direction of having a rational human mind, abstracted from materiality, seduced into a virtual world, and before long losing any embodied knowing, such as the pleasure of being able to ride Craig's motorbike. She wanted Emily to be situated in, and formed by, the contingencies of the world beyond her head, accepting and learning from the *heteronomy* that challenges us.

That way, Emily was less likely to become a fragile solipsistic self who shies away from emotional engagement and moral judgement. Maddy knew what Crawford meant when he talked about the self at the centre of a little 'me-world' (Crawford 2015, p.70). How, when we walk the streets of a city looking at GoogleMaps we are a pinpoint at the centre of the screen before us, immersed in layers of representation, seduced into self-centredness, insulated from the people and things around us. It can be a chore to look up and have to engage, to attend to the weather, or make eye contact. Or read a real map.

As Maddy looked to an AI future, she wanted an education that provided know-how on the basis of a broad and deep cultural literacy. Know-how that nurtured what was distinctively human, enabling moral reasoning, emotional intelligence, and the cultural knowledge that would locate Emily in history, enabling the past to inform her present and guide her future. She wanted Emily to have the opportunity for the creative engagement with the world around, inspiring metaphorical and artistic understanding, and the pleasure of skilled proficiency. An education that emphasised the formation of the person through the development of habits of heart, mind, soul and body, that would go some way towards building a fully rounded person, someone who was full of character.

Chapter 8

Thoughtfulness

A naked thinking heart

In the poem entitled 'The Blossom', John Donne describes his lovesick state, as he stays at Montgomery Castle in the last years of the sixteenth century, and is in love with a woman there. He ponders whether he should return to London and put on a witty, defended show, or stay in this vulnerable discomfort, in the vain hope the woman will have pity on him. He wants to stay, against his better judgement, and contemplates splitting himself, leaving the most important part of him behind. He suspects, however, that she is callous, and would not recognise – or if she did, would despise – what he calls his 'naked thinking heart', stripped of the rest of his body. He addresses that heart of his:

> Well then, stay here; but know,
> When thou hast stay'd and done thy most,
> A naked thinking heart, that makes no show,
> Is to a woman but a kind of ghost.
> How shall she know my heart; or having none,
> Know thee for one?
> Practice may make her know some other part;
> But take my word, she doth not know a heart.

Leaving to one side the story of the love behind the poem, now lost in time, it's intriguing how Donne refuses, with these words, to split himself, even as he contemplates it, into the usual dichotomy between heart and mind. The common assumption we make today is that our hearts feel, our minds think. Usually we take the heart to be the seat of emotion: and so we talk of the heart, broken in grief or love. It's the heart that feels, is torn in two, pumps faster when excited, or angry. It's hot and fiery, in contrast to the rational mind, which is cool and focused.

Donne is true to his classical education. Many philosophers, like Aristotle, thought differently. They believed it was the heart that was the organ that thought and reasoned – and also felt emotion – whereas the brain was not involved. It was Galen, one of the earliest Greek medical writers, who believed that the heart was the seat of the emotions, alongside the liver which was the place of the passions; that the brain was where reasoning happened. Donne recovers a heart that is thinking.

It's naked too.

Vulnerable, with all the rawness of that sense of exposure that comes when you are infatuated with someone else, his heart is holding together all sorts of feelings and trying to make sense of them. It's as if the poem is written from this naked thinking heart, not from his mind at all. We shouldn't be fooled, though. Donne's mind is definitely there, as he pours all his clever wit and skill of construction into the lines and form of the poem, intensifying, and no doubt relieving, some of the pressure and burden of his emotion, in good cathartic fashion.

Emotional intelligence

This chapter considers what it means to be a thoughtful person. Donne's naked thinking heart takes us straight to the wholeheartedness of it. A thoughtful person explores an issue, or listens to someone, without falling into that false dualism between mind and heart. Thoughtful people will bring a naked thinking heart in attention to the situation; open and vulnerable to what they are receiving, thinking with real emotional intelligence. Analysing what they hear, perceive and notice, they are thoughtful with compassion and carefulness about what direction or outcomes might be appropriate. Thoughtfulness requires attention born of humility and experience. It also involves – usually – anticipating and putting into practice the appropriate action and response.

John Donne's naked thinking heart helps us to hold together heart and mind. Thoughtfulness also helps us through other dualisms that can occur. Between thought and action, for instance. When people are described as 'thoughtful', often it's because they have done something with care and consideration for another person. The thoughtfulness has manifested itself in some action or other.

Thoughtfulness means also going beyond the narrow rationalism of so much 'thinking' today. As Jordan Peterson says:

> You might start by *not thinking* – or, more accurately, but less trenchantly, by refusing to subjugate your faith to your current rationality, and its narrowness of view. This doesn't mean 'make yourself stupid.' It means the opposite. It means instead that you must quit manoeuvring and calculating and conniving and scheming and enforcing and demanding and avoiding and ignoring and punishing. It means you must place your old strategies aside. It means, instead, that you must pay attention, as you may never have paid attention before. (Peterson 2018, pp.17–18)

There's a difference between rationalism and rationality. Peterson is talking about rationalism here – the narrow thinking that dismisses things it can't grasp. True rationality brings wise reasoning, or reasonableness, to the matter. With this understanding of reasonable rationality, faith in God is more than possible. Faith is reasonable – a fact that most rationalists don't get. It's at the heart of another dualism that 'thoughtfulness' challenges – that which is often assumed to exist between the left and the right hemisphere of the brain. Iain McGilchrist's important book *The Master and His Emissary* (2010) explores this further.[1]

---

1   www.ted.com/talks/iain_mcgilchrist_the_divided_brain

Iain McGilchrist's great metaphor

We met Iain McGilchrist in the Introduction, and the legend told by Nietzsche, about a ruler usurped by his emissary, which McGilchrist uses as a metaphor for his fears of a LH takeover of the wisdom of the RH in our brains and in Western culture today. In the story, the land becomes a tyranny and eventually collapses in ruins. McGilchrist uses this as a metaphor to describe the relationship between the two hemispheres of our brains. Instead of the common assumption that the RH and the LH do different things, McGilchrist argues that they attend to the world in mutually compatible ways. If one operates without the other, then the overall picture is lost. Latest research has found that both hemispheres contribute to all aspects of our experience of the world and what we do with that experience, but in different ways. The LH is not the dominant one, but is extensively dependent on the RH, and we dismiss its significance at our peril.

With his experience as a psychiatrist, McGilchrist writes convincingly about the pathologies of a society where the LH has the ascendency, losing what the RH knows.

Indeed, most of the remarkable things about human beings, the things that differentiate us from the animals, depend to a large extent on the right hemisphere...for instance, imagination, creativity, the capacity for religious awe, music, dance, poetry, art, love of nature, a moral sense, a sense of humour and the ability to change their minds. In all of these (though as always both hemispheres undoubtedly play a part), the principal part is played by the right hemisphere, usually involving the right frontal lobe. Where the left hemisphere's relationship with the world is one of reaching out to grasp, and therefore to *use* it, the right hemisphere's appears to be one of reaching out – just that. Without purpose. In fact one of the main differences between the ways of being of the two hemispheres is that the left hemisphere always has 'an end in view', a purpose or use, and is more the instrument of our conscious will than the right hemisphere. (McGilchrist, 2010, p.127)

In four or five chilling pages, McGilchrist asks: 'What would the left hemisphere's world look like?'(McGilchrist 2010, p.428ff). It's not difficult to apply these words to the education system today.

We would lose the broader picture, substituted for a more narrowly focused, restricted, but detailed, view of the world, making it difficult to maintain a coherent overview. The LH craves the appearance of clarity and certainty. With ever more narrowly focused attention, the LH leads to increasing specialisation, so knowledge becomes information, not wisdom. The LH dismisses everything outside its limited focus; the RH's 'whole picture' is simply not available to it. Skills and judgement, expertise, which come slowly and silently with practice, are discarded for quantifiable and repeatable processes, which can be regulated by administrators.

McGilchrist goes on to describe how the material and embodied world becomes increasingly abstracted and reified, so we see ourselves in conceptual, virtual ways, and as things, represented to ourselves. Fewer people find themselves doing work involving contact with anything in the real, 'lived' world. More and more work is overtaken by the meta-process of documenting or justifying what one was doing or supposed to be doing. Technology flourishes, as an expression of the LH's desire to manipulate and control, accompanied by a vast expansion of bureaucracy and systems of abstraction. The LH seeks measurable outcomes, with everything analysable into its constituent components, and so blotting out 'the awe-inspiring business of conscious human existence'. The 'mystery of being' gives way to a preference for technical problems for which solutions can be found.

Philosophically, the world becomes fragmented with bits and pieces thrown randomly together. Morality comes down to utilitarian calculation; at worst, enlightened self-interest. A depersonalisation of relationships between people, and between people and place, becomes the norm. Paranoia, lack of trust and resentment become pervasive within society, between individuals, and between government and people. Governments seek control through constant monitoring, controlling individuals as interchangeable equal parts in a mechanistic system, playing down individual responsibility.

The LH likes things to be explicit and clear, in a world marked by ever-increasing legislation, a 'network of small complicated rules', as de Tocqueville describes soft despotism.[2] As it becomes less possible to rely on a shared and intuitive moral sense, or implicit contracts between individuals, such rules become ever more burdensome. Being in control becomes the highest goal. Unlike at other times, when the RH has been more ascendant and death was accepted as omnipresent in life, the LH view is that death is the ultimate challenge to its sense of control.

The LH world deliberately undercuts what it doesn't understand, particularly a sense of awe and wonder. It tends to be over-explicit in its language of art and religion, showing a loss of their vital, implicit and metaphorical power. Religion becomes mere fantasy. The RH is drawn forward by exemplars of the qualities it values, whereas the LH is driven forward by a desire for power and control.

In a LH world, it becomes hard to discern value or meaning in life at all. A sense of nausea and boredom before life leads to a craving for novelty and stimulation. People become spectators rather than actors. Art becomes conceptual and loses the power of metaphor: Visual art lacks depth, music is reduced to little more than rhythm; concept comes to dominate.

In such a world, says McGilchrist:

> Cultural history and tradition, and what can be learnt from the past, would be confidently dismissed in preparation for the systematic society of the future, put together

---

by human will. The body would come to be viewed as a machine, and the natural world as a heap of resource to be exploited. Wild and unrepresented nature, nature not managed and submitted to rational exploitation for science or the 'leisure industry', would be seen as a threat, and consequently brought under bureaucratic control as fast as possible. Language would become devoid of any richness or meaning, and suggest a mechanistic world, with no overall feel for its metaphorical qualities.

This is what the world would look like if the emissary betrayed the Master. It's hard to resist the conclusion that his goal is within sight. (McGilchrist 2010, p.434)

A left hemisphere takeover?

McGilchrist has important things to say to the education system in a digital age. His analysis of the danger of a LH takeover rings true. It's not always been the case: McGilchrist argues that through the ages, the RH has predominated at times – at the time of the Renaissance, and during the Romantic era, when the arts, nature and religion offered apprehension of the other.

However, the arts and religion have too often participated actively in the betrayal of the Master, argues McGilchrist. Instead of their essential role in enabling the RH to encounter the other, metaphor and rich language have been stripped, in a LH tendency towards clarity and literalism. The rich traditional language of worship is replaced by formulaic, accessible words that lack any poetry. We fail to honour the metaphor, and the way it grows in meaning, with moral and emotional power, referred to the body, embodying the word.

Morality, according to McGilchrist, belongs with the RH, for it 'sees more of the picture, and it takes a broader perspective that characteristically includes both its own and the left hemisphere's, is more reciprocally inclined, and more likely to espouse another point of view' (McGilchrist 2010, p.86).

McGilchrist is at pains to emphasise that we need both hemispheres, but he makes the important claim that currently the ascendency of the left is cutting us off from important sources of knowledge. 'It is the right hemisphere which is responsible for maintaining a coherent, continuous and unified sense of self,' he writes (McGilchrist 2010, p.88).

Attending to the other

How do we attend to the other that the RH is able to apprehend? For without it the LH spirals down into a vortex of over-attention to detail, unable to free itself from the trap of instrumentality and reification. This applies to the 'self' too, raising the question: 'How do we free ourselves from the trap of excessive attention to self?' Education systems that focus on 'the unique child' are in danger of intensifying self-consciousness into hyper-consciousness, so self-reflexivity sharpens into mental illness, as McGilchrist has observed through his professional career. How do we challenge the LH preoccupation with creating a new humanity through AI? And how do we sustain a sense of the unique gift of human life that is ultimately mysterious and unable to be captured or controlled?

Drawing on McGilchrist's work, it's clear that an over-dependence on LH approaches, predominant in contemporary society, leads to an education system that is obsessed with what can be measured and monitored, in a constant, self-referential, process-driven mindset. Such a LH preoccupation, by a thousand cuts, closes down the engagement of the human person with all that stretches knowledge, character and horizons. Without the whole picture that the RH can apprehend, we are in danger of educating future generations into an impoverished humanity that fails to live up to all that the human spirit can be – full of character and able to think big thoughts.

Music (again)

Thoughtfulness engages both the left and the right hemisphere. Interestingly, when we play a musical instrument, both hemispheres of the brain are engaged as LH attention is given to detail as music is read, and the RH interprets the music and makes a coherent whole into a performance. Music education should be more highly valued than it is. Susan Hallam MBE published a report entitled *The Power of Music* in 2015.[3]

Hallam comments that the brain responds quickly to engagement with music, which has a significant impact on brain structure, with the changes reflecting what has been learned and how it has been learned, with skills transferable to other activities.

The Power of Music provides comprehensive research findings to support the assertion that musical training and expertise has multiple educational benefits across a range of cultural, emotional and social domains, including enhanced language and literacy skills, memory and mathematical ability, and a range of intellectual proficiency.

There are differences in the frontal cortex of musicians and non-musicians, which is the area of the brain which is implicated in the regulation of attention and self-regulation. Research shows that participation in formal early music education is linked with better self-regulation skills in infants and pre-school children, building positive attitudes towards school and better attendance, helping to re-engage disaffected students, including those in the criminal justice system. Music enhances self-confidence and increases motivation to engage in education, employment or voluntary activity. It strengthens social cohesion and inclusion, and psychological well-being.

---

3   Susan Hallam, MBE, *The Power of Music: A research synthesis of the impact of actively making music on the intellectual, social and personal development of children and young people*, published in Great Britain in 2015 on behalf of the Music Education Council by the International Music Education Research Centre (iMerc), Department of Culture, Communication and Media, UCL Institute of Education, University College London.

Children who engage in musical activities report a sense of accomplishment, enhanced determination and persistence, and more ability to cope with anger and express their emotions effectively.

Other benefits of music include discipline, time-management, relaxation, coping with difficulties, communication, and the ability to work and play with others. There are health benefits too, with music invigorating the immune system, reducing stress, anxiety and pain. Given all these benefits, it's not surprising that the report recommends greater musical education in schools.

Synaptogenesis

Synaptogenesis occurs as a result of musical activity. The plasticity of the brain and its ability to develop particular neural pathways is due to disciplined repetition of practice and activity is particularly evident in learning music, which means each individual has a specific learning biography. Active engagement with music impacts significantly on brain structure and function, changing it permanently, and enabling those developed skills to be transferable to other activities, most obviously language proficiency. The more rapid cortical thickness following musical training also develops motor planning and co-ordination, visuospatial ability and emotion and impulse regulation. The report gives evidence for the power of repeated action and practice to form patterns in our brains which then hard-wire particular behaviours. These are processes we've examined already as we've looked at how the human brain and the computer learn.

Making meaning

A rich, thoughtful engagement with the world takes practice, when both the LH and the RH are engaged with making meaning. We are readily seduced by stuff that engages our attention, offering easy gratification. Learning music, the art of reading, sticking with stuff that takes grit, offers so much more.

When we are dominated by a LH approach, information is more valuable than knowledge. Reading for information rather than knowledge causes a decrease in sustained attention characterising people's literary skills and habits.

> Books *stand* for knowledge, new ideas and the inventiveness of the human spirit and imagination. Will the Digital Native in the future appreciate such a non-interactive object with its fixed time and place, its unchangeable story locked away in its fragile pages? (Greenfield 2014, p.235)

Greenfield is not sure that the impact of classroom teaching that relies over much on screen engagement is beneficial. She comments that it's interesting that there are 160 Waldorf schools in the USA which subscribe to a teaching philosophy focused on physical activity and learning through creative, hands-on tasks. All digital devices are banned, as the school credo is that computers inhibit creative thinking, movement, human interaction and attention spans. The *New York Times* reported that the Waldorf school in Los Altos, California, was, tellingly, popular with the very Silicon Valley parents who were themselves immersed in the digital industries (Greenfield 2014). She comments: 'The difference between silicon and paper, the distractions of multi-tasking and hypertext, and the tendency to browse rather than to think deeply all suggest fundamental shifts in how our brains are now being asked to work' (Greenfield 2014, p.245).

Our thoughtfulness – ability to think deeply and holistically about a situation, or a subject, with concentrated attention is threatened by this. As Greenfield goes on to say:

> There's a danger that growing numbers of us are taking the more straightforward path and thinking increasingly like a computer, the more we interact with and adapt to its algorithmic mode of functioning determined by digital

cultures; so our brains will function more like suboptimal computers. (Greenfield 2014, p.247)

If Ray Kurzweil's prediction, throughout his writing, is correct, that digital devices will one day supersede the human brain, then we are at danger of losing the breadth and depth of thoughtfulness – such as produced *War and Peace*. Or John Donne's poetry.

Conclusion

Thoughtfulness is more than mindfulness: it enables the human person to bring both the LH and the RH to attend to the world in a way that makes metaphor, art and literature meaningful. Music, particularly, offers much to education, as the musician uses both hemispheres of the brain at the same time, in a way that is unusual in any other discipline. To be thoughtful is to refuse polarisations between mind and body, reason and emotion, thought and action, but to bring a wholehearted attention to whatever is under consideration, including the virtual world of the digital age. Education enriched by thoughtfulness enables the RH to see the coherence of the whole and resist the LH drive to control and measure, to test and examine.

Thoughtfulness:
from conscious incompetence to unconscious competence

Culture: What literature, music, art best express thoughtfulness? How might children engage and respond with appreciation?

Character: What habits could children practise deliberately to be thoughtful?

Call: As a way of understanding the profession of teaching as a vocation, what more could the headteacher and staff do to model thoughtfulness?

- Describe the times and places when you are a naked thinking heart, with your RH more engaged than your LH.

- Thomas Merton wrote of the importance of 'active contemplation'. Listen here: www.youtube.com/watch?v=jdeFNrKZ7LI. What contemplative practices might you explore further? Tending the roses? Long slow walks? Baking bread?

- Richard Rohr is a contemporary contemplative. Visit his blog here: https://cac.org/category/daily-meditations

- If you are a parent or a teacher, how might you engage children in thoughtful action and develop further their sense of attention?

Chapter 9

Fruitfulness

In his speech to the American Enterprise Institute, 2014, Bill Gates said:

> Software substitution, whether it's for drivers or waiters or nurses…it's progressing. Technology over time will reduce demand for jobs, particularly at the lower end of the skill set…20 years from now, labor demand for lots of skill sets will be substantially lower. I don't think people have that in their mental model. (Gates, quoted in Cameron 2017, p.1)

Machines are now workers

The world of work is changing, and will change more in the foreseeable future – and beyond. Martin Ford argues that automation challenges one of our most basic assumptions about technology that machines are tools. This is no longer true: machines are themselves now workers. The impact of the digital age is happening exponentially fast, too, affecting work as we know it; not helped since the 1970s by the fall in real terms of wages and soaring income inequality because profits are largely absorbed by business owners and investors (Ford 2015).

The impact of automation on jobs is already deep, and will extend further. Some are optimistic: Tegmark says that 'if we can figure out how to grow our prosperity through automation without leaving people lacking income or purpose, then we have the potential to create a fantastic future with leisure and unprecedented opulence for everyone who wants it' (Tegmark 2017, p.118). However, the statistics are sobering on the current impact on work of automation. The indications are that automation will increasingly continue to fulfil tasks and roles currently performed by humans, to the extent that many will need to find new purpose and occupation.

This chapter considers the nature of 'work' and suggests a change of approach that offers a deeper appreciation of what it means to be occupied fruitfully. To see work and occupation in terms of 'fruitfulness' is to come at it from a different angle – with a different imagination. One that is needed in today's world. How our education systems respond is crucial, because it won't be the case that acquiring more transferable skills will automatically protect effectively against job automation in the future (Ford 2015). It's likely that we're going to need a fundamental restructuring, if prosperity is to continue. And a reappraisal of what prosperity is.

One of the main reasons to work is to provide income. Given the enormous profits and surpluses that automation delivers, a redistribution of the wealth generated would make sense – as many are increasingly saying.

Why work?

Dorothy L. Sayers, during the Second World War, addressed just such questions about the nature of work. She wrote this:

> Work is not, primarily, a thing one does to live, but the thing one lives to do. It is, or it should be, the full expression of the worker's faculties, the thing in which he [sic!] finds spiritual, mental and bodily satisfaction, and the medium in which he offers himself to God. (Sayers 1942, p.12)

She restates a key thought, from her Christian understanding, that work is a creative activity undertaken for the love of the work itself. She hoped that the wartime experience would lead to a post-war reconception of work, away from the need of the consumer to earn money, and into a greater appreciation of the human fulfilment that comes from doing well a thing that is well worth doing.[1]

The fundamental changes that are ahead raise profound questions about what it means to be purposeful and productive, taking us to the heart of what work provides, psychologically, socially and emotionally as well as materially. A rethink of the nature of work is necessary. Humanity is predominantly shaped today by the need to be useful in a utilitarian, instrumental way, which means we miss what it might look like to be full of human character as fruitful, creative beings. The digital age could provoke a reimagining of what it means to be human, drawing on aspects of the creative, artistic human character.[2] With proper resources to enable a good basic standard of living, a more adventurous exploration of what 'occupation' means could re-invigorate the human spirit and offer paths through life that are fruitful in ways we have forgotten, or are yet to find out. This could include a range of different ways of volunteering within civic association and social organisation, to serve the common good, for example. It could involve learning from the wisdom of the religious life, where monks and nuns have been contemplating the nature of work since Benedict wrote his Rule in the sixth century.

The indications so far are that computers and robots are not very good at emotional intelligence. To date, they don't perform well at tasks requiring the ability to negotiate carefully, and make complex judgements required to relate with people. The indications are that our education systems need to take this on board as we look to the future. So as we anticipate the impact of the digital age, and explore the notion of 'fruitfulness', the question before us is what sort of education is required

---

1   See also John Hughes (2007).
2   J.M. Keynes argued in the 1930s that the working week would shrink to 15 hours and we would all become civilised folk of leisure.

to enable young people and adults to live fruitful lives? How might education enable someone to be full of character as they contribute fruitfully to the world?

Decimation of jobs

The changing face of work due to increasing automation is already affecting certain occupations more obviously than others. Robert Peston draws on research that is grounded in what is already happening, rather than some of the crazier projections of futurologists. He quotes Stephen Hawking:

> The automation of factories has already decimated jobs in traditional manufacturing, and the rise of artificial intelligence is likely to extend this job destruction deep into the middle classes, with only the most caring, creative or supervisory roles remaining. This in turn will accelerate the already widening economic inequality around the world. The internet and the platforms that it makes possible allow very small groups of individuals to make enormous profits while employing very few people. This is inevitable, it is progress, but it is also socially destructive. (Stephen Hawking, quoted in Peston 2017, p.210)

The US Federal Reserve Bank of St Louis categorises work in four ways: Firstly, there is 'non-routine cognitive' work, which includes managerial occupations, academics, professions; second, thre is 'non-routine manual', like nurses, carers and those who carry out physical and emotional jobs which are not routine-predictable; third, there is 'routine cognitive' work, such as book keeping, data processing, administration; and fourth, there is 'routine manual', which pulls in occupations such as manufacturing and transport (Peston 2017, p.212).

These different categories are affected differently by the impact of automation. Statistics show that routine manual work accounted for 26 per cent of all jobs in 1983 in the USA, which has fallen to 20 per cent today. Routine cognitive work has fallen from 28 per cent to 22 per cent in the same period. Non-routine manual work has risen from 16 per cent to 17 per cent, and non-routine cognitive occupations have risen as well, from 30 per cent to 40 per cent.[3] From this research it's evident that it's the non-routine work that computers don't do is where humanity should be focusing into the future.

This is borne out by other US research where it's argued that current technology (that is, automation at today's sophistication) could already be adapted to cover 45 per cent of the tasks people are remunerated for now. This means that 60 per cent of all occupations and 78 per cent of all routine-predictable physical work could see 30 per cent or more of their activities automated, which in itself represents 18 per cent of all labour in the US economy – able to be automated. That's what's possible now; not in some future scenario. The impact is likely to be profound on occupations such as manufacturing, food service, accommodation and on semi-skilled work such as welding, cutting and soldering.

In the UK, according to Andrew Haldane of the Bank of England,[4] it's not only non-cognitive routine work that will be affected. Cognitive routine work is also likely to be devastated. Accountancy, for instance, faces a 95 per cent probability of vocational extinction. As Peston comments: 'According to the Bank, a staggering 15 million British jobs are at risk of automation and 80 million American jobs. Which means 47 per cent of all those currently at work in the UK could see themselves made redundant' (Peston 2017, p.222). Peston warns that 'Governments should be agonising at breakfast, lunch and tea over what to do about robots' (Peston 2017, p.223).

---

3   The researchers comment that it's likely that this is both a cause of and reaction to the soaring numbers in higher education over that period of time: there are now 20 million at American universities, compared to 2.4 million after the Second World War; and in the UK we now educate 2 million, which is up from 130,000 in 1970.

4   Andrew Haldane, 'Labour's Share' speech at the Trades Union Congress, London, November 2015.

No Luddite response, though

These advances in automation need to be embraced. Peston points out that there is evidence that the problem with British manufacturing is not too much automation and too many robots, but too few. Manufacturing employment fell sharply in most developed countries between 1996 and 2012, but it fell least where investment in robots has been greatest. That implies that the competitive advantage of using the new technologies outweighs the job displacement.[5] The AI revolution comes at a time when Britain lags seriously behind in productivity.

Productivity is a key indicator of a nation at work. Haldane argues that the priority is to produce progressively more, because only then can we earn more – by getting better at making and selling goods and services (Haldane, cited in Peston 2017). Good levels of productivity indicate an economy that will make everyone richer. Productivity is a measure of efficiency, of management, of skill levels, and of the quality and capabilities of the capital resources. Today, those capital resources are mainly networked computers and robots.

Crisis in productivity

There's been a crisis in productivity, however, since the financial crash of 2008, particularly in Britain. The reasons are complex. Poor infrastructure doesn't help, nor does the fact that management does not compare well with other comparable nations. London finance is strong, but otherwise there is insufficient business dynamism, poor resource and support allocation, and business doesn't receive the investment it needs to survive and grow. The London-based financial services industry has become far too good at financial engineering at the expense of providing patient or long-term capital, with banks and investors hopeless at distinguishing between better

---

5   'Robots at Work', LSE Centre for Economic Performance, March 2015, cited by
     Peston (2017, p.215).

and worse companies (Peston 2017). Liam Fox, in a speech to the Conservative Way Forward Group in September 2016, said: 'This country is not the free trading nation it once was. We have become too lazy, and too fat on our successes in previous generation' (quoted in Peston 2017, pp.137–8). Fox claims that there is a general tolerance of mediocrity. We hoped that foreign businesses would bring in higher standards, but that hasn't happened, and we depend on dangerously few world-class companies.

Britain's poor productivity is down to a vast number of sub-standard firms. The technological revolution is real and spectacular for the minority of superstar companies, with the rest trapped 'in a clunky analogue world pondering during their tea breaks whatever happened to Teletext' (Peston 2017, p.140). The Bank of England says a staggering third of British companies have seen no productivity increase since 2000. The lack of exposure to competition and poor use of global supply chains means we are ill-prepared to meet the challenges of Brexit, which will only put a brake on the much-needed productivity revival in Britain as it will increase the costs and friction of doing business with our most important current market (Peston 2017).

There's a real need to address the issues here, as the deep divisions that became clear with Brexit reveal great regional disparities in income and an over-reliance on the financial industry at the expense of investing and innovating in other areas of business. Sir Charles Mayfield, who chaired a Productivity Commission, advocated that companies should measure their productivity and working practices against benchmarks for their industries and learn from each other. Boosting relatively low productivity especially outside London, would probably do more to mend the fractures and restore some sense of shared purpose than any other initiative (Peston 2017).

The myths of developing global markets are deceptive, and won't get Britain out of the productivity mess it's in. As *The Economist* notes:

Brexiteers dream of freedom from the European Union's shackles, imagining plucky British negotiators forging new trade deals with America, China and India. Reality dictates a different set of priorities. Britain already has around 40 free-trade agreements through its membership of the EU. None will survive Brexit automatically. Deal preservation lacks the glamour of deal creation, but it is a more urgent task.[6]

A deep-seated rethink about work

The increase of automation is inevitable. It will either exacerbate the current divides, or will be the opportunity for a major and deep-seated rethink about work, productivity, and social division. It seems sensible to argue that the vast fortunes made by technology companies needs to be more readily available to support initiatives to build a fairer, more cohesive society, otherwise a future world in which there is little proper work and insufficient income for many will be even more unjust and unstable than it is currently. This makes no sense for the future well-being of everyone, whatever their career and job prospects are. A future of less work with even wider wealth differentials would be disastrous. A world of impoverishment and rising unemployment is not a sustainable future. Enforced leisure is not the answer. A foretaste of that is apparent in the USA, where depressed, low-income communities are torn apart and anaesthetised by opioids.

Universal Basic Income

To face this challenge, Peston is not alone in commending that the owners of wealth generated through AI are taxed sufficiently to provide a Universal Basic Income, set at a high-enough level to guarantee a decent way of life for all. He believes it's going to be important to consider giving people income without jobs.

6   *The Economist*, 10 February 2018, p.26.

We want jobs, he says, because they can provide us with income and purpose, but given the opulence of resources produced by machines, it should be possible to find alternative ways of providing both the income and the purpose *without* jobs. He advocates redistributing a small share of the growing economic pie to enable everyone to become better off.

Not only *can* we do this, but we *should* do this. It's a moral imperative to share the wealth generated by increased automation.

Tegmark also explores different proposals for wealth-sharing. One way would be for everyone to receive a basic income, with no preconditions or requirements. There are a number of small-scale experiments in Canada, Finland and the Netherlands. Or governments can help citizens by providing free or subsidised services. 'Even in a future where machines can outperform humans at all jobs,' Tegmark suggests, 'governments could opt to pay people to work in childcare, eldercare, etc., rather than outsource the caregiving to robots' (Tegmark 2017, p.126ff). He is clear that there's enough wealth to make everyone better off in the coming digital age – even though he recognises that there's strong political disagreement about whether it should happen. He also recognises that the current trend in the USA appears to be in the opposite direction, with some groups of people getting poorer decade after decade.

> Policy decisions about how to share society's growing wealth will impact everybody, so the conversation about what sort of future economy to build should include everyone, not merely AI researchers, roboticists and economists. (Tegmark 2017, p.128)

All the evidence is that greater equality makes democracy work better. Where there's a well-educated middle class, the electorate is harder to manipulate, and it's tougher for small numbers of rich people or companies to have undue influence. A fairer redistribution of wealth can open up other possibilities. Peston writes:

Life would then be about volunteering to make our communities more humane, caring and safer; and the enjoyment of culture. Failure to change our welfare safety net into a satisfying way of life would have only one outcome. We would all become Luddites – and justifiably so. (Peston 2017, p.225)

Education has a crucial role to play

How does education need to change to meet the challenges ahead?

Education needs to equip young people for a fast-changing world where there may be much less work, at least as it has been traditionally understood. It would suggest we need a broad education that enables a deep hinterland of cultural, emotional and moral knowledge. Deep hinterlands give us the resourcefulness that enables the imagination to flourish, enabling high performance in the non-routine jobs that will survive the automation revolution. Emotional intelligence and imagination help people to work well in teams, with flexibility and agility of mind and heart. Education should be focusing on what enables young people to grow in wisdom.

This requires really good teachers, and I'm with Peston when he reckons teachers' pay should be trebled, to ensure the brightest and best are engaged in preparing the next generation for life, work and occupations that aren't 'work' as it's been understood (Peston 2017).

As AI develops, the human ability to reflect consciously and imaginatively, and morally, is what will sustain a humane future, which will benefit not only human persons, but also contribute to the humanising of digital learning. As AI takes off, fuelled by the incredible resources now allocated to teach computers to learn and understand language, for instance, we need a broad understanding of 'intelligence' that mirrors human wisdom, not a LH narrow approach that is merely utilitarian and instrumental.

So the education system needs to strengthen those who will fare best in non-routine work, whether it is cognitive, or non-cognitive. Those working with people will be least affected by automatisation. Tegmark gives this career advice to anyone facing questions of future career possibilities: Does it require interacting with people and using social intelligence? Does it involve creativity and coming up with clever solutions? Does it require working in an unpredictable environment?

The more questions that receive the answer 'yes', then the better the career choice will be. Safe bets include becoming a teacher, nurse, doctor, dentist, scientist, entrepreneur, programmer, engineer, lawyer, social worker, clergy minister, artist, hairdresser or massage therapist (Tegmark 2017).

Teaching

Peston says – good news for any teachers reading this book on education – that the sector least at risk of automation is education, because there will continue to be a need for teaching that offers and instils deep expertise and complex interaction with people. Teaching needs to be valued as a career that can shape the future more than most (Peston 2017).

> Our schools are teaching the wrong things, they are creating a generation of young workers vulnerable to being made irrelevant and unnecessary by the machines. Maths, reading and writing are vital for living, but not so much for earning a decent living, because machines can already do all basic information management and processing much faster and more accurately than us. What machines can't do – and quite possibly never will be able to do – is negotiate, build relationships, empathise, instil confidence, win trust, create great art, write moral philosophy, dream, or any of the other emotional and intuitive activities that are central both to highly paid careers and the sheer joy of being alive. (Peston 2017, p.223)

He bemoans the narrow criteria for measuring students' success, with schools almost entirely focused on compelling children to get the best possible grades in exams that themselves measure a very inadequate set of skills. There's no encouragement here for creativity, flexible thinking, the ability both to lead and work in a team, with the capacity to listen, observe and adapt. These are all aptitudes that the workforce of the future – if it is to stay human and humane – will require. He calls for a revolution in education, concerned about how unfit for purpose our schools are, and writes:

> Our children are being trained with military dedication to do jobs that robots and algorithms can already do. Obviously, everybody needs to be literate and numerate, simply to get the most out of life. But jobs that rely heavily on literacy, numeracy, processing and analytical skills now require almost no human involvement. Even if lots of those jobs – in administration, manufacturing and assorted service – are still done by humans, they won't be much longer. (Peston 2017, p.231)

So what would an education look like that forms young people for what computers can't do? Yes, it would emphasise creativity, flexibility and emotional engagement. More than that, though, an education for the future would aim at what a fruitful life looks like, understanding productivity in ways that move us on from the traditional understanding of work towards a deeper appreciation of the human spirit and what enables it to flourish. Fruit grows when the shoots and roots are green and deep – deep in the rich soil of the wisdom of emotional and moral knowledge born of cultural literacy.

Fruitfulness is different to productivity

A fruitful life is one in which deep learning enables human beings to develop creativity, to gain satisfaction through interaction with other people, to develop a sense of adventure, to support occupations and leisure and to strengthen the desire to serve the common good through volunteering. Feeding the imagination by providing a deep hinterland is the best gift of a good education.

To strive, to seek, to find and not to yield

When I was a teenager, I was inspired by a poem by Tennyson to understand my whole life differently. It stirred in me an adventurous spirit that has never gone – the spirit to see knowledge as always beyond the narrow horizons I (or anyone else) might construct.

The poem tells the story of Ulysses, an old king now, who is restless with his settled life, matched with an aged wife, doling out laws to a people who hoard and sleep and feed and do not do much else. He wants to travel again, to sail with his old mariners, to respond to the lights, the deep, the slow moon climbing. He yearns to leave behind the prosaic, dull life of being a king, handing over responsibility to the capable hands of his son Telemachus, so he can experience life to the lees, to the dregs, through the arch where gleams the untravelled world whose margin fades forever as he moves.

Now, it might be that this poem of Tennyson is about dying – about the final journey we make – and if it is, then the truth of the poem remains as powerful. For if life holds such adventure, and if death is merely a continuation of that human impulse to live as fully as possible, then it's never too late to seek a newer world. The poem calls into question the narrowness of our horizons in life – and perhaps in death too – and inspires the reader to see and know as much as possible, to travel and become part of all that we meet – to strive, to seek, to find and not to yield, as the poem concludes. I thought to myself, aged 15, that I would like to be able to look back on my life as an old person, and be a grey spirit who still yearned in desire to follow knowledge like a sinking star beyond the utmost bound of human thought.

The poem offers a hinterland of rich imagery that is best understood if the reader is already familiar with Homer's epic poem *The Odyssey*. It inspires with a vision that looks at life as full of possibilities and promise, to be grasped with both hands, whatever our circumstances and prospects. It challenges us to make the most of our lives as a gift. How we understand 'work' is fundamental to that.

Quality of life

What contributes quality of life? To recap from the Introduction, it might look something like this: we want to have a good, happy and secure family life, with a continuing network of friends. We want fulfilling work that feels worthwhile. We want to make a difference to human welfare, to the common good. And often people will also say they want a life that enables loss and darkness to be held, so that we are not overwhelmed with a sense of chaos, or collapse. To flourish is to be able to acknowledge the depths of the human condition, its bleak places and sad times, within a greater sense of fullness.

To prioritise such things in life takes us away from a narrow concern with income, to consider seriously a renewed impetus to civic associations, hobbies and lifelong learning, belonging to clubs and movements, and other institutions that develop social interaction and strengthen society.

A fruitful life

What might a fruitful life look like?

Crawford says we live too much in our heads anyway, given the temptations and seductions of the virtual world. He advocates going in the opposite direction entirely, and developing occupations that enable humanity to encounter the world as real, for in that there is pleasure, he says – the deep pleasure of wonder and gratitude of developing skills to make things and create. Acquiring such skills takes us away from being occupied by manufactured realities that simply distract us. It is not that in becoming skilled one somehow becomes immune to distraction, he says, but the well-being that comes from a real skill with real, material stuff enhances life (Crawford 2015). This is to focus seriously on non-routine, non-cognitive work and occupations that are less affected by automation.

Paul Tough (2012) and Angela Duckworth (2017) write of how character is formed by the deliberate practice of acquiring skills and knowledge, such that one achieves a sense of 'flow'. Tough writes about the thrill of watching the leading chess teacher we met in Chapter 5 impart her joy in the game to pupils, who otherwise would not have engaged. Here was that sense of flow, of doing something well when you've practised until it is second nature:

> You simply don't experience flow if you aren't good at something – I will never feel it at the chessboard. During one conversation, I asked Spiegel whether she ever felt that her students were sacrificing too much to succeed at chess. She looked at me like I was crazy. 'What's missing from that idea is that playing chess is, like, *wonderful*,' she said. 'There's a joyousness to it. That's when you're happiest or that's when you're most you or that's when you feel your best...there's nothing else [you]'d rather do.' (Tough 2012, p.137)

And Susan Greenfield, also, commends developing non-cognitive, non-routine occupations, through the real contact of real people doing real things:

> Even the most diehard digital zealot cannot escape the simple fact that every hour spent in front of a screen, however wonderful, or even beneficial, is an hour spent *not* holding someone's hand or breathing in sea air. Perhaps even simply being at ease and happy in total silence could become become a rarefied commodity that, instead of being a normal part of the human repertoire, will find itself on a wistful wish list of the future. (Greenfield 2014, pp.20–1)

A fruitful life looks beyond mere productivity, towards other goals and skills, the achievement of flow in something you're good at, the engagement with people. This can come through serious playfulness as explored in Chapter 5 – and particularly, perhaps engagement through concern with the environment or by caring for other people and their needs. This is to stir new generations to a concern beyond themselves.

iGeneration's attitudes

In her work on the iGeneration, Twenge (2017) found students were less likely to be engaged with the social problems of the nation and the world, or do anything to help the environment. iGen'ers want a job that makes enough money. They are not so interested in a job that is interesting, where you can learn new things and see the results. They are less interested in making friends at work and are less entrepreneurial than Millennials. She finds that iGen'ers see more barriers in their way to success, and are also more likely to say that they think getting the job they want will involve too much work. There's a disturbing lack of enthusiasm here amongst iGen'ers for work which reflects the uncertainties that lie ahead for that generation, given what is predicted for the work economy over the next few decades. If you're facing the prospect of a significant drop in largely routine jobs, then it's not difficult to see how a sense of hopelessness and apathy can set in.

However we look at it, the key question of human worth is fundamental, and disassociating that sense of worth from precarious work becomes increasingly necessary if we are to look to a future that provides a sense of well-being for the majority, rather than merely the lucky few who have paid employment. Our education systems need to address these issues as a matter of urgency by having in mind not simply the paid jobs that are likely to survive and flourish, but also the wider notion of 'occupation' as time used positively, with a sense of worth and purpose. A keen imagination needs to be brought to this issue as a real priority. Here, the notion of fruitfulness seems a good place to start.

Thinking outside the box

It's valuable to think outside the box, and one way to do this is to listen to the reflections of men and women who live in religious communities, where work plays a crucial part within an overall framework of communal living, study, prayer and worship. This life has seen a decline in numbers since the 1960s, but still many are called to join the significant number of monasteries and convents that thrive throughout the world. Many trace their traditions to St Benedict, who has been called the Father of Western Monasticism. He wrote a Rule for living in a religious community in the sixth century, which is still followed today, and which has much to say about work and occupation that can help us to consider fruitfulness in different ways to those prevalent in today's Western culture.

Learning from the religious life

There's plenty of literature around for those who want to explore further what motivates those who lead the religious life. It's important to recognise that people who choose to make lifelong vows within religious communities choose to do so freely and only after a lengthy period of discernment. They see themselves as dedicating their lives to God in a way that enables them to focus attention away from self-absorption and towards the needs of the world, which is simply realised in a life of prayer for others.

Those embarked on a religious life will usually belong to one of a number of traditions which take their name from their founders – for example, the Benedictines follow the rule of Benedict; the Franciscans, the way of life outlined by Francis of Assisi in the twelfth century; the Dominicans, or Order of

Preachers, the teaching of Dominic.[7] The Cistercians were founded in France at the turn of the eleventh century, following the teaching of Bernard of Clairvaux, who sought to reform the Church of his day by a closer adherence to the teaching of the Benedictine Rule. In the seventeenth century, there was a further reform movement, which led to the Order of Cistercians of the Strict Observance (OCSO) who are commonly called Trappists, after their founding abbey of La Trappe, in France. Perhaps the most famous Trappist was the theologian and mystic Thomas Merton, who entered the Abbey of Gethsemane in 1941, where his writings and letters to world leaders are amongst the best spiritual and social works of the twentieth century. Merton's most widely read work remains his autobiography, *The Seven Storey Mountain*, which informed and inspired many to seek a deeper life of spiritual fulfilment than was evident in the world. One of the key characteristics of the Trappists is the silence that is shared by Cistercian and Benedictine monasteries.

I'm drawing on the writing of Charles Cummings OCSO, who is a Trappist monk at Holy Trinity Abbey in Huntsville, Utah. His book *Monastic Practices* is a good introduction to the life of a religious in the Benedictine tradition (Cummings 2015). In it he writes:

> The image of the cowled and hooded monk gazing placidly across a lake, with nothing to do all day but contemplate eternal verities, is pure myth. The cloister walls contain their own variety of workaholic while concealing him from the world's view. Contemplative leisure is available in our monasteries but so is work, and it is often work that prevails. There is always work to be done, and nearly all of it can be justified as a means of self-support or a service to others. (Cummings 2015, p.61)

He describes a triple base to the life: sacred reading, manual work and liturgical prayer. All are needed to sustain a healthy

---

7   A notable exception in the UK is the Community of the Resurrection (CR), which was founded by Charles Gore in 1892. See www.mirfield.org.uk

life, and although it's our concern with what he has to say about work that will preoccupy us here, one or two reflections on what he says about reading.

Slow reading

The way a religious reads is different to our usual utilitarian, information-acquiring way. It takes time to be fruitful. Cummings writes:

> Speed reading is useful, and even necessary, for digesting the contents of textbooks, periodicals, or newspapers. But when the time for sacred reading comes, I have to be able to read slowly and patiently, in a relaxed and open spirit, ready to 'taste and see how good the Lord is.' (Psalm 24.8)

He continues to tell the story of Sidney Piddington, who spent three years in a Japanese prisoner of war camp, where he disciplined himself to linger over every page:

> Not only did slowing down make the book last longer but as a bonus Piddington discovered that the practice lifted him above the sordidness and senselessness of prison-camp life and put him into a more humane world; super-slow reading preserved his sanity, his human dignity, and his inner freedom. (Cummings 2015, pp.10–11)

This might seem like a waste of time, to read again and again, slowly, very slowly, the words before you, but it is a discipline that bears fruit. It enables a deep listening to be learned, and those who develop the practice can become 'more generous, considerate, gentle and less selfish, cranky, gossipy, touchy' (Cummings 2015, p.18). Although a religious person will usually turn to the Bible first of all, it doesn't matter what the reading material is. It can inspire a greater engagement with the natural world, art and music, and can become deeply playful and joyful. It might seem like a waste of time, but that is the point. This sort of reading is simply for its own sake, with no practical goals, or books to get through, or purpose beyond a deep appreciation of what the words are saying, their meaningfulness. It is a RH way of reading, of simply reaching out, with no end in mind.

This gives us some understanding of how 'work' is viewed within a religious community.

Work belongs to the rhythm of a fully human life

Cummings writes:

> By our work we intend to accomplish something good for others or ourselves. Without this intention of doing something useful, we are simply playing, not working. When monks and nuns work they tend to put themselves wholeheartedly into their task and to accomplish it fairly well. They take pride in their creative accomplishments and rightly so. Without the sense of personal creative involvement, work becomes sheer drudgery. Putting these elements together, we may describe monastic work, in general, as creative effort for useful purposes. (Cummings 2015, p.44)

Since the beginning, when Benedict wrote his Rule, manual work has been a crucial aspect of the life of a religious and has been seen as belonging to the essential rhythm of a fully human life. According to Cummings (2015, p.49): 'It is natural for human beings to want to work, to enjoy working, to experience the normal satisfaction of a job well done.' Because of the support of the community, work becomes productive, but not for financial wealth or income. Instead it leads to a sense of fulfilment, relaxation and contentment. It will be engaged, usually, with the soil, producing food; and today in ways which honour the environment, it is restorative rather than exploitative or rapacious of the land.

Much monastic work is hidden. It's not done to attract attention, but is done because it needs to be done, quietly and simply, without fuss. It is a form of active contemplation, as Thomas Merton[8] described it. Cummings says this:

> Monastic life gives me licence to be creatively inactive and at leisure with God. Contemplation is a functionally useless form of creative involvement. Long ago the Roman philosopher Cato said, 'Never is man more active than when he does nothing'. Doing nothing make be harder for me than doing something, but it is no less valuable. In monastic life I can rejoice in my opportunity to do nothing and produce nothing. (Cummings 2015, p.55)

There are strong links here with the sort of playfulness explored in Chapter 2, and self-forgetfulness. Cummings continues: 'Self-forgetful service of the community is, like prayer, a movement out of myself toward the other, a movement of giving, of love' (Cummings 2015, pp.57–8).

It makes life worth living – when the person slows down and works in a leisurely, balanced and humane way, with proper rest, and a sense of purpose – which for the religious is given as seeking God. The idea of God that lies behind this approach is a God who delights in being creative. That delight is captured in various places in the Biblical texts: Psalm 104, for instance, or the Book of Job, chapter 38, where God is portrayed as creating with a wild joyfulness, gratuitously, wastefully even.

Conclusion

Whether the person believes in God or not, there is value in absorbing the wisdom of this approach to work. It broadens purpose to include wider horizons, which challenge the human person to seek a sense of fulfilment that isn't dependent on a narrow understanding of work that is merely about purpose, utility or instrumentality. In a world where those who have

8   Thomas Merton OCSO (1915–68) was a Trappist monk of American nationality. He was a successful writer, theologian, mystic, poet, social activist, and student of comparative religion.

work, work too hard, and those who haven't, or are threatened by the impact of automation, face poverty and abjection, a different vision is needed: one where work is decoupled from income, and which puts human dignity at its heart, reimagining the true fruitfulness of the human person.

Fruitfulness:
from conscious incompetence to unconscious competence

Culture: What literature, music, art best express fruitfulness? How might children engage and respond?

Character: What habits could children practise deliberately to be fruitful, looking towards a humane future?

Call: As a way of understanding the profession of teaching as a vocation, what more could the headteacher and staff do to model fruitfulness?

- Write your own obituary with fruitfulness in mind.

- From roots, to shoots, to fruits, what does fruitfulness mean in your life, now?

- Develop the art of reading slowly by taking a book you have already enjoyed and reading it again, as if it were the only book in the world.

- If you are a parent or a teacher, how can you encourage the children in your life to practise fruitfulness, in ways that will be relevant when they retire?

Chapter 10

Fullness

Maddy's first degree was in theology, and every so often she takes herself off for an evening at the university where she studied. It's a visiting lecturer from the USA on this occasion. In her vibrant and engaging style, she is talking about '*The Fullness of God*'. Maddy takes notes.

There is always more

The lecturer began by talking about Stephen Hawking who had just died. His atheism (declared in 2010 in his book *The Grand Design*) was based on the assumption that, given the laws of physics, nature generates itself into existence, so there is no need for a creator. He had argued that philosophy was dead too, as it had not kept up with modern developments in physics.

The theologian challenged this. Hawking had overstepped a barrier, dismissing theology without having read what theologians actually say. He had assumed that religious believers see edges between time and eternity, as if the universe were 'like a model railways track', with God's role 'to set the train going'.

The speaker thought Hawking had misunderstood what theologians said about God. God couldn't be understood as the one who sets procedures, like time, in process. God is, instead, equally at work in all moments. She thought Hawking had done the theologian a favour, given them the opportunity to clarify that God could not be confused as one more cause in a chain of causes. God had to be thought of differently. The language of physics didn't work for how religious people think about God (Davison 2017).

There are always more questions – even beyond those that Hawking asked; more to understand about existence than the laws of physics can comprehend.

The speaker said there are two propositions to kick off with:

- Whatever we feel, think, imagine, or care – there is always more.

- There is nothing more than the fullness of God.

She quoted from the Bible, some words attributed to the apostle Paul:

> I pray that you may have the power to comprehend, with all the saints, what is the breadth and length and height and depth, and to know the love of Christ that surpasses knowledge, so that you may be filled with all the fullness of God. (Ephesians 3, 18–19)

She then asked her audience to imagine all the galaxies, known and unknown, stretching over vast expanses of space. The tiniest nano-particle, a quark, a neutrino – too small to be seen, but detectable all the same.

She told them to think of all the advances of science, in any direction, small or great; to think of the boundless extent of all there is.

Or to contemplate the inner life of humanity, the heights and depths of the human heart and mind. To think of the most sublime experience they ever had. Filled with overwhelming joy; moved by some wonder of the natural world; or ecstatic as they listened to a fine piece of music. Wonderful though it was, there is always more.

Or the utter depths of depravity and cruelty. Evil beyond words. There's always more of that too, sad to say, she said.

Wherever we go, as human beings, we can never come to the end of the experience of our hearts, minds, souls or strength. Whatever branch of human understanding, the ground is endless in what we can explore, the depths and heights we can reach.

There is always more.

We arrive at one of the great debates of our age. Is experience, as human beings understand it, all that there is? Is it a finite infinity that expresses merely the limit of humanity? Or is there reality beyond the utmost bounds of human thought, beyond what can be known or experienced? A reality that surpasses human understanding of all that is? Some say yes. Some call this transcendent other, God.

They say that God isn't a thing alongside other things in that vast universe of thought, of expanse, of divergence that humans experience (Shortt 2016). God can't be identified or located through human faculties alone. God isn't something the human understanding can grasp, capture and then say, 'Now I've got God!'

God as transcendent other will always be ineffable, beyond, beneath, behind, before the seemingly endless reaches of human understanding. Whatever we imagine, or think, or feel, there is always more.

However, there is nothing more than the fullness of God; otherwise, of course, it isn't God. The speaker then asked: 'Why talk of the fullness of God? Rather than just "God"?'

Because, she said, 'fullness' gives a sense of endless, overflowing abundance that is a more adequate way of accounting for the 'something more' that is behind the experience of the common yearning for fulfilment, for flourishing.

This experience is the *je ne sais quoi* of art, or beauty, where the human spirit is ecstatic, speechless, unable to capture experience, aware of something more than can be understood. It escapes human control, the grasp of human reach, this experience of amazement, wonder, enchantment – call it what you will. The idea of the fullness of God captures its plenitude, its abundance. In this fullness belongs that experience which won't go away, of awe, wonder, enchantment. In it are found the goals of human life which cluster around words like 'fulfilment', or 'flourishing'.

The speaker referred to Charles Taylor, the Aristotelian philosopher who argues in *A Secular Age* that a yearning for a sense of fullness informs the aspiration to human flourishing.[1] The sense of fullness is felt even by those who dismiss the existence of God (whom Taylor calls exclusive humanists), as much as those who contemplate a transcendent other.

Amazement, wonder, enchantment

Some will explain the experience of amazement, wonder, enchantment – and the speaker said let's call that 'AWE' – within an exclusively humanist frame, reducing such experience to materialist explanations. These debates began before Charles Darwin, but he certainly stirred things up.

The mention of Darwin prompted the speaker to diverge into a brief comment on Creationism. She said there were still Christians and other religious people in the world who believe that the universe and all life originated from a specific act of divine creation, as described in their ancient writings. They read the book of Genesis and argue that it is literally true in all it says. 'Creationists' reject the scientific theory of evolution as it was most famously developed by Darwin in the mid-nineteenth century. Creationists hold that evolution, as a theory, cannot adequately account for the history, diversity and complexity of life on Earth. They argue that there is a qualitative difference between humanity and animal.

---

1   Taylor, C. (2007) *A Secular Age*, published by the Belknap Press of Harvard University Press, Cambridge, MA.

Creationism and endogenous retroviruses

The debate continues, she said, but since the Genome Project[2] there is absolute evidence of the common gene heritage between human and animal. Rather wonderfully, the evidence comes through retroviruses, which insert themselves into our genes, and once they are there, remain for ever. They can be traced back and be shown to be held in common with other species. Some permanent or endogenous retroviruses (ERVs) are so ancient that they predate our most recent cousins – such as chimps, gorillas and other primates. This science gives incontrovertible evidence that yes, we are descended from a common ancestor with other species. Darwin was right. The Creationist position really has no basis.

But does that mean that everything can be explained solely by scientific, materialist evidence? Is the experience of AWE merely a sophisticated firing of neurons in the brain? The humanist and atheist Raymond Tallis, for example, argues against the reductionism of popular writers like Dawkins and Dennett, who give a materialist explanation to everything. The speaker drew attention to Tallis's[3] *Michelangelo's Finger: An Exploration of Everyday Transcendence*, where Tallis highlighted our ability to point and therefore to understand other points of view, to share experience beyond our own, realities that are not merely immediate to us. This enables an everyday transcendence, without recourse to God, Tallis argued, stopping short of an explanation of transcendence that goes beyond the bounds of human thought, as Frances Young (2013) has argued in *God's Presence*.

The speaker said she wasn't convinced, though. Are the arguments of people like Raymond Tallis sufficient? He still

---

2   The Human Genome Project (HGP) was an international scientific research project with the goal of determining the sequence of nucleotide base pairs that make up human DNA, and of identifying and mapping all of the genes of the human genome from both a physical and a functional standpoint. The project formally launched in 1990 and was declared complete on 14 April, 2003.

3   Raymond C. Tallis (born 1946) is a philosopher, poet, novelist, cultural critic and a retired medical physician and clinical neuroscientist.

doesn't answer the question 'why?' 'Why can we point?' Is it adequate to account for the experience of AWE to deny, out of court, a transcendent reality that summons that experience from us? The speaker thought not. She thought that the experience of AWE is more easily explained, if not understood, if one accepts the existence of God. It's more difficult if one doesn't.

She said we lost our sense of enchantment with the dawning of modernity. Now, in our modern and post-modern state, we take for granted that human rationalism will be able to extend the bounds of human mastery over all things. Our modern self-confidence drives out the AWE that belonged to an enchanted age. Wonder was the hallmark of enchantment, a state in which we are comfortable with not-knowing, but that wonder has evaporated in the cold light of modernity. The speaker said we haven't lost it entirely, though, this AWE – for it breaks through every so often and surprises us. That's just the point. For what can account for it adequately, within the humanist frame? She repeated that she was yet to be convinced by their arguments.

In modernity, mastery usurped mystery

She said we needed to recover a sense of AWE. There are those who are crying out aloud for it, as they observe and lament the degradations that the modern human now inflicts on the natural environment. Our will to power and knowledge has had a devastating effect. What would it be for humanity to become again enchanted? We need to rediscover the joy and hope, the wonder and patience that accompanies AWE if we are to care enough to save the planet from human greed and mastery. The recovery of a sense of mystery at the natural world is necessary if we are to cease our destruction of habitat and species in the service of human greed.

Re-enchantment

The speaker referred to Michael McCarthy, who commends a
sense of joy. Like other natural writers, he encourages humanity
to recover wonder. This can only happen if we remember how to
see things, treat things, not as the means to human flourishing,
but for their own sake. The speaker quoted a passage from
McCarthy's book *The Moth Snowstorm* in which he described a
blackcap singing in a tree:

> Here was this God-given, blossoming snow-white tree, which
> was breathtaking in its beauty; and here was this God-given,
> breathtaking sound coming out of it. This tree, this tree of
> trees, was not just an astonishing apotheosis of floral beauty. It
> now appeared to be singing.
>
> The rational part of me couldn't cope. It was all too much,
> and it fell to bits. I had gone way past simple admiration into
> some unknown part of the spectrum of the senses, and there
> was only one possible response: I burst out laughing. And
> there, in the exquisite fullness of the springtime, was the joy
> of it. (McCarthy 2016, p.154)

'And there, in the exquisite fullness of the springtime, was the
joy of it,' the lecturer repeated.

It is a sense of fullness that so often describes the experience
of AWE. A fullness that overflows the normal boundaries of the
self into something delicious, exciting, unmistakeable. Lovely,
good and true in a way that can't be explained, but takes us
into an ineffable realm. A realm where poetry comes into its
own, and language opens out beyond control to dialogue with
others, to seek to express a sense of praise and thanksgiving to
the transcendent other (which some people call God).

Sonderegger

The speaker spoke of the work of Katherine Sonderegger,
who has written an exhilarating book in which she describes
the encounter of Moses with God, in a burning bush that is

never consumed. God is both the flames and the burning, and both continue without destruction. Moses asks God: 'Who are you?' God responds, 'I AM WHO I AM' (Sonderegger 2015, p.81). God's being is God. God's doing is God. Perhaps it helps to think of 'God' as a verb rather than a noun, or a name, the speaker said. There is no difference between God and who or what God is or does. The best word to use of God is love. God is love. A love that is all in all.

When we begin to see God as ultimately different in this way, our attitude to God changes. No longer do we project onto God our modern and post-modern understanding of having, being and doing as autonomous selves who hold onto their will to power and mastery, and the assumption that knowledge is power. Instead of asking 'What am I getting out of this?' we are able to surrender to the otherness of the God of love who shapes our being and our doing in our humility. Then a sense of wonder begins to return.

It is an abundant world in which the self abides, a world that tells us of God's fullness.

The speaker said that it's not the case that God is other than God's fullness. God's essential nature is full, abundant. God is love; continuing to create and sustain all that is. Everything is in the fullness of God. Everything lives and moves and has its being in the fullness of the God who is love.

The speaker began to draw to an end. She said again that in an exclusively humanist world it is difficult to account for a persistent intimation of something sublime, or transcendent, behind the beauty of Bach's music, or the intricacy of a spider's web, or the dawn coming up over the sea. Such things can be explained in any number of ways, rationalistically. But there is something irreducible about a transcendent fullness that breaks through the confines of an exclusively humanist approach, if we have eyes and ears to see and hear. She said the onus was on those who take an exclusive humanist approach to give an adequate account of the glimpse of something other, the intimation of glory that emerges in the most mundane, daily, ordinary, simple sight or sound. For her, and for others too, the exclusively humanist world didn't cut the ice when it comes to AWE. That world view and its explanations were simply not adequate to her rational, aesthetic, sensitive and sensate experience that pointed her beyond, to a love that passed human understanding.

She said: 'With all my rationality and aesthetic sensibilities, it makes much more sense to stop in awe, wonder and enchantment, love and praise of a God in whose fullness is beyond anything I can conceive. Here I stand under the glory that is God, content with my own not-knowing and unknowing. I wonder, and am enchanted, and don't need to explain.'

Pleroma

The speaker finished by reading a poem by Malcolm Guite:[4]

> More than good measure, measure of all things,
> Pleroma overflowing to our need,
> Fullness of glory, all that glory brings,
> Unguessed-at blessing, springing from each seed,
> Even the things within the world you make
> Give more than all they have, for they are more
> That all they are. Gifts given for the sake
> Of love keep giving; draw us to the core,
> Where love and giving come from: the rich source
> That wells within the fullness of the world,
> The reservoir, the never-spent resource,
> Poured out in wounded love, until it spilled
> Even from your body on the cross;
> The heart's blood of our maker shed for us.

('Good Measure', Guite 2016, p.47, used with permission)

Maddy left, rather more moved than she had expected to be.

---

4   Guite, M. (2016) *Parable and Paradox*. Norwich: Canterbury Press.

When she got home, she went to find Craig to tell him about
it, but he was engrossed with Emily, planting out seedlings, so
she joined in. It would wait.

Chapter 11

Truthfulness

Enlightenment Now

As I write, Steven Pinker has just published his latest book, *Enlightenment Now* (Pinker 2018). It's a convincingly good read. Pinker betrays the power of ideology, though: how, when you have a set of fixed beliefs, they cloud your whole perspective. For him, everything that predates the Enlightenment is suspect. There might be one or two good things to come out of the Dark Ages (so-called), but not many. His ideological frame (Enlightenment: good; Dark Ages: bad) shapes what truth looks like. As far as it goes, *Enlightenment Now* tells the truth. But it would have been a more truthful book if it had acknowledged other things.

Nick Spencer has written a good review.[1] He describes how Pinker presents graphs showing human progress on life expectancy, child mortality, maternal mortality, infectious diseases, calorie intake, food availability, wealth, poverty, extreme poverty, deforestation, oil spills, protected areas, war, violence, homicides, battle deaths, famine deaths, pedestrian deaths, plane crash deaths, occupational accident deaths, natural disaster deaths, deaths by lightning, human rights, state executions, racism, sexism, homophobia, hate crimes, violence against women, liberal values, child labour, literacy, education, IQ, hours worked, years in retirement, utilities and

---

1   Nick Spencer is Research Director at the think tank Theos. See www. theosthinktank.co.uk

homework, the price of light, disposable spending, leisure time, travel, tourism…and much else besides. It's an impressive and invigorating story of progress.

Spencer has one major problem, though: Pinker glosses over stuff that doesn't fit into his overall upwards narrative. Climate change becomes a minor bump in the road, easily addressed by carbon trading and nuclear power. Inequality as 'not a fundamental component of well-being'. He is generally a bit too willing to dismiss the lives of people in the past as nasty and brutish just because they were shorter. He glosses over sweatshops, online searches for bestiality, decapitation videos and child pornography, declining levels of social mobility in the West.

Pinker's understanding of the Enlightenment is too vague, as well. His take is ahistorical and at times verges on caricature. Spencer argues that Pinker's assertion is untenable that human co-operation, natural rights, or international peace were undreamt of before 1750. Schools, hospitals and charities are hardly 'institutions of modernity' but have a long history through the Middle Ages. The very idea of progress is dependent on the linear idea of history that Christianity bequeathed to the West. Spencer quotes David Wootton's review of *Enlightenment Now* in the *Times Literary Supplement* that 'the only major claim not supported by a graph (or indeed much evidence of any kind) is the assertion that all this progress has something to do with the Enlightenment'.

Pinker refuses to recognise anything negative coming from the Enlightenment – like the workhouse, slave trading (which was finally abolished due to the efforts of Quakers and Evangelical Christians rather more than Enlightenment philosophers and deists). Political governance emerged from models of congregational governance with a long history predating the Enlightenment. According to Spencer:

> In short, Pinker's progress *ex nihilo* from the Enlightenment doesn't add up. Had he been more attentive to the historical

peculiarities and details of what happened in England in 1688, the rest of Europe after it, and the rest of the world after that, he might have seen the 18th century as the period not of a new and unprecedented start, but one in which Enlightenment philosophers, politicians, investors, and inventors picked up and built on the existing institutions of European order, which had been slowly crafted over centuries.

It stretches the imagination too far to say the Enlightenment was an atheist movement, as Pinker clearly strains to claim. His understanding of Christian ethics is little short of a caricature. To claim that 'theistic morality' is 'the idea that morality consists in obeying the dictates of a deity' is wilfully ignorant.

Why is Pinker so blind about Christianity? It's not difficult to see why. Christianity itself has been a fixed idea for centuries in the West. It was the dominant mindset that most just accepted as the way things were – 'We are a Christian nation.' It was massively disrupted during the twentieth century, though, starting with the slaughter of the First World War, which turned over the comfortable complacencies of the late-Victorian and Edwardian world. Those who survived the trenches found it difficult to believe, anymore, in a God who had allowed that carnage to happen.

Ideological frames

The point to make is: what we know to be true belongs within the ideological frame we have. We don't always choose our ideological frames. Sometimes they are imposed on us. Totalitarian regimes are the obvious examples. Other ideologies are more subtle. Most of us are shaped by ideology – it's difficult not to be. When it's a benign ideology, it feels like your own skin. It's the normal, taken-for-granted assumptions we make, the unconscious bias and the values we hold with those around us. It's the dominant current mindset and we accept it without question.

Then – as Pinker does – we often turn a blind eye to inconsistencies; those annoying facts that challenge the mindset we hold. Most often we choose to live with the inconsistencies and find justification for them, or we simply ignore them.

'We live in the Free World.' That's an ideological statement, if ever there was one. A classic example of inconsistency to that 'Free World' ideology is the continued existence of Guantanamo Bay and all it stands for. Ostensibly a lock-up for those who threaten the Free World, it breaks the morality of human rights by imprisoning people without due justice, without proper attention to the rule of law, and so it undermines any claim that the Free World has to moral superiority. Most people know that, but choose to ignore it. Their ideological frame is not significantly disrupted.

That same ideological frame is likely to have changed after 9/11 to incorporate a sense of the rightness of a 'war against terror'. For those who belong in that ideology, the mindset of 'The West against the Rest' has become a given since that fateful day in 2001. If you question prejudice against Islam in such ideological communities, you will stir convictions and beliefs that are Islamophobic, and often downright racist, betraying an ideological frame that sees 'truth' in a particular way.

On the other hand, if you're a Muslim in the West, it can often be difficult to be seen at all as a human being, let alone as a humane neighbour living alongside people of difference. And that experience of prejudice can very quickly drive you, or your offspring, towards ideological Islam, where the 'truth' is that the West is bad, corrupt, exploitative, post-colonial and still fighting the crusades (Fergusson 2017; Sudworth 2017). Opposing ideologies become entrenched and polarised, in a vicious circle of mutual and wilful misunderstanding.

Tribal belonging

Ideology is everywhere – it can be understood as the mindset of the tribe to which we belong. Most of us belong to one tribe or another, and often to many different tribes at the same time. They give us our identity, or identities. It can be an interesting exercise to identify them, and the ideological baggage that comes with them: football club; political or interest group; school and university; pro-Trump; pro-National Rifle Association (NRA); climate change denier; the Brexit tribe; the Remoaner tribe. Political parties and sport are the obvious tribes, and today social media creates tribes too, which are reinforced by echo chambers that determine what or who we listen to or respond to on Twitter, Instagram, Facebook.

Each tribe has its own culture and way of talking. To challenge the tribal political correctness can get you into trouble. Long after he left office as the Education Secretary of State in 2014, say 'Gove' in a group of UK teachers, and see what happens.

Identifying the ideological frames we live with, and seeing them for what they are, is a step on the road of self-understanding. This is not to rid ourselves of them, necessarily: They might be a very good way of framing things. Many of the tribes we belong to are benign, even positive – they give us a sense of belonging and incorporate us into wider society through associations. However, when we recognise our tribal belongings and ideological frames, we can grow out of them if they serve us badly. When we see how tribal we are, we can understand our unconscious biases and how we are prejudiced. We can grow through an inadequate way of seeing things in a bigger frame.

What is truth?

It's important to start here with some comments on ideology as we explore 'truthfulness' in this chapter. Because many will say that 'truth' is nothing more than what is claimed to be true within any particular ideology. They will say, 'All "truth" is contextual', embedded within culture, or tribe, or ideological frame, and there's nothing more, no Truth with a big 'T'.

I'm going to argue differently to this. I'm going to claim that there *is* such a thing as Truth. Although I don't think it's possible to define it, it can be recognised – if not, then we wouldn't be able to tell truth from untruth. Lying would be meaningless. We know a truthful person – someone with a true character; even though it might be difficult to define what it is about her that makes us say 'she's truthful', we can still recognise it when we see it.

Truthful people seek to know the ideological frames that shape what they take to be 'true', and will want to transcend those ideological belongings, particularly when they are no longer adequate. What replaces the old will be another ideological frame, which will also need to be transcended in turn. That's OK. It's the truthfulness of the intention that's important here, the intention which urges that person onwards, restless within any ideology with its particular framing of 'truth'. To be truthful in this sense is to want to live within ideological frames and tribal belongings which are as true to reality as possible. It's to bring a hermeneutic of suspicion to one's current fixed ideas and be prepared to seek a more truthful way of seeing the world.

To be a truthful person is also to value Sincerity and Accuracy as virtues. I've capitalised the words because Bernard Williams does so in his book *Truth and Truthfulness* (Williams 2004). More about Sincerity and Accuracy later.

The desire to be truthful

To want the best possible – the truest – framework with which to view the world and reality is to be self-critical. It's to examine your ideological commitments and to be prepared to discard them in favour of better ones.

I think of the times when I had views I'm now ashamed of. In the 1970s, when I was a teenager, a group of university students came for lunch. I made some disparaging comment – as a joke, haha – about Jewish people. I didn't realise that a couple of the students were Jewish. They were gracious. I have never made an anti-Semitic comment since (though I am, at times, critical of the state of Israel). My ideological world view changed fundamentally that day.

I want to grow more truthful, closer to the Truth, the older I get. That desire itself is a truthful desire.

It takes imagination, to grow in truthfulness.

Reading novels is a great way to develop the imagination so we grow in truthfulness. It enables us to explore different ideological frames. All good art does this. Film. Poetry. Art. Music.

The truth of novels

Novels – because they take relatively longer to read (a day, a week, a month) – offer us a sustained experience of a different ideological framing of the world. The length of time is important. You find yourself absorbed as the author creates particular characters who betray by their actions and thoughts the peculiarities of their time, culture and customs. To engage with the novel is to be stirred out of our existing, perhaps complacent, mindset; the novel cam lead us to consider other horizons, deepening our understanding, giving us insight by stimulating our imagination. We are invited by a skilful novelist to view our own lives, our usual mindset or frame of reference, as if from outside, and to seek a more truthful way of understanding experience (de Botton 1998).

Take Iris Murdoch's *The Sea, The Sea*, for instance (Murdoch 1999). It's a great book about self-delusion, about ego, about fantasy. It captures brilliantly how the main character, Charles Arrowby, is gradually brought to a greater self-awareness, and truthfulness. Or is he? We're left wondering – especially when we contrast him with his cousin James, who personifies truthfulness as the events of the novel unfold. It's a book that leaves you wondering about yourself. About your own ego, self-delusions and fantasies. Your ideological frame shifts as you read.

Truth is never a possession

To look at things this way, Truth is never a possession. Ideologues characteristically claim 'truth' as theirs: They are right, and everyone else is wrong. Often they will hijack religion to give extra authority to their dominant truth claim – and it's not difficult to think of examples in today's world. When this happens, it can be deeply frustrating for religious people; hard for them to disassociate themselves from the ideologues and say, 'That's not what our religion teaches!' Too often, wider society doesn't get any further than to dismiss all religion as ideological, and violent to boot. It serves the ideologues when this happens, for they will want to polarise people into 'us' and 'them'. Then the Truth suffers. It becomes more difficult to be truthful when you're forced into one camp or the other. Someone I know says, 'I never do binaries.'

No one – religious or not – is free of ideology. A key difference is this, though: Truthful people, whether religious or not, will not be afraid to question their own ideological assumptions – even the religious claims themselves – because they know that, ultimately, Truth does not belong to any person, tribe, or ideology, and is bigger than their doubt.

And, yes, ideological assumptions are present within any global religion.

Take Christianity. There are many Christian 'tribes', and they can differ fundamentally from each other. The difference between a US 'Bible-belt' Christian, for example, and a Russian orthodox priest leaves you wondering how they can both claim Christian allegiance. The wisest of each will understand that Christianity is bigger than their own ideological frame – that they are shaped by the culture and society, history and community to which they belong. So, religious people will always be embedded within culture, and will express the ideological assumptions, the taken-for-granted mindset, even prejudices, that belong to that culture. If they are astute, they will realise that the culture isn't everything; that their religion gives them the wherewithal to transcend and critique their culture, in truthful pursuit of the Truth.

Truth, then, is something to seek, rather than possess. It is beyond our grasp. It's also undefinable. Anyone who claims they have the 'truth' is being (knowingly or unknowingly) untruthful.

Truth vulnerable to power

When 'truth' is reduced to a cultural phenomenon and is no longer understood as bigger than any culture, then it will always be vulnerable to power. Pseudo-truth will become the possession of the most dominant person or group. That dominance may be based on personality, or strength, or articulacy, or any other factor that gives the powerful the edge over others. Then the 'truth' of what that powerful person says will carry the day. If, within that culture there is no other recognised truth to witness to, then there will be no other ground upon which to argue or resist. There's a long tradition of speaking truth to power: of holding the powerful to account from a position of relative weakness, but that requires a confident belief that there is the Truth to appeal to.

Speaking truth to power

It's important to bear witness to and believe in Truth as beyond ideology and culture. When the reality of Truth is questioned – as with the language of 'post-truth' – then culture or society is in danger. Its members no longer have ground on which to imagine that things could be different. In a 'post-truth' world, it becomes impossible not to simply concede to those who are dominant – like the wealthy, or those who hold an ideological grip on others. The language of 'post-truth' needs to be resisted, for the sake of Truth and truthfulness, to enable humanity to imagine how it can be different, to bear witness to other and better ways of being humane in today's world.

What is Truth? Pontius Pilate asked this of Jesus, standing before him at trial. Jesus made no response to this cynical Roman leader who had seen it all and who knew that power and Roman ideology were all that mattered; that truth spins to suit the needs of the powerful. Today, the same cynicism threatens hope and belief in the possibility of a more truthful way. Cynical talk of 'post-truth' simply plays into the hands of the dominant. Opposition and resistance become eviscerated.

Instead of listening to the most articulate, or the wealthiest, or the most powerful, the truthful seeker-after-Truth will have ears and eyes for the views expressed that are modest, thoughtful, careful, ones that don't just follow the latest trend or the dominant ideology. To be truthful and seek after the Truth means you might end up questioning the current assumptions. To think critically means you're not content with what everyone else thinks, as the Truth will always be beyond.

Truth and truthfulness

Bernard Williams engages with those who don't think Truth exists, but who nevertheless value truthfulness. He asks: 'If you do not really believe in the existence of truth, what is the passion for truthfulness a passion for? Or – as we might also put it – in pursuing truthfulness, what are you supposedly being true to?' (Williams 2004, pp.2–3).

Without a belief in Truth, he thinks there can only be 'a deconstructive vortex', a descent into nihilism. He sees that nihilistic slide in his own academic world as a retreat from professional seriousness, through professionalisation, to a finally disenchanted careerism. A lack of belief in Truth means seriousness goes. You can see this in education. Instead of a truthful pursuit of Truth within education and learning, there's an insidious turn towards instrumentality and utilitarianism, where, for example, education isn't an end in itself (for the sake of truth) but a means to an end – a good career, more money.

Truth, as the RH might comprehend it, becomes victim to the LH's impulse to operationalise it.

Those who don't believe in the existence of truth Williams calls 'truth deniers'. Many deniers look back to Nietzsche – though Williams says this isn't really fair, as Nietzsche didn't stop believing in truth, but only in the Christian metaphysical view, with its roots in Platonism. Williams is keen to protect Nietzsche. Whatever way you look at it, though, there's plenty of quotable material in Nietzsche's writing to support a truth denier, to whatever degree of nihilism she or he wants to go.

But let's take Williams' perspective as a way to understand Nietzsche more deeply. Anyone interested in truthfulness needs to engage with Nietzsche and his profound critique of truth claims.

Nietzsche

Williams quotes Nietzsche:

> Truth has had to be fought for every step of the way, almost everything else dear to our hearts, on which our love and our trust in life depend, has had to be sacrificed to it. Greatness of soul is needed for it, the service of truth is the hardest service – for what does it mean to be *honest* in intellectual things? That one is stern towards one's heart, that one despises 'fine feelings', that one makes every Yes and No a question of conscience! (Nietzsche, from *The Anti-Christ*, quoted by Williams 2004, p.13)

Nietzsche here commends an approach which seeks truth, not in what is comfortable and dependable like the little pleasures and habits of life, but in a constant honesty that drives out the old 'fine feelings' and delicate questions of conscience. That whole approach to being 'truthful' needs to go, says Nietzsche. Instead truth must be sought in a radical denial of the deceptions and self-deceptions (as he saw them) of Christian morality.

Nietzsche's experience of Christian morality was intense and smothering – enough to make anyone want to break out. He couldn't see anything remotely 'truthful' in the petty, claustrophobic culture in which he was nurtured, where it was all too obvious that anyone seeking to help someone else out of Christian charity was really serving her own needs; where the injunction to forgive seemed weak and manipulative. The Christianity in the society of late-nineteenth-century Germany in which Nietzsche grew up showed no signs of transcending its cultural embeddedness. It would not have been difficult to reject the empty morality that cloyed around him.

Top of the list of what Nietzsche rejected was the Christian claim that truth was divine:

> you will have gathered what I am getting at, namely, that it is still a *metaphysical faith* upon which our faith in science rests – that even we knowers of today, we godless anti-metaphysicians, still take *our* fire, too, from the flame lit by the thousand-year-old faith, the Christian faith which was also Plato's faith, that God is truth; that truth is divine. (Nietzsche, from *The Gay Science*, quoted by Williams 2004, p.14)

For Nietzsche, courage was required to counter the age-old truth claims of Christian Platonism. It took courage to reject the cultural assumptions and strive for another world view – or no world view at all, for Nietzsche wanted freedom from any and all ideological frames. He didn't trust any of them. Always restless, he pursued the truthful dismantling of human constructions wherever he found them, not least within himself. He asked:

> How much truth does a mind endure, how much does it *dare*? More and more that became for me the measure of value. Error (faith in the ideal) is not blindness. Error is *cowardice*. (Nietzsche, from *Ecce Homo*, (the preface), quoted by Williams 2004, pp.15–16)

It's hard not to honour his project to strip away all the accretions of the past and find truth in the purity of the hero's courage that always sought to be beyond good and evil, beyond any all-too-human claim to have arrived at the truth.

Williams says complex debates continue about what Nietzsche understood truth to be. Nietzsche's project of truthfulness, to shed the tired cultural lies and falsities of the cultural ossification of Christianity that he saw all around him, is clear. Williams says he held onto truth – I'm not so sure. He quotes Nietzsche:

> What then is truth? A movable host of metaphors, metonymies, and anthropomorphisms: in short, a sum of human relations which have been poetically and rhetorically intensified, transferred and embellished, and which, after long use, seem to people to be fixed, canonical and binding. Truths and illusions we have forgotten are illusions; they are metaphors that have become worn out and have been drained of sensuous force, coins which have lost their embossing and are now considered as metal and no longer as coins. (Nietzsche, from *Truth and Lies in a Non-Moral Sense*, quoted by Williams 2004, pp.16–17)

Williams explains that this nihilistic view is from an early essay and that the mature Nietzsche was more prepared to affirm the existence of truth. Whatever. It is the case that Nietzsche's writings as a whole have left an inspiring legacy for truth deniers. Williams himself claims Nietzsche to his own view that truthfulness doesn't hold water without a notion of truth. I'd agree with this – and go further: that Nietzsche doesn't persuade me out of the sense of affirming the existence of Truth as Christian Platonic thinkers have argued down the centuries, and continue today (Davison 2019).

The truthfulness of God

To believe in the existence of Truth as a key aspect of the nature of God makes real sense to me. As such it has to be unknowable (but not unrecognisable) to humanity. It is a quality to aspire to, seeking to grow in truthfulness towards the Truth. It offers always a critique of the untruthfulness of current situations and circumstances, such that, with Nietzsche, we can be restless to discard what is not honest.

If all our 'fullnesses' come to ultimate realisation in the fullness of God, and in so far as we participate in God, we grow in fullness of character. Then to share with others an understanding that the pursuit of Truth is a joint enterprise is sensible; that we seek the same Truth, even though we will come from a wide (sometimes extreme) variety of viewpoints and ideological positions. Despite our differences, we share the same truthful desire to seek Truth, and in that Truth we understand each other better, knowing that only in God is full understanding and unity to be attained. If I know that someone I disagree with, or who holds violently different views to me, is also seeking the Truth alongside me, then I can listen more readily, and engage without fear that a great, critical depth of difference between us will not polarise us.

Instead of the otherness of 'us' and 'them', of 'me' and 'you', we then seek what we have in common. We can resist the tribal identities and the fragmentation of Truth, and, instead, seek to understand what the Truth might mean in our lives, enabling us to grow out of our current ideological viewpoint towards a wiser, broader, deeper horizon, shared by others.

This is actually a clear refutation of Nietzsche's position and Williams' view of Nietzsche's position. In the wrong hands, Nietzsche can lead to a place where Truth is less than culture, and then it can be a tool the powerful can use to shape society. Nietzsche understood truth to be universal, but not transcendent. I'd hold that it's important to affirm the transcendent nature of Truth, eternally beyond our capacities, and not within our grasp. If Truth transcends humanity, then in humility we do not end up relying on our own strength, nor do we despise weakness, as Nietzsche did.

Accuracy and Sincerity

Williams expands two basic virtues of truth: Accuracy and Sincerity, which are both important to a truthful disposition.

Let's take sincerity first. For people to be truthful, a culture of trustworthiness needs to be in place, where trust has intrinsic value and isn't merely a utilitarian commodity (Williams 2004, p.92). Sincerity is embedded in other virtues like trustworthiness and honesty; and as such it contributes to character. Williams describes it thus: 'Sincerity consists in a disposition to make sure that one's assertion expresses what one actually believes' (Williams 2004, p.96).

He has a long debate with Immanuel Kant's assertion that lying is always wrong and argues that there are circumstances when it's important to take into account what people deserve, and when deception might be the best option, or evasion, or silence, in order to keep someone's secret, or to protect someone from another's dishonesty. All such circumstances taken into account, the disposition of sincerity is one to cultivate.

Accuracy is also a virtue. To be accurate means the development of skills and attitudes that resist laziness, eagerness to please, self-deception. To cultivate accuracy means a person is prepared to stick at it, sometimes against resistance and opposition, in order to get things right. It's a matter of conscience, honour and self-respect (Williams 2004). Both accuracy and sincerity are virtues that build truthfulness.

Beyond human constructions and cultural captivities

This chapter has explored the power of ideology and, despite Nietzsche's vehement denial of the Christian and Platonic understanding of Truth, I've argued that it makes sense to continue to believe in Truth as existing beyond human constructions and cultural captivities. I've said that to grow in truthfulness is to be self-critical of one's own ideological frames and tribal belongings, and to be prepared to shed the skins of previous world views so to inhabit ones that approximate more closely to the Truth, even though that Truth is not definable, or attainable in life.

We've seen how Bernard Williams describes the relationship between the Truth and truthfulness, and how he commends two virtues of truth, accuracy and sincerity. These are dispositions, or characteristics – and yes, in an education that will develop a person as full of character, sincerity and accuracy are important virtues to acquire.

Fake news

These virtues of Truth become increasingly important in a digital age. There is serious concern about how to ensure social media users can differentiate between fact and fiction; and more broadly, how any society can judge the reliability of data that's used.[2]

In April 2016, the UK's House of Commons' Science and Technology Committee persuaded the government to establish a Council of Data Ethics to examine ethical problems brought about by the information revolution. In September 2016, Amazon, DeepMind, Facebook, IBM, Microsoft and Google created a new ethical body, the Partnership on Artificial Intelligence to Benefit People and Society. The Royal Society, the British Academy and the Alan Turing Institute, the national institute for data science, are working on regulatory frameworks for managing personal data, and in May 2018, Europe's new General Data Protection Regulation came into effect, strengthening the rights of individuals and their personal information.

Work also needs to be done in schools to enable students better to differentiate truthful claims made on social media from sensationalist, post-truth misinformation. The development of

---

2   www.theguardian.com/media/2016/jul/12/how-technology-disrupted-the-truth

critical skills to identify fake news needs to be a priority.[3] To that end, in September 2017 the UK All-Party Parliamentary Group on Literacy launched the Commission on Fake News and the Teaching of Critical Literacy Skills in Schools, following the publication of a new report from the National Literacy Trust, the *Fake News and Critical Literacy Evidence Review*, which highlighted how children and young people in England do not have the necessary skills to identify fake news.[4]

In November 2017 a UNESCO conference was held in Rabat, Morocco, on Media and Information Literacy (MIL),[5] prompting countries to ensure that MIL is on the curriculum of their schools.

Such initiatives indicate the growing awareness of the value of accuracy and truthfulness to societies. Without it, trust is eroded – both personally between people and in the institutions that enable a society to function. Truthfulness breeds trustworthiness – essential if a society is to flourish.

A person without qualities

In 2015 Dan Ariely wrote a book entitled *The Honest Truth about ishonesty: How We Lie to Everyone – Especially Ourselves*. Now a Netflix documentary, he offered a well-received argument on the importance of telling the truth, and why people don't. The *New York Times* criticised him for not exploring enough the wider implications of that loss of trust on society, and so decided that 'its findings don't add up to more than a sardonic

---

3   www.tes.com/news/school-news/breaking-news/pupils-lack-critical-literacy-skills-identify-fake-news

4   See https://literacytrust.org.uk/policy-and-campaigns/all-party-parliamentary-group-literacy/fakenews for the Commission on Fake News. The Commission relies on information gathered in autumn 2017, to find out what children know about fake news and to measure their ability to spot fake news, where critical literacy skills are already being taught and what support teachers need to improve the teaching of these skills. The results will be published in summer 2018.

5   https://en.unesco.org/news/building-momentum-media-and-information-literacy-mil

gloss on a provocative subject.[6] Again, though, the conclusion to be drawn is the importance of truthfulness – for individuals, and for society.

Simon Blackburn quotes Robert Musil's 1961 book, *The Man without Qualities*, giving a characterisation of someone who can't be trusted:

> And now just run your mind over the sort of man he is. He always knows what to do. He can gaze into a woman's eyes. He can exercise his intelligence efficiently on any given problem at any given moment. He is talented, strong-willed, unprejudiced, he has courage and endurance, he can go at things with a dash and he can be cool and cautious – I have no intention of examining all this in detail, let him have all these qualities! For in the end he hasn't got them at all! They have made him what he is, they have set his course for him, and yet they don't belong to him. When he is angry, something in him laughs. When he is sad, he is up to something. When he is moved by something, he will reject it. Every bad action will seem good to him in some connection or another. And it will always be only a possible context that will decide what he thinks of a thing. Nothing is stable for him. Everything is fluctuating, part of a whole, among innumerable wholes that presumably are part of a super-whole, which, however, he doesn't know the slightest thing about. So every one of his answers is a part-answer, every one of his feelings only a point of view, and whatever a thing is, it doesn't matter to him what it is, it's only some accompanying 'way in which it is,' some addition or other which matters to him. (Musil 1961, p.71)

To be a person without qualities, without character, is to live in the modern world without scruple or a sense of responsibility to others. The truth of the description stands: a description of someone lacking in humanity, lacking in Truth.

---

6   www.nytimes.com/2015/05/22/movies/review-dis-honesty-the-truth-about-lies-assumes-everyone-tells-them.html

Conclusion

To be full of character, truthful and trustworthy, is to develop the virtues of accuracy, so information you develop and pass on can be trusted, and sincerity, so you are able to speak your mind truthfully. It's to know when to employ critical thinking skills – on social media, and in conversation with others – so you can differentiate between what is trustworthy and truthful and what is not.

To develop as a truthful person is to recognise a deep connection between truthfulness and the Truth as something that exists and is recognisable, even though we can't grasp or define it. Truth transcends our tribal belongings and ideologies and enables us to critique current circumstances and seek a more truthful world.

Truthfulness:
from conscious incompetence to unconscious competence

Culture: What literature, music, art best express truthfulness? How might children engage and respond with appreciation?

Character: What habits could children practise deliberately to be truthful?

Call: As a way of understanding the profession of teaching as a vocation, what more could the headteacher and staff do to model truthfulness?

- Bernard Williams has a long debate with Immanuel Kant's assertion that lying is always wrong, and argues that there are circumstances when it's important to take into account what people deserve, and when deception, or evasion, or silence, might be the best option, to keep someone's secret, or to protect someone from another's dishonesty (Williams 2004). Taking all such circumstances into account, truthfulness can be a habit of the heart. Work out for yourself when you think it is acceptable to lie, such that you could explain to a child you know and still affirm the importance of truthfulness.

- Recall a time when you have spoken truth to power.

- If you are a parent or teacher, research the latest on MIL, and do what you can to be ahead of the game in your school or at home.

Chapter 12

Hopefulness

Hope is a thing with feathers

Emily Dickinson captures something quintessential about hope in her characteristically intense little poem, '"Hope" Is the Thing with Feathers', which you can find here.[1] The poem suggests a small bird – a linnet, perhaps – singing away for all its worth. Perching in our soul, it sings our yearning for a better world without words, communicating with all the power of the music of birdsong the sweet sound that comes to us from darkest experience. A still, small voice of hope. It's a fragile, vulnerable sound, but persistent. Despite all our doubts and fears, our sense of hopelessness even, it continues to sing. It is a promise, however difficult things are, that asks nothing, but gives hope to live by.

Angela Duckworth, in her book *Grit*, says character virtues are life goals that develop with maturity. Duckworth says of grit that it increases with age, it grows with us. 'Over time we learn life lessons we don't forget,' she says, 'and we adapt in response to the growing demands of our circumstances' (Duckworth 2017, p.89). Hopefulness, she argues, defines every stage of a gritty life. It's about learning how to keep going even when things are difficult, through all doubt (Duckworth 2017).

Looking towards the future – as parents, as teachers – and bringing children up to be resourceful and fruitful, means

---

1   www.poetryfoundation.org/poems/42889/hope-is-the-thing-with-feathers-314

we need to have done some serious thinking about how to encourage them to want to change the world for the better. Duckworth describes how to enable young people to gain expertise in tackling hard problems. She says it takes time – longer than most people imagine: 'Grit is about working on something you care about so much that you're willing to stay loyal to it. ... Not just falling in love, [it's] *staying* in love' (Duckworth 2017, p.54).[2]

Hope is not easy optimism

It's a challenging world in which to sustain hope. For it to be real hope, hope that doesn't collapse into false optimism, or sinking pessimism, we need to take seriously the severity of the threats that face us. Hope is not easy optimism, but a deep wisdom that recognises the promise implicit in all things, situations and people. This promise is the promise of fulfilment; an ultimate faith that, as Julian of Norwich said, 'all shall be well and all manner of thing shall be well'. As Duckworth insists, it's only when 'you keep searching for ways to change your situation for the better, you stand a chance of finding them. When you stop searching, assuming they can't be found, you guarantee they won't' (Duckworth 2017, p.178).

Duckworth speaks of how children learn from an early age to overcome adversity, if they are enabled to do so. She explains:

> If you experience adversity – something pretty potent – that you overcome on your own during your youth, you develop a different way of dealing with adversity later on. It's important that the adversity be pretty potent. Because these brain areas really have to wire together in some fashion, and that doesn't happen with just minor inconveniences. It isn't enough to tell someone they can overcome adversity. For the rewiring to happen, you have to activate the control circuitry at the

---

2   See her TED talk at www.ted.com/talks/angela_lee_duckworth_grit_the_ power_of_passion_and_perseverance

same time as those low-level areas. That happens when you experience mastery at the same time as adversity. (Duckworth 2017, p.190)

She recognises that it's 'difficult for kids in poverty. A lot of helplessness experiences. Not enough mastery experiences. They're not learning "I can do this. I can succeed in that"' (Duckworth 2017, p.190).

What is it to be hopeful? It's to see the world with a different perspective, with eyes trained to see hopes – and fears – in another light. Those who have religious faith can be at an advantage. The Christian, for example, will understand hopes and fears in the light of the narrative of the life, death and resurrection of Jesus Christ.

What Christians believe about hope

The frame of faith, hope and love is not simply a perspective, though. It's not just another way of seeing the world, like putting on a pair of specs. It is more profound than that. It comes from participating in the life of God. A Christian will say that in God she lives and moves and has her being, and from that belonging she receives the radically different perspective of hope.

Participation in God is participation in fullness or abundance, beyond our wildest imagining. Christians believe that the nature of that abundance is love. God's love was revealed in the creation of all things, and also, particularly, in the life of Jesus Christ, in his self-sacrificial death and then resurrection. Christ's death was a death for others, that the world might know that death is not the final word.

The resurrection of Christ shows what the life of participation in God is like. Christians believe that participation in God holds them and takes them through life and death. The apostle Paul wrote: 'We do not live to ourselves, and we do not die to ourselves. If we live, we live to the Lord, and if we die, we die to the Lord; so then, whether we live or whether we die, we are the Lord's' (Romans 14.8). The Christian belongs in God, and as he participates in God, he shares in the fullness of life and of being that transcends death. In that abundance is fulfilment; all personal fullnesses become abundantly full in the fullness of God. To be full of character is to participate in God.

Hope for fulfilment

Christians believe that God became human in Jesus Christ so that all humans may know that they participate in the love of God – however much they might turn away from that life and love. God became human and therefore confirmed that all the material world, the real world around us, is good, very good – as declared in the account of the creation in Genesis. God became human, Christians believe, so that humans might dwell in Christ as Christ dwells in God. This belonging begins at baptism when the person receives God's grace. The life of faith begins at that point, and if someone is regular in worship, he is strengthened by prayer and the sacrament of Holy Communion.

The bread and wine, which Christians believe becomes the body and blood of Christ, is spiritual food that sustains the person. As they eat and drink, they are renewed in their belonging in the body of Christ, dwelling and participating in God. At baptism, and through the sacraments as they grow in the life of faith, the Christian also receives the Holy Spirit, who inspires and confirms her in faith, hope and love. The Holy Spirit comforts when in doubt and despair, strengthening and praying through the person with sighs too deep for words. The Christian participates through faith in the God who is Father, Son and Holy Spirit.

Both the thing hoped for, and the promise

Christians believe that everything has its being through participation in God. God also holds all time, from the beginning, in the present, and into the future. Christians see themselves as drawn, as they participate in God, from God to God. So they say of Christian hope that it is both the thing hoped for, and the promise that inspires the hope.

Participation in God means the Christian frames her life crucially – literally through the cross – in the light of the resurrection of Jesus Christ from the dead. The cross represents all that is deadly in the world; torture, evil, negativity, pain and suffering. Whether that deadliness is observed, or suffered, the Christian still hopes, for there is life beyond any suffering and death. Hope shapes the present in the light of the future that is promised by God. Hope also enables the story of the past to be told in a certain light, enabling thankfulness for what has been, what is, and what is to come.

Christians believe that Christ is at the beginning of all things, is with the world now, and will be at the end of time. Alpha and Omega, Christ is what Christians know of God. Christ is also the promise of God; he is the peace left with us, and peace to come. The future draws the world towards itself. As the German theologian Jürgen Moltmann says, in Christ 'the hidden future already announces itself and exerts its influence on the present through the hope it awakens' (Moltmann 1967, p.18).

The word 'promise' is important here. When we are promised something, we can rely on it. Christians hold that Christ's whole life was one of promise – the promise of participation in God where we find our ultimate fulfilment, joy and peace. That promise shapes our lives and orientates us to the future. This is a personal promise, so what each person has been, is and hopes to be is shaped in response to the God of love. Discipleship, or following the way of the Christian, is to learn to live righteously in God's eyes, which means seeking to do right by others, in the world, fulfilling God's will for our lives.

Hoping against hope

There will always be a conflict for the Christian between the promise of God, and the state of the world, the tension between present experience and future hope. That will mean, often, that Christians find themselves hoping against hope. They will seek to glimpse the resurrection when experience is dark, and when it seems all life is hanging on the cross. It's then that Christians believe it's important to know their participation in the God who promises resurrected life and thereby sustains hope.

Participation in God gives the deep assurance that the conflict between present experience and future hope of the fulfilment that is to come will be resolved. Any fears, whether the personal burdens of guilt, shame or failure that can submerge the person in despair, or fears for the world that can result in feelings of helplessness and apathy (such as the impact of climate change, the terrifying possibilities of a digital future, the hatred and terror that infects the world) – all our fears are taken and held in God. They are held where hope has meaning, between what is and what can be. We are held in the tension between the sorrow, dangers and suffering of the present age and the promise and hope that all will be well.

Jürgen Moltmann comments: 'Those who hope in Christ can no longer put up with reality as it is, but begin to suffer under it, to contradict it. Peace with God means conflict with the world' (Moltmann 1967, p.21). And so, he says, the Christian Church should be a constant disturbance in human society, towards the realisation of righteousness, freedom and humanity here in the light of the promised future that is to come. The Church is committed to answer for the hope that is in it. The promise of hope sets the agenda of mission.

Profound hopelessness is hell

Christians often struggle to live in a world which has very different perspectives, either now largely rooted in atheism, or alongside people of other faiths, and therefore then often become defensive, or swayed in and out of the knowledge of the God in whom they participate. They find themselves losing the sense of God's promise when trying to make sense of the complexity of today's world and succumbing to a sense of hopelessness. Profound hopelessness is hell: not for nothing did Danté write over the entrance to the underworld 'Abandon hope, all ye who enter here.'

To sustain hope against hopelessness, it's important to resist that hell. That's why worship, prayer life and the sacraments are so important to the Christian, for worship is participation in the God in whom we live and move and have our being. It refreshes the hope, which becomes again the mobilising and driving force of faith, the eyes and ears attentive to God's promise as the Christian reflects on human nature, history and society. Attending to God's promise means turning to face into God's future and seeing the present in the light of God's future, known in the resurrected life. That life is participating in the fullness of God, drawn ever more deeply into the ultimate fulfilment that awaits all that is.

Not utopian

Christians believe that what is hoped for in any situation is not something human beings can achieve by their own effort, but only by hopeful participation in the promise of God. Human utopias will always collapse eventually – most often, as the twentieth century showed, in terrifying dictatorships or regimes of terror. Instead, participation in God leads us on, one hopes, by the creative, inventive imagination of a love that can transform situations and people.

It takes practice to be a hopeful person

How might someone with a hopeful character live fruitfully in today's world? It takes practice to be a hopeful person. As Duckworth emphasises, 'Experts do it all over again, and again, and again. Until they have finally mastered what they set out to do. Until what was a struggle before is not fluent and flawless. Until conscious incompetence becomes unconscious competence' (Duckworth 2017, p.123). She recommends three things that help cultivate a sense of purpose. Firstly, it's good to reflect on how the work you're already doing can make a positive contribution to society; second, to think about the small but meaningful ways current work can be enhanced by connection to core values; and third, to find inspiration in a purposeful role model (Duckworth 2017).

Habits of hopefulness need particular deliberate practice today. It's much easier to be cynical and hopeless, to despair and give up. Hopefulness does not come naturally. We need to train ourselves, or be trained, in hopefulness. How can we practise hopefulness?

Long live the weeds and the wilderness yet

It's hard for me, for example, not to despair when I consider the environment and the impact of climate change. As Gerard Manley Hopkins writes:

> *What would the world be, once bereft*
> *Of wet and of wildness? Let them be left,*
> *O let them be left, wildness and wet;*
> *Long live the weeds and the wilderness yet.*

(Manley Hopkins, 'Inversnaid', 1881)

Christians and people of faith are not as central to environmental causes as they should be, given that most religious traditions offer insights and wisdom about the natural world. The role of prophet for today's world more often belongs with nature writers. There is a great potential, though, for faith traditions to bring a sense of hopefulness, working in partnership with anyone whose love and concern for the natural environment is deep. So many nature writers use virtues that might be more easily identified with faith: Michael McCarthy (2016) commends the importance of joy; Andrew Balmford (2012) writes about hope; George Monbiot (2013a) talks of a long-term patience; and others write with such love and passion for the natural world, that habits of hopefulness can only contribute to the struggle to find a sustainable future.

We can start by inspiring young people and children with a love of nature, into hopeful habits of care and stewardship. As George Monbiot suggests, we need to rewild the child.[3]

Rewilding the child

From an early age, parents and teachers can find time to engage with the natural world as the best way to enable children to develop a passion for it, and to work hard to build a sustainable future. Love of the natural world starts by reading aloud, stirring the imagination; and then walking, and naming the trees, the flowers, the birds, to pass on a knowledge of the environment (MacFarlane and Morris 2017).[4] To listen to the wind, hear the birdsong, is to receive natural beauty as a gift. To learn to be still and see a kingfisher, hear a cuckoo, watch a molehill moving. To know a robin's nest, and watch a frog in a pond. To be attentive, immanent and sensitive to the world is a gift to learn with the young people in our lives. There is literature and poetry galore to inspire habits of hopefulness. John Clare wrote of his hiddenness in nature as he listened intently to the nightingale, making himself unnoticed in the world, his self no longer the centre of attention, but apprehended by the otherness of the world.[5] It is with such experience that God can become known.

---

3   www.monbiot.com/2013/10/07/rewild-the-child
4   See also www.actionforconservation.org
5   In his poem 'The Nightingale's Nest', Clare describes how he creeps stealthily through brambles and undergrowth to watch a nightingale on her nest. His hiddenness is a recurring theme: 'All seemed as hidden as a thought unborn.' See www.poemhunter.com/poem/the-nightingale-s-nest

Contemporary writers who celebrate wildness seek to re-engage the imagination in nature, to reconnect with the ancient land and the patterns and rhythms of the seasons. This does not view nature as something to be exploited, but seeks enchantment.

George Monbiot writes:

> Environmentalism in the twentieth century foresaw a silent spring, in which the further degradation of the biosphere seemed inevitable. Rewilding offers the hope of a raucous summer, in which, in some parts of the world at least, destructive processes are thrown into reverse. (Monbiot 2013a, p.9)

The hope of a raucous summer. There is a deep note of hope that runs through much nature writing, to counter the profound, realistic anxiety that knows the environment is under intense and growing pressure from anthropogenic impacts.

Stewardship

Habits of hopefulness can also draw on the Bible. Often, in current green thinking and writing, Christianity is criticised for giving us a legacy of exploitation over nature. An article written in 1967 by the medieval historian Lynn White is still widely quoted; he is thought to argue that the 'dominion text' of Genesis 1.28 ('have dominion over the earth and subdue it') was at the root of the ecological crisis, because it licensed humanity to regard the earth as its possession, to exploit and turn to material advantage. In fact, he went on to express hope that Christianity would again celebrate its myths and offer a progressive lead in reverence of nature.[6] Benedict, for example, interpreted the 'dominion text' to understand human beings as gardeners, to serve and keep creation. The concept of stewardship is central. The rich resources of the Judaeo-Christian tradition offer

---

6   White, L. (1967) 'The historical roots of our ecological crisis.' *Science 155*, 1203–1207.

much to inspire humanity into hopefulness, with responsibility and a sense of stewardship, on the basis of the principle that what humanity has received should be handed on to future generations in a better state than received.

Psalm 104 is a song of praise to the God who is wrapped in light as in a garment, who rides the wings of the wind. And the myriad diversity of the created world is there: the leviathan, playing in the deep; the coneys, the animals of the forest, the birds of the air. And from the rich gifts of creation, humanity is satisfied. Meat, vegetables, wine, oil, bread. What more could humanity need? The God portrayed has love that reaches beyond the farthest star; is deeper than the deepest ocean; is greener than the greenest green. A God whose glory fills the earth.

Hopefulness can be grounded in the God who creates with a wild patience, despite human sin. The promise of God is that good can come from bad, like the rainbow that shines through the rain. Such hopefulness can inspire people to change. It's easy to feel rather desperate when we think about the environment. But habits of hopefulness can lead to repentance and change, living into the future in accordance with God's desire that humanity live in harmony with the world around, confident and hopeful in God's promise.

Getting real rather than virtual

Habits of hopefulness keep humans engaged in the real world, interacting with real people. From a theological perspective, it is to understand how participation in God means not to depart from this world into virtual reality, but immersion in the materiality of the world around. This is to take the Christian understanding of the incarnation seriously. Christians believe that God became a human being in Jesus Christ, which was the greatest affirmation we can have of the material world around us – the world of stuff, of resistance – of reality rather than virtuality. As we attend to the world beyond our heads we find ourselves. In *The World Beyond Your Head*, Crawford (2015) commends the discipline of skilled practice to remind us of the reality of the world. Habits of hopefulness enable us to get real rather than virtual.

Habits of hopefulness are strengthened, too, through deliberate practice. Duckworth writes:

> Make it a habit. Figure out when and where you're most comfortable doing deliberate practice. Once you've made your selection, do deliberate practice then and there every day. Why? Because routines are a godsend when it comes to doing something hard…when you have a habit of practicing at the same time and in the same place every day, you hardly have to think about getting started. You just do. Daily rituals. In their own particular way, all experts…consistently put in hours and hours of solitary deliberate practice. They follow routines. They're creatures of habit. (Duckworth 2017, p.139)

Recollecting the presence of God needs to be a habit in the same way, for that is how hopefulness grows, as God's promise of the fulfilment of all things is recalled. Hopefulness can be encouraged by speaking the promise of peace and love into times and places of despair and hopelessness, to remind others that suffering isn't how it's meant to be; that despite the awfulness of present experience, the promise is secure; that all will be well, and all manner of thing will be well. Many Christians pray daily, and there's a good app here that can be downloaded for free.[7]

Habits of hopefulness can be helpfully developed within the frame of Christian faith, which offers the promise of resurrected life within the fullness of God. Christians see signs of hope all around as they seek and know the real; learn to trust in the future and not to despair. Hope gives and gives and gives, and asks for nothing in return. It is a gift when viewed from participation in the great promise of God.

---

7   www.churchofengland.org/prayer-and-worship/join-us-in-daily-prayer

Conclusion

This chapter on hopefulness has drawn most explicitly on Christian theology. Hope has been differentiated from optimism, and we've explored how it can face into the darkest experience and despair, because it looks to a future that holds out the promise of fullness of life. Hope is different to the impulse that stirs utopian visions.

The question of climate change was addressed, and how to encourage children to be hopeful by engaging with the natural world, developing habits of stewardship and involvement with the reality of the world around them.

Hopefulness:
from conscious incompetence to unconscious competence

Culture: What literature, music, art best express hopefulness? How might children engage and respond with appreciation?

Character: What habits could children practise deliberately to be hopeful?

Call: As a way of understanding the profession of teaching as a vocation, what more could the headteacher and staff do to model hopefulness?

- Duckworth says grit depends on not giving up a sense of hope. Recall a time when you didn't give up, and what you gained from the experience.

- Learn Dickinson's poem '"Hope" is a thing with feathers'.

- Find a project or organisation to join that will make the world better.

- If you are a parent or teacher, read *Battle Hymn of the Tiger Teachers* (Birbalsingh 2016). Does it leave you hopeful or in despair for the future of education in the UK?

- Inspire a child you know to garden.

- Learn 12 native trees of England and teach them to a child.

Chapter 13

Fulfilment

Pope Francis, *Laudato Si*

It's Easter Week, and Maddy and Craig have invited Benji and Dan, Caz and Jonty, Sam and Natalie around for the evening. It's the second time they've met since the New Year, with a really stimulating discussion of Iain McGilchrist back in February. Now they are reading something Craig recommended – much shorter, which was a relief. He was interested in what they made of Pope Francis's *Laudato Si*, and as it was easily downloaded, he'd suggested that.[1]

Jonty always went for the obscure. He noticed reference to a Frenchman, Teilhard de Chardin, who had written in the early 1920s how there was an underlying unity to all things. He was intrigued by the description of the love of God which spends itself again and again for the creation. Teilhard de Chardin put God's sacrificial love at the heart of things.

What impressed Jonty was the way Teilhard de Chardin showed reverence of the created order, and the forces of generation, degeneration and regeneration in the world. He understood more how a Christian mystic thought of self-sacrificial love that lives, dies, and lives again as a process that overflows in abundant life, renewing the face of the earth.

---

1   http://w2.vatican.va/content/francesco/en/encyclicals/documents/papa-francesco_20150524_enciclica-laudato-si.html

Dan remarked on how Pope Francis offered something into the profound anxiety of culture, nations and the world, and Maddy agreed that it left her hopeful. Whatever signs of disaster there were in disrupted weather patterns, in the pollution of the oceans with all that plastic, reading Francis was to be reminded again of the imperative of self-sacrifice that lies at the heart of the love of God in Jesus Christ. He explained how Christians repent, and try to change, seeking to live in accordance with God's desire, in harmony with the world around. How important it was to keep alive hope, joy, patience. That faith in the God who loves and gives in order that humans might have life. 'I have come that you might have fullness of life,' said Jesus (John 10.10).

Self-sacrifice: a new asceticism for today

Caz wondered what ascetic traditions were, that stressed self-control and self-discipline. It sounded like such traditions offered a training of the appetites of the self towards ends other than self-gratification. Instead of self-fulfilment, asceticism trains the desires towards fulfilment in some larger goal, a greater story. And so people through the ages have been prepared to sacrifice themselves for their country, or for their friends. She'd watched the 2011 film *Of Gods and Men* recently, and had been really moved by the story of these Christian monks in Algeria, who had embraced life and the call to be ascetical, whatever the personal outcome.[2]

Treading lightly on the planet

Craig wanted to know what asceticism meant for them, in today's world. He said how difficult it was to change the habits of a lifetime; the habits of hedonism, consumerism, narcissism. It was to change the whole mindset, so instead of asking 'What's

---

2   www.theguardian.com/film/2010/dec/02/of-gods-and-men-review

in it for me?' or 'Where are my creature comforts?' or 'How can I get more?' it's about resisting the temptations of the world and pervasive advertising. This was to turn abstinence into a virtue, so we don't eat as much, become vegan or vegetarian, don't have new clothes every season, or travel abroad at every opportunity. It's to learn to be ascetic: developing the habits of a different way of life based on the virtue of less is more. Fasting, disciplined prayer and praise, self-sacrificial giving to those in need. He thought that might be to understand more about abundant life.

The fullness of God

Sam was intrigued by the idea of the fullness of God, of thinking about life differently to it being 'just my life', but something more, something richer and fuller. Like the difference between adding 'fulness' to a word and making it more of a state of being than the simple word 'mind', or 'peace' or 'joy'. So, instead of simply experiencing joy, I am in a state of joyfulness. Fullness gives this. 'It grows the word, somehow,' he said, 'just like we grow from joy to joyfulness.' He wondered whether all words found their ultimate meaning in the fullness of God.

Maddy tried to explain the lecture she'd heard. How nothing is beyond the fullness of God, no evil, or cruelty even – everything is taken into the fullness. Nothing is beyond the reach of God; nothing excluded from that fullness.

Maddy said Christians believe that they grow into that fullness as they worship. As they gather together, they are taken up into the fullness of God. They experience forgetfulness of everything that doesn't matter. Thoughtfulness, faithfulness, joyfulness grows. In self-forgetfulness, the self grows into God's fullness.

Full of character

Natalie followed carefully. She was interested in what it meant to say that someone was full of character. That it could never be fully achieved, of course, but is only ever partially realised, although we do have an idea of what it is. If you want fullness of life, then it's both before you, and yours already. To desire fulfilment is to have the idea of fullness in our minds and hearts so we can describe the yearning to others and they can understand. She thought it was a small step to go from an idea of fullness to imagine God as the fulfilment of fullness, where our partial fullness has its place, with potential to develop into greater fullness.

Even though she didn't go to church much, Maddy said that she'd been impressed, when she'd studied theology, by the idea that loving and worshipping God was the ultimate end of our lives. Worship, the time when people bring the best of themselves, seeking to understand more clearly and deeply the fullness of God that rounds human life in ultimate love.

That was the essence of their conversation, anyway. There was lots of other banter, and Emily came down a couple of times to find out what was going on.

The second time, they all went out to look at the stars, and Benji pointed out the Plough and the North Star.

Praise be to you...

Pope Francis had chosen *Laudato Si* as the title of his paper on care for our common home, because it is the opening of St Francis's hymn of praise to creation.

Written in the thirteenth century, its words take the reader into a state of thankfulness. Thankfulness for Brother Sun, for Sister Moon and the stars, Brother Wind and Sister Water. Brother Fire and Sister Mother Earth, for Sister Bodily Death from whom no one living can escape.

The canticle sets the human person within the world of natural beauty, where all is given by God, and for which thankfulness is the response.

In each of the 'fullnesses' considered here – thankfulness, self-forgetfulness, carefulness, playfulness, resourcefulness, thought-fulness, fruitfulness, truthfulness and hopefulness – there's been a basic assumption made: that the human person finds fulfilment not in pursuing the belief in her own autonomy, but in embracing and being shaped by that which is other to self. It is to be willing to be formed by that which is heteronomous to the self.

Thankfulness begins the intimation that we are heteronomous, rather than autonomous, when we say thanks for everything with a sense of gratitude for gift. A gift is the most immediate sign of that which is other to us: It is not our own but is given to us, in love and generosity, and as we receive it, our sense of autonomy is challenged and changed. As we say 'thank you', we acknowledge the otherness of the gift and giver; we engage heteronomously.

Heteronomy is there in Chapter 2 on self-forgetfulness, with its exploration of the prevalence in today's Western culture of the autonomy that so shapes the anthropology (the understanding of what it means to be human) that is the legacy of the Enlightenment and permeates modernity. Instead of being caught up into the vortex of me, myself, I, in an endless pursuit of self, where autonomy is prized above all, a different self emerges when heteronomy is embraced. When the self seeks to lose itself in caring for the other, in giving oneself for the good of others, in surrendering the self into a greater good – for example, a family, a school, a choir, sports team, or something more abstract, like an education – then it finds itself in that surrender.

We need to retain some sense of autonomy, of course, in order to judge for ourselves what can be trusted – and partly the reason why heteronomy is so difficult today is because it's so difficult to trust. Look at how people in the twentieth century were swept up by disastrous ideologies that destroyed lives and truthfulness. Look at some institutions today that have purported to care – social care services, the Church, charities – and have failed with terrible hurt and damage done to vulnerable young people and adults. Trust is very difficult today. But it's essential if the human self is going to grow through relationships with others. Such trust begins when the institutions prove their trustworthiness, and when people begin to trust them. That's always going to be a risk, though, because no institution is completely infallible. There will always be individuals who have evil designs and are clever at manipulating systems and the vulnerable to their own ends.

So to allow the self to be shaped by the other is a risky thing to do, and takes *phronesis* – the wisdom that comes from experience that enables the self to judge carefully and clearly what leads to fullness of life, and what diminishes it. That's a lifetime process, and begins with the carefulness that a baby and infant experiences from his earliest days.

The experience of carefulness, the playfulness of childhood, and the resourcefulness that comes as childhood becomes adulthood, are all shaped by the relationship between self and other. When this relationship is one of trust, within a context of love and generosity, then the self grows in reciprocity, trust and responsibility. Part of that process is the wisdom to cope when things go wrong; when we're let down, or betrayed or abandoned, or deceived and our trust is destroyed. To recover from such experience, depending on the severity of the experience, is sometimes incredibly hard, even impossible – and survivors emerge often scarred or traumatised for life. It can be hard, even impossible, to take the risk ever again on heteronomy. Autonomy can seem the only option, closing down into self, trusting only self. But those who find themselves, lose themselves.

Thoughtfulness is when we engage our full attention, using both the left and right hemispheres of our brains, towards the other; when we attend not just to the particular and detailed – the next thing that needs to be done, the tactics and strategies that will achieve our goals – but also to the other that encounters us as we reach out in openness to the world. Thoughtfulness is to anticipate the needs of others around us, because we've put ourselves in their shoes as far as we are able, imagining what they are feeling, thinking, experiencing, and seeking their good. Thoughtfulness takes us out of ourselves and builds trust, as we become trustworthy in the eyes of others. There's a lovely story of a Chinese man who was learning English. One day, his teacher asked him what had been the happiest moment of his life. He pondered for a long while. And then he smiled and said, 'Once, my wife went to Beijing and she ate a meal of duck and other delicacies. When she returned, she would tell me often about the delicious duck.' The happiest moment in his life was her trip and the eating of the duck.

To see our lives in terms of fruitfulness is to bring a different perspective to what we contribute through work, relationships, education; it's to want to be fruitful so our lives offer something to others, to the common good, towards making a better world. The goal here is not self-fulfilment or aggrandisement, but to find ourselves in what we bring to fruition. The religious life has a great deal to show us here: that fruitfulness is ultimately shaped by our engagement and surrender to the other that some call God; which can look like a waste of time and effort but which, instead, frames all time and effort by a larger story.

Being truthful is to recognise, ultimately again, that there is a Truth that transcends our own supposedly autonomous being. This means that what we assume is our own truth is always alongside the truth of others in a morally relativistic world. Any conception of truth is dependent on an underlying reality that holds the truthfulness of all there is in one unity, such as the wise and mystics have apprehended through the ages. To accept the heteronomy of that Truth is to find a sense of hopefulness.

Hopefulness in today's world is hard – there is much to cause anxiety, most particularly the impact of climate change, and the global insecurities that threaten stability and peace in longstanding and intractable tensions born of historic evils. It's hard, but possible if life is seen as ultimately belonging within a fullness in which we live and move and have our being.

This book began with those fears, and the anxiety of bringing up a child today to be wise, with dignity and hope. Ultimately, this is best undertaken by embracing heteronomy, a life that is shaped by the other.

Conclusion

This book is written to provoke a deeper thoughtfulness about education and how it can be enriched today for digital generations who want a humane future; it is not a how-to manual for teachers. It doesn't offer strategies to enhance leadership, or performance, or provide the know-how to run a MAT. It doesn't explain what mentoring is or commend consultancy to overstretched headteachers. Nor does it have a linear argument, presented in an accessible style with text boxes, different examples and anecdotes.

Instead, it's written with today's parents in mind. To be a parent, with a child about to start school, is momentous. It's to let go of someone you love, partially anyway, into a system that will be at least as formative as you have been. It's to raise your head and look into the future.

Mostly, when we raise our heads and face into the issues and challenges that humanity is up against and the world suffers, we very quickly duck down again. It's understandable, because most of those challenges we can't do very much about: climate change, increasing world instability, economic polarisation, the impact of automation. Given that's the case, the best place to concentrate, it seems to me, is on the quality of our human personhood, on what makes us full of character. So that whatever happens, at a personal, or global level, we have the dignity to live fully and courageously, with an understanding of fulfilment, flourishing and abundance of life that transcends our hopes and fears.

There are some key themes that run through the chapters.

What the 'self' is, and how best to find ourselves today. How not to find the self in an unquestioned *autonomy* of the self, but rather in taking the risk of *heteronomy*, with the humility to allow the other to change us and shape us.

McGilchrist's use of the distinction, yet indivisibility, of the left and right hemispheres of the brain, to describe culture today is the greatest metaphor around, I believe. Like all good metaphors, it is rooted into materiality.

Materiality, too – I've tried to take us back to an engagement with the real stuff of the world around us, following Crawford's insight that what we attend to makes and shapes us, and that too much attention to the virtual world of the internet and the digital age is not doing us any good. Again, to be *heteronomous* selves, rather than *autonomous* selves, is what's commended here. Particularly as we consider the alarming self-preoccupations and absorption of so many today, young and old. It's not popular, to see narcissism in others, and it's not comfortable to see it in myself, but the old myth has perennial truth – that too much attention to the self is self-destructive. Brooker's *Black Mirror* is prophetic.

And then there's automation and machine learning, and the crossovers between how humans learn and the deep learning that algorithms now achieve. This brings a renewed focus on how our brains develop from the earliest days through lifelong learning, as synaptogenesis occurs and neural pathways are formed, shaping us into particular knowledge, habits and patterns of behaviour and characteristics. This book is about education; about what formation means and how much more we can learn from how we learn about being human. About our personhood, and living life to the full. About being more than clever in a narrow, focused, LH way.

Having a child who is about to start school concentrates the mind on all this and more. The nature of work and what

makes for fulfilment through fruitful occupation are going to
be much more important questions as automation reduces the
opportunities for paid work, particularly in predictable, routine
tasks, though we shouldn't be surprised at the sophistication
of the deep reinforced learning of algorithms and what they
can do, in exponentially fast ways. The cleverness of robots is
already surpassing our abilities. That's not going to stop.

Decoupling work from income seems the obvious thing to
do. I'm aware that introducing Universal Basic Income is highly
political and probably won't happen, but like many people, not
least the RSA,[1] I believe it should happen and is affordable.
Whether it's introduced or not, how people spend their time
fruitfully and meaningfully, is going to concern humanity in
Western cultures more and more. Whether this means we are
witnessing the beginning of the end of the economic system
called 'neoliberalism', and if so, what replaces it, is a hugely
important question, beyond the scope of this book, but relevant
nonetheless.

To have a four-year-old child, like Emily, is to wonder
about such things. What she will face for employment – which
is a necessary aspect of the fulfilled and flourishing life – in 15
or 16 years' time.

There are many reasons to take seriously the educational
approach of E.D. Hirsch. The most important reason is because
he champions the acquisition, accumulated through more than
a decade of school and college, of a cultural hinterland that not
only enriches life, but also enables children to make sense of the
cultural codes and knowledge that lie behind the information,
skills and processes that they encounter as they grow up. This
is particularly important for children from minority cultures,
who can struggle to understand the significance of what they
are learning (or not) at school if they don't have the taken-
for-granted hinterland that is often assumed to be in place.

---

1   Royal Society for the encouragement of Arts, Manufactures and Commerce. See
     www.thersa.org

To be taught, in the 'naturalist' belief that originated with Rousseau, which goes hand in hand with the 'progressive' educational ideology that he spawned, is not to provide that hinterland. So it isn't there, for most kids anyway, unless their home life has invested time and effort to do the groundwork. This isn't elitist; it's merely saying that life is richer and fuller when we know more. Education means and offers more, too. It's the duty of parents and educators to pass on knowledge and a cultural hinterland to children in a disciplined and systematic way, so they get the picture.

I'm very aware of the way religion in general, and Christianity in particular, is understood as a toxic phenomenon today that should simply be allowed to die, or kindly be put to sleep. I think differently: that good religion (and I know there's lots of bad religion around) has tremendous resources to bring to the consideration of what it means to be fully human. I hope I'm writing not for the convinced, but for those who are open-minded and want to understand more about what motivates sane and thoughtful people still to believe in God. The sense of something that transcends life and experience is the place where I began, through the awe and wonder that was inspired in me by the natural world and the stars. The apprehension that there is a reality that is other to me and to all that there is, an other that isn't a thing alongside other things in the world, is behind my understanding of pleroma, of fullness and abundance.

Good religion knows how much it owes to good philosophy, and Christian Platonism understands the relation between God and everything else as a relationship of participation. We (and everything else) are real in so far as we participate in the reality of God, who is beyond human understanding, reason and conception, and is best known as love. God's love is revealed by studying the life, death and resurrection of Jesus Christ, and allowing ourselves to be inspired by the Holy Spirit.

If Christian Platonism gives the framework to understand the fullness in which we are truly thankful, self-forgetful, careful, playful, resourceful, thoughtful, fruitful, truthful and full of hope, then the thought of Aristotle gives us the focus on becoming virtuous. Aristotle put enormous store by friendship and the good life, which he called *eudaimonia*, and the practical wisdom or *phronesis* that enables us to make good choices and grow in virtue, in good character, as individuals and as members of society. The Christian tradition (and other religions) goes a step further and emphasises how important it is to contribute self-sacrificially out of love for our neighbours, so we are shaped by our concern for the other, and particularly those in need, who are vulnerable and forgotten by the powers of the world. An Aristotelian ethic, coupled with Christian morality, runs through the book like letters through a stick of rock.

Maddy and Craig's daughter is named Emily for a very good reason. I'm bold enough to want to answer Rousseau back.

Bibliography

Ariely, D. (2015) *The Honest Truth about Dishonesty: How We Lie to Everyone – Especially Ourselves*. London: HarperCollins.

Arthur, J., Kristjánsson, K., Harrison, T., Sanderse, W. and Wright, D. (2017) *Teaching Character and Virtue in Schools*. London and New York, NY: Routledge.

Balmford, A. (2012) *Wild Hope: On the Front Lines of Conservation Success*. Chicago, IL: University of Chicago Press.

Bayley, J. (2003) *The Iris Trilogy: A Memoir of Iris Murdoch*. London: Abacus.

Birbalsingh, K. (ed.) (2016) *The Battle Hymn of the Tiger Teachers*. Woodbridge: John Catt Educational Ltd.

Blackburn, S. (2014) *Mirror, Mirror: The Uses and Abuses of Self-Love*. Princeton, NJ: Princeton University Press.

Bostrom, N. (2014) *Superintelligence, Paths, Dangers, Strategies*. Oxford: Oxford University Press.

Bowlby, J. and World Health Organization (WHO) (1952) *Maternal Care and Mental Health: A Report Prepared on behalf of the World Health Organization as a Contribution to the United Nations Programme for the Welfare of Homeless Children* (2nd edn). Geneva: WHO. Available at www.who.int/iris/handle/10665/40724, accessed on 12 July 2018.

Brooks, D. (2012) *The Social Animal*. London: Short Books.

Brooks, D. (2015) *The Road to Character*. London: Allen Lane.

Cameron, N.M. de S. (2017) *Will Robots Take Your Job?* Cambridge: Polity Press.

Carr, N. (2015) *The Glass Cage: Who Needs Humans Anyway?* London: Vintage.

The Church of England Education Office (2016) *Vision for Education, Deeply Christian, Serving the Common Good*, GS 2039, July 2016. See www.cefel.org.uk/vision

Cobb, E. (1977) *Ecology of Imagination in Childhood*. London: Routledge & Kegan Paul Ltd.

Crawford, M. (2015) *The World Beyond Your Head: How to Flourish in an Age of Distraction*. London: Penguin Random House.

Crittenden, P.M., Dallos, R., Landini, A. and Kozlowska, K. (2014) *Attachment and Family Therapy*. Maidenhead: Open University Press.

Charles Cummings, OCSO (2015) *Monastic Practices*. Athens, OH: Cistercian Publications.

Cunningham, H. ([1995] 2005) *Children and Childhood in Western Society since 1500*. Harlow: Pearson Education Ltd.

Davison, A. (2017) 'Looking Back toward the Origin', in G.A. Anderson and M. Bockmuehl (eds) *Creation ex Nihilo: Origins, Development, Contemporary Challenges*.South Bend, IN: University of Notre Dame Press.

Davison, A. (2019) *Participation in God: A Study in Christian Doctrine and Metaphysics*. Cambridge: Cambridge University Press.

de Botton, A. (1998) *How Proust Can Change Your Life*. London: Vintage.

Duckworth, A. (2017) *Grit: Why Passion and Reslience Are the Secrets to Success*. London: Vermilion.

Fergusson, J. (2017) *Al-Britannia, My Country: A Journey through Muslim Britain*. London: Bantam Press.

Field, F. (2010) *The Foundation Years: Preventing Poor Children from Becoming Poor Adults*. London: H.M. Government.

Ford, M. (2015) *Rise of the Robots: Technology and the Threat of a Jobless Future*. New York, NY: Basic Books.

Gavin, A. (2012) *The Child in British Literature: Literary Constructions of Childhood, Medieval to Contemporary*. New York, NY: Palgrave MacMillan.

Gerhardt, S. (2015) *Why Love Matters: How Affection Shapes a Baby's Brain*. London and New York, NY: Routledge.

Tim Gill ([2007] 2009) *No Fear: Growing Up in a Risk Averse Society*. London: Calouste Gulbenkian Foundation.

Greenfield, S. (2014) *Mind Change, How Digital Technologies Are Leaving Their Mark on Our Brains*. London: Penguin Random House Ltd.

Guardini, R. (1997) *The Spirit of the Liturgy*. New York, NY: The Crossroad Publishing Company, trans. Ada Lane, 1997. (First published in German in 1918 and in English in 1930.)

Guite, M. (2016) *Parable and Paradox*. Norwich: Canterbury Press.

Harari, N.Y. (2015) *Homo Deus: A Brief History of Tomorrow*. London: Harvill Secker.

Hirsch, E.D. ([1987] 1988) *Cultural Literacy, What Every American Needs to Know*. New York, NY: Vintage.

Hirsch, E.D. (1996) *The Schools We Need: And Why We Don't Have Them*. New York, NY, and London: Doubleday.

Hirsch, E.D. (2006) *The Knowledge Deficit: Closing the Shocking Education Gap for American Children*. New York, NY: Houghton Mifflin.

Hofstadter, D. (2007) *I Am a Strange Loop*. Cambridge, MA: Basic Books.

Hughes, J. (2007) *The End of Work: Theological Critiques of Capitalism*. Blackwell: Oxford.

Kurzweil, R. ([2005] 2016) *The Singularity Is Near: When Humans Transcend Biology*. London: Viking Penguin.

Kurzweil, R. ([2012] 2014) *How to Create a Mind: The Secret of Human Thought Revealed*. London, Viking Penguin.

Lammy, D. (2011) *Out of the Ashes, Britain after the Riots*. London: Guardian Books.

Louv, R. ([2005] 2010), *Last Child in the Woods: Saving Our Children from Nature-Deficit Disorder*. New York, NY, and London: Atlanta Books.

Luce, E. (2017) *The Retreat of Western Liberalism*. London: Little, Brown Book Group.

Macfarlane, R. and Morris, J. (2017) *The Lost Words: A Spell Book*. London: Hamish Hamilton.

McCarthy, M. (2016) *The Moth Snowstorm: Nature and Joy*. London: John Murray Press.

McCullough, M.E., Emmons, R.A. and Tsang, J. (2002) 'The grateful disposition: A conceptual and empirical topography.' *Journal of Personality and Social Psychology 82*, 112–127.

McGilchrist, I. ([2009] 2010) *The Master and His Emissary: The Divided Brain and the Making of the Western World*. New Haven, CT, and London: Yale University Press.

Moltmann, J. (1967) *Theology of Hope*. London: SCM Press.

Monbiot, G. (2013a) *Feral: Searching for Enchantment on the Frontiers of Rewilding*. London: Allen Lane.

Monbiot, G. (2013b) 'Our children are just not wild enough.' *The Guardian Weekly*, 11 October 2013, p.19.

Monbiot, G. (2017) *Out of the Wreckage: A New Politics for an Age of Crisis*. London: Verso.

Morgan, N. (2017) *Taught Not Caught: Educating for 21st Century Character*. Woodbridge: John Catt Educational Ltd.

Moss, S. (2012) *Natural Childhood*. London: National Trust. Available at www.nationaltrust.org.uk/documents/read-our-natural-childhood-report.pdf, accessed on 9 June 2018.

Murdoch, I. ([1978] 1999) *The Sea, The Sea*. London: Vintage.

Musil, R. (1961) *The Man without Qualities* (vol. 1). London: Martin, Secker & Warburg.

Palmer, S. (2006) *Toxic Childhood: How the Modern World Is Damaging our Children and What We Can Do about It*. London: Orion Books

Parkin, S. (2017) *Death by Video Game: Danger, Pleasure, and Obsession on the Virtual Frontline*. London: Serpent's Tail.

Peston, R. (2017) *WTF: What Have We Done? Why Did It Happen? How Do We Take Back Control?* London: Hodder & Stoughton.

Peterson, J. (2018) *12 Rules of Life: An Antidote to Chaos*. London: Penguin Random House.

Pinker, S. (2018) *Enlightenment Now: The Case for Reason, Science, Humanism and Progress*. London: Allen Lane

Roberts, F. and Wright, E. (2018) *Character Toolkit for Teachers: 100+ Classroom and Whole School Character Education Activities for 5- to 11-Year-Olds*. London: Jessica Kingsley Publishers

Sacks, J. (2000) *Celebrating Life: Finding Happiness in Unexpected Places*. London: Fount.

Sayers, D.L. (1942) *Why Work? An Address Delivered at Eastbourne April 23rd 1942*. London: Methuen & Co. Ltd.

Sayers, D.L. (1948) *The Lost Tools of Learning*. London: Methuen & Co.

Shortt, R. (2016) *God Is No Thing: Coherent Christianity*. London: C. Hurst & Co.

Skeels, I. (2013) *St Cuthbert's Wild School for Boys*. CreateSpace.

Sonderegger, K. (2015) *Systematic Theology, Volume 1, The Doctrine of God*. Minneapolis, MN: Fortress Press.

Spencer, N. (2016) *The Evolution of the West: How Christianity Shaped Our Values*. London: SPCK.

Spufford, F. (2014) *Unapologetic: Why, Despite Everything, Christianity Can Still Make Surprising Emotional Sense*. London: HarperCollins.

Storr, W. (2017) *Selfie: How We Became So Self-Obsessed and What It's Doing to Us*. London: Picador.

Sudworth, R. (2017) *Encountering Islam: Christian-Muslim Relations in the Public Square*. London: SCM Press.

Taylor, C. (2007) *A Secular Age*. Cambridge, MA and London: The Belknap Press of Harvard University Press.

Tegmark, M. (2017) *Life 3.0: Being Human in the Age of Artificial Intelligence*. London: Penguin Random House.

Tough, P. (2012) *How Children Succeed: Grit, Curiosity, and the Hidden Power of Character*. London: Houghton Mifflin Harcourt Publishing Company.

Twenge, J. ([2006] 2014) *Generation Me*. New York, NY: Atria Books.

Twenge, J. (2017) *iGen: Why Today's Super-Connected Kids Are Growing Up Less Rebellious, More Tolerant, Less Happy – and Completely Unprepared for Adulthood*. New York, NY: Atria Books.

Twenge, J.M. and Campbell, W.K. (2013) *The Narcissism Epidemic: Living in the Age of Entitlement*. New York, NY: Atria Books.

Ward, F. (2013) *Why Rousseau Was Wrong: Christianity and the Secular Soul*. London: Bloomsbury.

Watkins, P.C., Woodward, K., Stone, T. and Kolts, R.L. (2003) 'Gratitude and happiness: Development of a measure of gratitude, and relationships with subjective well-being.' *Social Behavior and Personality 31*, 431–451.

Williams, B. (2004) *Truth and Truthfulness*. Princeton, NJ: Princeton University Press.

Williams, J. (2018) *Stand Out of Our Light: Freedom and Resistance in the Attention Economy*. Cambridge: CUP.

Winnicott, D.W. (1969) *The Child, the Family, and the Outside World*. London: Penguin.

Winnicott, D.W. (1971) *Playing and Reality*. London: Penguin.

Young, F. (2013) *God's Presence: A Contemporary Recapitulation of Early Christianity*. Cambridge: Cambridge University Press.

Index